1 a

Rolling Breaks

ROLLING BREAKS
and Other
Movie Business

by Aljean Harmetz

ALFRED A. KNOPF
New York
1983

THIS IS A BORZOI BOOK
PUBLISHED BY ALFRED A. KNOPF, INC.

Library of Congress Cataloging in Publication Data

Harmetz, Aljean.
Rolling breaks and other movie business.

1. Moving-picture industry—United States—Addresses, essays, lectures. 2. Moving-picture producers and directors—United States—Addresses, essays, lectures. 3. Moving-picture actors and actresses—United States—Addresses, essays, lectures. 4. Screen writers—United States—Addresses, essays, lectures. I. Title
PN 1993.5.U6H35   1983   384'.8'0973   82–49190
ISBN 0–394–52886–7

Manufactured in the United States of America

FIRST EDITION

To Seymour Peck, a great editor
and a great gentleman,
with love

Rolling Breakeven: The point in the life of a movie when receipts have covered expenses (production, advertising, publicity, distribution fees . . .) and rolling break participants—actors, directors, etc.—begin to receive their share of profits, if any. It is the "breakeven" that rolls away when any new expenditure is made. (For example, the moment a rolling break participant is paid his first share of the profits, the breakeven rolls away—indeed disappears—and none of the remaining participants can be paid their shares until more box-office receipts come in and a new breakeven point is established.)

Acknowledgments

I would like to thank the people I write about—the studio executives, actors and actresses, technicians, writers, publicists, producers, and directors. They have been more than my sources. They have been my teachers, and I want to acknowledge my gratitude to all of them.

Many of these articles were first printed in *The New York Times,* and I would especially like to thank three editors at that newspaper: my immediate editor, Sy Peck, who never tampered with an article to demonstrate his own power and never changed a sentence without improving it; deputy managing editor Arthur Gelb, whose insightful ideas for articles show up more than once in this book; and executive editor Abe Rosenthal, who hired me and encouraged complete coverage of Hollywood.

In addition, my gratitude to:

My editor, Vicky Wilson, who shaped the form of Rolling Breaks, my husband, Richard S. Harmetz, whose encouragement has never failed me, my friend Mae Howard, who kept the house running, my sons, Anthony and Daniel, who lived through the original writing of these articles, and my daughter, Elizabeth, who survived the nights and weekends I spent reshaping them.

Contents

Introduction

I spent my thirteenth and fourteenth summers stuffing pictures of Lana Turner, Esther Williams, June Allyson, and Van Johnson into envelopes. I was very good at my work, often stuffing 3,000 envelopes a day, and my fingers were always covered with paper cuts.

I wanted to be a movie star more than anything in the world. The closest I came was when my mother, who worked in the wardrobe department at MGM, got me an audition with director Mervyn Le Roy. I did a splendid Cockney accent. When I was done, he thanked me, and that was that.

I was a fat, introverted little girl with seven years of dramatic lessons behind me and no future. And every day I spent my lunch hour pretending to be what I could never become.

I would wander through the 39 acres of Chinese villages, small-town railroad stations, bridges, lakes, streets that had one corner in Paris and the next in New York, artificial trees and plaster-of-Paris mansions that made up MGM's Lot 2. I ate my carrots, cottage cheese, and hidden candy bars at the foot of staircases that went nowhere, in front of doors that opened to nothing.

Today's children—including three of my own—hardly understand the desperate passion I felt about being a movie star.

They are the children of tape decks and television—not of the Rialto, the Nu-art, the Bijou, the Warners Beverly, and the Loew's State. They learn about life from the anarchy of album cuts and from the real wars in living color that invade their living rooms at 7 p.m. every evening. My generation learned about love and marriage, heroism and cowardice, second-hand —on slightly used celluloid. "When you want to send a message, send it by Western Union," Sam Goldwyn once said to justify sailing his glittering entertainments down our Saturday afternoons. But we cheated Goldwyn. For us, every Saturday afternoon was a message. We are the depositories of a hundred thousand such messages.

All the events of the real world filtered down to us through the personalities of movie stars and, in the dark of a hundred movie theaters, we learned what was worth doing and the style in which to do it. From Marilyn Monroe's moist lips to Marlon Brando's torn T-shirt to Jimmy Dean's rebellious slouch, the movies were our primer on what to desire. After the movie was over, we parked our cars on some deserted street and spelled out our lessons on warm bodies.

The Hollywood in which I grew up no longer exists. When I began writing about Hollywood in the mid-fifties, I was told quite solemnly by an MGM publicist that "No MGM star drinks, smokes, uses bad language, or has sex—even with her husband." The studio, in loco parentis, taught its stars how to walk, how to fence, how to behave in public and in private— approving or disapproving their choices of houses and husbands. "They said I was a disgrace to the studio because I came into the commissary in denims," Peter Lawford once told me. "They said Robert Taylor wore a suit and a tie and a pin through the collar even when he wasn't working. They were very high on pins through the collar."

Now Lot 2 has been sold for a housing development and movie stars live their lives as they please. To the almost complete indifference of their employers, actors and actresses snort cocaine, protest United States government policies in Latin America, and have children months or even years before they decide to get married.

Sometimes vicious, often tyrannical, and always dictatorial (even if benevolent), the crude immigrants who built movie empires at least loved movies passionately. If Harry Cohn bragged that he judged the worth of a film by whether his ass fidgeted while he was watching it, his judgment was not the impersonal result of research done among the "proper movie-going age group" in a suburban shopping center. Perhaps the movie industry has always been three-fourths industry and one-fourth art and I was merely deceived by my own passionate adolescent response. Today the prevalent language of Hollywood is that of accountants. *Bottom line, software, ancillary rights, protecting the downside, rolling breaks, gross participation* are the dusty words that choke the tongue. The men who run the studios are, for the most part, journeymen—at United Artists today, at 20th Century-Fox tomorrow. As Billy Wilder says, "You remember from when they were mailboys at William Morris or MCA." Like the rest of American businessmen, they are concerned with short-term performance and the long run be damned. If they prove inept as studio presidents and are fired, their golden parachute allows for a lucrative independent production arrangement.

Right now Hollywood is poised at the edge of a technological revolution. Video cassettes, videodisks, subscription television, DBS, pay-cable, satellite transmission, SMATV are fancy new wrappings in which movies will be delivered. What I wonder is whether there will be anything inside the wrappings that is worth looking at.

I am inordinately curious—I might have been happiest as an archaeologist—and I keep fingering a subject until I understand everything about it. In his 1961 *The Fifty-Year Decline and*

Fall of Hollywood, Ezra Goodman described the Hollywood press corps as "a second-rate fourth estate subsisting—with negligible exceptions—on press-agent handouts of mostly trumped-up tales, freeloading (another name for payola) and general incompetence." But the basic seriousness of personality that often makes me a drab companion allowed—or, rather, forced—me to scrutinize seriously an industry that thrived on fiction and hyperbole. The schizophrenic gulf between the artist and the industry, between the romantic figures who stride across the screen and the manipulations behind the screen, can be glimpsed between the lines in the pieces collected here.

My first published work was a poem in the *Atlantic Monthly*, my third an article in *Modern Screen*. Writing for the fan magazines allowed me to earn as I learned how the industry worked. Writing for the fan magazines was also a quick immunization. Hollywood has always tried to seduce the press, just as its success lies in seducing the public. Fan magazine writers were treated with an unpleasant mixture of largesse and contempt. My *market*, not my skill, determined my status then and now. The memories of my days at *Motion Picture* and *Photoplay* make it easier to remind myself that *The New York Times*, not Aljean Harmetz, is being courted. I watched other fan magazine writers become appendages to one starlet or another, happy to spend Sundays beside an actor's swimming pool and glowing with the appositive "Friend." That I resisted is due less to strong character than to the weaknesses of my personality— an innate mistrust and an old dog's fervor for my own hearth. I came close to the border once. Being something of an age with Natalie Wood, Nick Adams, and the "Rebel Without a Cause" alumni, I joined their lives for six months or so. To be a movie star's friend was heady but, in the long run, I found the superficiality and publicness of it uncomfortable.

I have no friends in the movie industry, although I have indulged myself with a dozen good acquaintants. Even that much is difficult. One studio head I like tremendously saw to it that none of his executives returned my phone calls for several weeks, recently, after I pointed out in print that three of his movies were in various kinds of trouble. After years of inventing the most outrageous lies and watching the press swallow them, Hollywood demands only good publicity.

If I were offered today what I wanted so desperately as a child, a chance to be a movie star, I think I would turn it down. To be a movie star was to hold a leash on life. It was an all-purpose American dream that encompassed everything— easy money, quick fame, unlimited power, accountability to no one, eternal happiness, and no prices to pay. Sooner or later I probably would have discovered that there are always prices to pay, but spending one's adult life as an observer of the film industry is a good way to temper excess romanticism.

Rolling Breaks

Mary Pickford—America's [Gothic] Sweetheart

The voice is cracked and faded, like a piece of velvet ruined by the sun. It has a musty, unused sound that is painful to hear.

The voice comes out of a black tape recorder manipulated by Buddy Rogers and stumbles through a little speech of welcome to 20 journalists gathered in the western bar at Pickfair.

Rogers, Mary Pickford's husband for the past 34 years, prefaces the recording with, "I said, 'Honey, all your friends are coming, all those wonderful members of the press.'" He confides, "And Mary's so happy you're all here."

The reporters stand awkwardly beneath 15 Frederic Remington paintings worth $25,000 each. One drinks champagne from a crystal-and-gold Louis XIV goblet. Two butlers and two maids serve hors d'oeuvres and the shrimp seem as big as lobsters.

The occasion is a press conference. Eleven of Mary Pickford's feature films and three of her Biograph shorts are being shown at the County Museum of Art. It is only the second time

March 1971

that the films have been shown publicly in the last 35 years.

The recording ends. Buddy Rogers presses the stop button. "And she's a million times better than that. A million times better than that. She's been sick, you know." He adds, gratuitously, "She was 'My Best Girl' in 1927 and she's still my best girl."

Upstairs, in the bedroom she has rarely left since an eye operation—was it two, three, or four years ago? She cannot quite remember—Mary Pickford waits for the journalists to leave. With their marriage 52 years ago, she and Douglas Fairbanks made movie actors socially respectable. Pickfair was a hunting lodge then owned by a Los Angeles banker who made the long journey from Los Angeles to Beverly Hills each weekend to shoot deer, fox, and mountain lion.

Long gone are the days when Mary Pickford and her guests would pack a picnic lunch and ride her horses through the mountains from Pickfair to the Pacific Ocean and pass only one house on the way. Long since departed for a more distant shore is the countess who asked to stay at Pickfair for three days on her way to Hawaii and stayed 11 months and insisted on champagne every morning. Dead, too, is Douglas Fairbanks.

Pickfair, 1971, is a museum surrounded by Beverly Hills. Of the original 15 acres only five remain. On what used to be the vegetable garden, five $70,000 houses have sprouted. The 1807 china that Napoleon gave Josephine is locked behind glass, and the Oriental Room is an attic of frozen mementos from Douglas Fairbanks's and Mary Pickford's 1926 trip around the world— a long corridor of swords and samurai sets and lacquered chests and teacups of deep rich blue. It would take a week to touch each piece of Pickfair's china, each figure of jade, each carved cupid at the bottom of a lamp.

Although more than 100 people were guests at Pickfair at three parties given by Buddy Rogers, none of them saw Mary Pickford. Not even her stepson, Douglas Fairbanks, Jr., who spent the week in the guest cottage. One of the last interviews she gave was in 1965 to Kevin Brownlow, the young English silent film historian. He has tried many times since to see her or talk to her on the telephone. She has always been "unavailable."

In 1971, Buddy Rogers is the master of Pickfair, and Mary Pickford is confined to the bedroom she had built for herself decades ago, with its five windows overlooking "all of Beverly Hills and all of Los Angeles." Buddy Rogers and Matty Kemp —her smiling, jolly business manager—insist that her health does not permit her to see anyone. Several, perhaps prejudiced, Hollywood sources say that it is more; that Buddy Rogers and Matty Kemp consider Mary Pickford and Mary Pickford's films their private domain.

Robert Cushman, a 24-year-old film student who has spent over two years studying her films and who wrote the program notes for the American Film Institute's tribute to Mary Pickford, wonders aloud.

"Miss Pickford loaned me her personal scrapbook and wrote letters to introduce me to people. Her letters to me ask me to come visit her at Pickfair. In one letter, she wrote, 'I've been wanting you to come to Pickfair for so long.' She sent me a beautiful gold watch, engraved, when I graduated from UCLA. But every time I call, her secretary tells me to 'try again some other time.' " So far, in two years of trying, Cushman has not been able to talk to Miss Pickford.

Buddy Rogers—tanned and manicured and topped by a mane of carefully combed white hair—stops his troop of journalists in the hall outside his wife's bedroom. "Darling, all your friends are here." He leans inside for a moment. The reporters at the head of the line hear a soft murmur. For those behind, Rogers interprets. "Give them what? Give them your love? Mary says to give you her love." There are echoes of both Edgar Allan Poe and Edgar Bergen in the performance. The journalists move on, each pausing for a moment to stare at the half-closed door.

Mary Pickford is 78 years old and she does exist. In each of the cities where the retrospective of her films will be shown —San Francisco and Dearborn, Michigan; Brighton, England, and London; Munich, Berlin, Belgrade, and Paris—one journalist will be allowed to telephone Pickfair. To reassure himself and his city of that fact.

Her best hour is from 1:00 to 2:00 p.m. On the day that I call, she is not quite awake at 12:30. I am asked to call back at 2:15.

Her voice is sweet and gentle and very, very old. It brings to the mind's eye lavender sachets and the young girl turning to dust once she has left the protection of Shangri-la in the novel *Lost Horizon.*

"Such a hullabaloo when I wanted to destroy my films. I had more letters telling me not to. Lillian Gish and I had the only argument we ever had. 'Don't you dare do that, Mary. They don't belong to you; they belong to the public. The public will be very upset.' I said, 'Well, time's passing and people will compare me to modern actresses, and I just don't want to do it.' I felt the films had served their purpose and I just wanted to get rid of them and I decided to burn them."

She claims that early in her career she burned a film. "The film was two-thirds finished. I called the director in and I said, 'I want that film burned today.' I thought it was dreadful. So they took it on the back lot and burned it. Everybody was very disturbed, but that didn't stop me." (She remembers the unfinished film as being titled *Secrets,* although it is no relation to the 1933 film by that name in which she starred with Leslie Howard.)

Four or five years ago she allowed herself to be persuaded not to order the films destroyed at the time of her death. So far the Mary Pickford Foundation run by Matty Kemp has spent approximately $200,000 making fine grains and dupe negatives on acetate safety film of 29 of her features and 28 of her Biograph shorts. She has donated 51 more shorts to the Library of Congress, which will preserve and restore them.

Yet she has seen none of her films "for at least twenty years. It made me so sad to look at them, you know. Because so many . . . so many . . . had died. Including my own family. And my friends."

She was always dissatisfied by most of her films. "I can't stand that sticky stuff, you know," she confides in a whisper. "I got so tired of being a Pollyanna. When I was making *Pollyanna,* a fly lit on the tablecloth and I scooped it up and said, 'Do you want to go to heaven, little fly?' And I smashed it. 'Well, now you have, little fly,' I said. And they left it in the picture."

She did not want to make *The Taming of the Shrew,* but Douglas Fairbanks insisted. She brought director Ernst Lubitsch to America to direct her in *Rosita,* but his cynicism and sophistication were incomprehensible to her. She is happy that *Rosita* is now decaying in a vault at Bekins' Storage. Thirty-eight years after her retirement from the screen, she remembers *Suds* (1920) and *Little Lord Fauntleroy* (1921)—in which as a 28-year-old woman she played both 10-year-old Lord Fauntleroy and his mother—and *Secrets* (1933) as her favorites among her films. "I think I wouldn't be embarrassed by *Secrets,* " she says of her last film. "Even now. Even today."

What is amazing is that she does not need to be embarrassed by any of her films. In the darkness of the County Museum of Art's Bing Auditorium, a nine-year-old son of McLuhan's Global Village—weaned on two decades of sadistic Warner Bros. cartoons and presently nurtured on "Love, American Style"— cried at the death of Mary's aunt in *Rebecca of Sunnybrook*

Farm (1917) and giggled with delight at the sight gag that ends *The Hoodlum* (1919). The adult audience at the retrospective echoed both his tears and his laughter.

Mary Pickford's title of "America's Sweetheart" and the subliminal memory of long golden curls conjure up stomach-churning images of honey and treacle and spun sugar candy. In reality, Mary Pickford's screen character was spunky, self-sufficient, headstrong, and mildly wicked. The little girl that she played in so many of her films stole a piece of blackberry pie in retaliation when she was unfairly refused dessert, manipulated more often by temper tantrums than passivity, and was quite likely to strike back with her fists when taunted. Even more surprising, Mary Pickford's acting was restrained and naturalistic.

Even the great director D. W. Griffith could not bully her into the overacting that was fashionable in the early decades of the silent film. She won the second Oscar given by the Academy of Motion Picture Arts and Sciences for Best Actress (for *Coquette,* 1928–1929).

Mary Pickford, Charles Chaplin, and D. W. Griffith were the three most important figures of the silent film era. Mary Pickford's influence on the era is almost indescribable—as is the money she earned from it. In 1914, she was being paid $104,000 a year. In 1919, she, Griffith, Chaplin, and Fairbanks founded United Artists to produce and distribute their own films. By 1923 her income was well over $1 million a year.

She was, quite literally, the first movie star. She supervised every aspect of her films. They were impeccably photographed and directed—by the finest Hollywood cameraman, Charles Rosher, and the best directors of the era, Sidney Franklin, Marshall Neilan, and Maurice Tourneur.

She retired, by her own choice, when she could no longer play little girls and adolescents. In 1965, she told Kevin Brownlow, "I left the screen because I didn't want what happened to Chaplin to happen to me. When he discarded the little tramp, the little tramp turned around and killed him. The little girl made me. I wasn't waiting for the little girl to kill me. I'd already been pigeonholed. I know I'm an artist, and that's not being arrogant, because talent comes from God. I could have done more dramatic performances that [sic] the ones I gave in *Coquette* and *Secrets,* but I was already typed." In 1971, she adds, "I always said I would retire when I couldn't play little girls any more, when I couldn't do what I wanted to."

She cannot remember when she last saw a movie, although Buddy Rogers says he runs current films often in the projection booth at Pickfair. She says, "I think the new pictures are disgusting. Very dirty. I've heard about them."

Nor does she watch much television, although "Buddy bought me a TV and it's wonderful. The color is so good." She looks through her five windows, and she reads. *"The Runner's Bible.* That's my favorite. It's not too hard to read, you know. Now this sounds very snooty, but I like Shakespeare and the Bible." And she misses Hedda Hopper. "I miss her because she and I used to fight. I didn't agree with her but I liked her. We fought in private. Publicly, she was always very sweet to me."

She does not go out any longer because "I had an eye operation. Double cataracts. That was upsetting. More to my nerves than to my eyes." If she did leave Pickfair, she would "not ever want to go back into the studios again. It's depressing. All those big stages empty. It's heartbreaking. I remember when there was nothing but activity and now you go into those black studios and nothing is happening. It's very sad."

There is a long pause and Buddy Rogers is suddenly on the phone. "I don't want her to tire too much, honey. She's doing just great. She's just sensational. But I don't want to tire her, sweet."

It is, quite obviously, time to say goodby.

"Nice to talk to you," Mary Pickford says. "I hope I'll see you."

Mary Pickford died May 29, 1979. Pickfair was sold to Jerry Buss, owner of the Los Angeles Lakers basketball team, for $5,362,000. Buddy Rogers built (and is living in) a small house on the Pickfair grounds.

Cocaine and Hollywood

The high that cocaine gives lasts 20 minutes and costs $20. In Hollywood, where it has been the chic luxury drug for the past six years, a growing number of producers, directors, and, especially, actors are now turning to it as their main energy source —even when they are working.

"I don't know a single major actor between the ages of twenty-four and forty-four, with the exception of Warren Beatty, who is not a coke user," said the owner of a trendy public relations firm. "The actresses use it less because coke is so self-destructive in terms of looks."

"Coke is the ambrosia of the gods," said one unit publicist. The gods to whom he referred are movie stars, and he had worked on two pictures back to back in which the male star carried a heavy coke habit. "Everyone walks in fear around coke. You're not relating on a human level any more. If you ask a question, you never know where the answer will come from or what paranoia or tantrums the question will produce."

"I started using coke in 1975, at the point when it became epidemic in Hollywood," said Hal Ashby, the director of *Shampoo* and *Coming Home*. "I stopped pretty quickly. I was making *Bound for Glory* and I became short-tempered. I'd get cross at Haskell Wexler [the cinematographer who won an Academy

Award nomination for *Bound for Glory*] for things that weren't his fault. It's not my nature to be curt and quick-tempered. I saw what was happening and stopped using it."

Unlike amphetamines, which it most resembles, coke is very subtle; and for better or worse, according to dozens of interviews with people in the industry, the creative decisions on a substantial group of recent motion pictures have been made under the influence of the drug.

The presence of the drug on movie sets is hardly a secret. According to a survey taken by the stunt women's subcommittee of the Women's Committee of the Screen Actors' Guild in the fall of 1982, 22 of 41 stunt women surveyed said they had been offered drugs on a set or location, and nearly 25 said they had worked with someone who was under the influence of drugs. More than a third of the women said they had witnessed drug dealing on a set, and nearly half added that they wouldn't automatically refuse a job simply because someone they had to work with was a heavy drug user.

Al Ebner, the unit publicist on *Close Encounters of the Third Kind,* first became aware there was a drug-related problem on the movie three weeks into the location filming. "I smoke pipe tobacco that isn't available in Wyoming," he said. "I asked for tobacco to be sent to me in the studio pouch. A week or ten days went by and it didn't show up. When I asked why, I was told that the studio was checking everything that went into the pouch because too much dope was being sent." Julia Phillips, the producer of *Close Encounters of the Third Kind,* has admitted that she began to snort coke on that movie and eventually spent more than $1 million on the drug.

Richard Watkins, an adjuster for Lloyds of London, has said the growing use of cocaine during the shooting of films had prompted some insurance companies to change deductibility and exclusion clauses on the Hollywood movies they insure in order to cut losses that they attribute to the drug. "Influenza," he said, was becoming a chronic excuse for actors who stay up all night using coke and are unable to report for work in the morning.

The children of actor Vic Morrow have filed a suit contending that illegal drugs may have been used when a helicopter crashed on July 23, 1982, during the making of a feature film, *The Twilight Zone,* killing Morrow and two Vietnamese children. Don Llorente, an investigator for the National Transportation Safety Board, acknowledged that he was investigating the possibility that cocaine was being used before the crash by people connected with the film but said he had as yet found no evidence of it.

Because cocaine is as illegal in Hollywood as it is elsewhere in the United States, with possession classified as a felony carrying a prison term of up to five years, any examination of its effects on movies must most often be shrouded in pseudonyms and appositives.

The director of an expensive musical that failed at the box office is alleged to have snorted, or ingested, cocaine routinely with his female star in her dressing room. An actor only agreed to do a film on location in Europe after being reassured that his weekly supply of cocaine—seven grams—would be brought to him. A star who has taken to trying to direct and produce his movies is floundering in quarrels and court cases because, according to an acquaintance, "he has shot his brains on coke."

A studio executive said cocaine was often used by "agents pitching properties to studio executives and free-lance producers pitching projects to studio executives." He said the usual procedure was "to snort in the car as you're parking it in the studio lot to get yourself up for the meeting. Meetings in Hollywood tend to last forty minutes, but a snort of coke is only good for twenty minutes. When it wears off, there's always a trip to the bathroom in the middle of the meeting."

The fact that cocaine is often snorted behind the locked

doors of bathrooms has had unexpected consequences. "People joke about the fact that they're embarrassed to go to the bathroom at parties," producer David Geffen said. Another producer said he acquired an unwarranted reputation for being a cocaine user when he had a siege of intestinal problems.

"If I didn't want to work again," a skilled craftsman said, "I would let you use my name." He told of an assistant director who was a conduit for cocaine on his last picture "until he went out of his head and they had to lock him in his hotel room for a few days. . . . The producer was on four or five different things," he added. "Whenever I went to talk to the producer, I didn't know if I was dealing with someone on Valium, someone on bennies, someone who had just been snorting coke, or a rational human being. In the end, most of us were fired from a picture that was hell."

Although articles about cocaine use in Hollywood have focused on glamorous figures such as directors and actors, there is actually endemic drug use among assistant directors, grips, camera operators, and other technical members of a movie crew. It is those technicians who are often said to supply a movie's director or star with drugs. In their survey, the stunt women blamed peer pressure, addiction to drugs, inability "to cope with the daily realities of life," and "boredom on the set" as reasons for the drug taking.

There was almost unanimous agreement among those interviewed that when the people in charge of a movie are heavy users of cocaine, the finished movie shows the effects. "When the director or stars or producer are on cocaine, they seem to have tunnel vision," said one studio vice president who described himself as a recreational user of the drug. "There's a party going on on screen, but the audience isn't invited. You can't enter into the logic of the film. The sin is the mess that results on the screen."

The huge cost overruns on some movies, including *The Blues Brothers* and *Heaven's Gate,* have been attributed in part to delays and the need for retakes caused by participants who were using cocaine. Cocaine use has been reported on a number of recent pictures that critics found incoherent or improvisational, including *Lookin' to Get Out, Goin' South, Under the Rainbow, Dr. Jekyll and Mr. Hyde,* and *Personal Best.* On the other hand, large amounts of cocaine on a set do not necessarily mean a movie will be a critical or commercial flop, as witness *Close Encounters.*

Glenn Jordan, director of *Only When I Laugh,* said he had "once worked with a cameraman who used cocaine. His work was sloppy because he was so hyper he didn't have the patience to refine it," Jordan said. "I don't think it's possible to maintain an important career if you're on coke."

"It's hard to be responsible when you're stoned," one producer said, adding that the director of his last movie was "incoherent because he was so out of his mind on coke. . . . Coke is a serious problem in Hollywood because there's no social pressure against it."

Among those their peers label as heavy users of cocaine are the current head of a major studio and two male stars whose screen personalities epitomize the perplexed, middle-class urban man. Both the latter seemed on the verge of becoming superstars in the early seventies. Instead, they have been dismissed as burned out and are hired only for unimportant movies.

Although the names of Hollywood's big cocaine users—and dealers—are only whispered, there are, of course, some matters of public record. According to the Los Angeles police, Richard Pryor was free-basing—distilling cocaine to its crystalline essence for smoking—when he burst into flame. Burned over the upper half of his body, Pryor survived. John Belushi did not.

He died naked on his motel room floor, said the Los Angeles coroner's office, of a "speedball"—an injection of cocaine and heroin into his veins.

In a number of other cases cocaine has moved from the privacy of being snorted in Beverly Hills living rooms onto police blotters. Producer Robert Evans pleaded guilty to possession of cocaine, although he was 3,000 miles away in California when his brother purchased five ounces of coke for $19,000 from undercover narcotics agents in New York in May 1980. Stan Dragoti, director of *Love at First Bite,* was arrested at the Frankfurt airport in West Germany and admitted his guilt, saying he had been driven to drugs by overwork and by the strain his wife, model Cheryl Tiegs, caused him by her highly publicized love affair with another man. Dragoti spent several weeks in jail, but his 21-month prison sentence was suspended. Evans got a suspended sentence in return for making an anti-drug television program.

Richard Dreyfuss, the Academy Award–winning star of *The Goodbye Girl,* wrapped his Mercedes around a palm tree in Beverly Hills one night in October 1982 and was charged with driving under the influence of drugs after a vial of white powder was found on him.

"I'm very glad I got caught," Dreyfuss said in an interview taped January 25, 1983, for Princeton University's nationally syndicated "American Focus" radio program. "I was certainly in possession of controlled substances. Without getting into anything theological, God turned over a car so I would stop and talk to him for a minute."

After an oblique reference to John Belushi with "Some people are not lucky enough to bottom out correctly," Dreyfuss added, "There's a tremendous fear that drives us and pain we are afraid to face."

Dreyfuss said he had pleaded innocent only so that he could

be placed in a drug diversion program. Early in March 1983, he was assigned to such a program for 24 months.

Actresses Louise Lasser, Linda Blair, Anjelica Huston, Gail Fisher, and Mackenzie Phillips have also been arrested on suspicion of possession of cocaine. In almost every case the arrest was an accidental by-product.

Miss Lasser, television's Mary Hartman, made a scene in a Beverly Hills store and a vial of white powder was allegedly found in her purse. The home of Miss Huston, daughter of director John Huston, was searched by authorities looking for evidence that Roman Polanski had committed statutory rape there. The house of Miss Fisher, best known as secretary to the television detective Mannix, was searched because the telephone company suspected she was using a device to avoid long-distance telephone charges. Eighteen-year-old Miss Phillips of television's "One Day at a Time" was found semiconscious in the street by sheriff's deputies.

Only Linda Blair, who at 13 played the girl possessed by the devil in *The Exorcist*, was deliberately investigated. Accused by the Florida police of being part of a cocaine ring, she eventually pleaded guilty to a misdemeanor—conspiring to possess cocaine. She was fined $5,000 and given three years' probation. One of the requirements of her probation was that she make four public appearances each year, warning young people about drug abuse.

The Anjelica Huston charges were dropped in return for her testimony against Polanski. Miss Lasser, Miss Fisher, and Miss Phillips were allowed to go into drug diversion programs. When such a program is completed, charges against a first offender are dropped. Miss Fisher also pleaded guilty to one of the telephone charges and was given a year's probation. The second charge was dismissed.

The actresses involved can rightfully attribute their arrests to bad luck, since insiders estimate that over half the actors and actresses in Hollywood have tried cocaine at least once.

"Why do I use cocaine?" said one top male movie star. "It was never a question of pressure. It was a question of having a good time. I've never known anyone who said, 'The pressure's intense. Let me have a snort.' If someone gives you drugs in 1968 and it's pleasant, you keep on getting high." Contrary to accounts that stars have easy access to cocaine, the actor said, "You don't get it as part of a deal. That's bullshit. You have to find your own. It can be embarrassing and dangerous, and it's never easy."

Although cocaine is not addictive, it is habit-forming. Its physical effects include a constantly dripping nose and damaged nasal membranes from snorting, one reason that "influenza" has become a common excuse. Two Beverly Hills plastic surgeons are said to do a handsome business in restoring burned-out noses. Belushi, who was on a cocaine, booze, and heroin binge during the last week of his life, exhibited the classic psychological symptoms of a coke freak at a party following a *Cat People* screening three days before he died. "He was hyper, overactive, verbal to the degree that you couldn't shut him up," said one observer. Because cocaine overexcites, most people temper the use of coke with alcohol. "You feel a mixture of being overheated and drunk at the same time," said one agent. The speedball of cocaine and heroin that killed Belushi would have had much the same effect. "The rush of the speedball," said the agent—who has never shot heroin, although he admits to shooting speed in the sixties—"is said to be sensational."

"Cocaine makes people feel good," said Dr. Ronald K. Siegel, a psychopharmacologist who operates a clinic that treats chronic abusers of cocaine. Most of his patients, among whom was Julia Phillips, have moved from snorting cocaine to freebasing, a habit on which, he said, they spend from $2,000 to

$12,000 a week. Dr. Siegel, like other experts, said that most people can use cocaine as a recreational drug without impairing their work or family life. But for most of those who have escalated to free-basing, he added, cocaine is the central focus of their lives. Said one producer, "You wouldn't believe how many changes in top-level jobs and in people's marriages are related to coke."

The drug is available at parties, although not in the gold bowls or generous quantities described in news magazine articles. Actually, said Michael Maslansky, a partner in a Hollywood public relations firm, "Coke is so expensive people turn into Scrooge where it's concerned."

Why aren't more people arrested? "You can't go to one of those big homes and knock on the door and say, 'We hear you're snorting coke inside,' " said Steve Walker, a Los Angeles narcotics detective. "These people don't buy their drugs on the street. They have more sophisticated ways of getting it, like having it delivered in limousines. That's what a lot of these limousine services do."

Five men have just been convicted of selling cocaine from a limousine, much as ice-cream vendors make daily rounds in a suburban housing tract. Lieutenant Frank Bridges of the narcotics unit of the Los Angeles Sheriff's Department said detectives had followed the limousine to the homes of "scores of Hollywood celebrities" in Beverly Hills, Bel-Air, and the hills above the Sunset Strip. "We came within an eyelash of prosecuting several Hollywood biggies," said Lieutenant Bridges, but there just wasn't enough evidence to stand up in court.

Creative artists have, throughout history, used artificial stimulants. Any number of alcoholic actors have given fine performances while besotted. *Kubla Khan* was created by Samuel Taylor Coleridge in an opium dream. Whether the effects of cocaine on heavy users will leach out and destroy the movies they write and direct and in which they act will be answered over the next few years.

Two vignettes:

On a location in the Southwest, the male star, a cokehead, was described by a co-worker as "crazed." The director tried to coax him onto the set because sunlight was precious on that location. The star had a tantrum and refused to work for the rest of the day.

On another location, in the Northeast, the male star was petulant and belligerent. He lashed out at people on the set and retreated to his dressing room to sulk.

Did their films change in adjustment to their drug-induced mental states? The only thing that is certain is that their careers weren't hurt.

"Nobody makes any moral judgments about cocaine because it's so widespread," said Dragoti. "If people are afraid to hire you, it's only because they're afraid you're out of control. After my arrest, I went into health—into tennis, jogging. I had a lot of meetings where people could see I was O.K."

As a final afterthought, he added, "Cocaine is no more widespread in Hollywood than it is in any other rich area, you know. Cocaine tracks affluence."

Ms. Rona:
Don't Call Her a Gossip

The telephone adorns Rona Barrett's ear like an earring. It is as ever-present an ornament as the three gold-and-diamond rings she wears on the carefully manicured fingers that encircle the receiver. It is also her tool and weapon.

"Power and money, Frank. That's your middle name. . . . How do you know I haven't called? I called you at home three times. . . . No, I didn't leave my name with your maid. She wasn't intelligent enough. It would have come out 'Joyce Haber.' I remember when you kissed a—— with her."

There are eight telephone lines into Rona Barrett's cinder-block office in the basement of the ABC studios in Hollywood. On this particular day—a busy one—a couple of assistants are fielding some 120 calls an hour for an average of two per minute. Rona chooses to handle 37 of these calls herself—from talent agents, publicists, producers, and studio presidents. Only rarely does she actually talk with the movie and television stars who

May 1979

are the usual subjects of her two three-and-a-half-minute news broadcasts each day on "Good Morning, America."

"Where did I get that information, Frank? I got it from a little birdie who left it on my Melba toast. At least I can say one thing for you: You've only faked out the exhibitors with your movies once."

Abruptly, the producer on the other end of the line hangs up. Rona is unperturbed. "He's not hanging up on me so much as on my genre."

At 42, Rona Barrett is, incontrovertibly, the mistress of that genre, the principal heir to Hedda Hopper and Louella Parsons not only in her ability to dig up the bones Hollywood has buried but in the bitchy, extravagant way she tosses those bones to the 6 million viewers she numbers as her audience. This talent has made Rona rich. She owns real property worth over $2 million. The three movie magazines that carry her name outsell all others. The best tables at the best restaurants are reserved for her.

If no rosebuds are strewn in Rona's path, everything else is. For a favorable review of a movie, she has been offered a ten-speed bicycle, a color television set, and a mink coat. And George Barrie, the perfume manufacturer cum movie producer, once sent her $1,500 worth of Fabergé for Christmas. Yet as insatiably ambitious as Rona is, her aspirations are for status more than material gain: She will accept nothing she has not earned. When Barrie wouldn't take back the perfume, she tossed it into the arms of her co-workers at the television station. The dozens of bottles of liquor that appear on her doorstep each Christmas are given away with the original tags still on them.

Rona has no illusion that the celebrities who curry her favor are her friends. "I have star acquaintances. I learned fifteen years ago that stars make lousy friends. About 99 percent of them have gutter smarts—and 100 percent are really insecure. The majority come from broken homes or alcoholic parents, and they're more neurotic than the average human being. They have a deep need to be noticed, to be loved, to be approved of. They've discovered that having ten people approve of what they do isn't enough; they need the love of thousands, hundreds of thousands, millions. Only a few of them are solid people. Gregory Peck. John Wayne. Michael Caine. The only thing John Wayne doesn't understand is why he can't keep a relationship going forever with one woman. And the way Caine suffered as a boy—starving and watching the bombs explode in his backyard . . . that somehow made him pull everything together.

"I can pick up the phone and dial the ten major stars and they'll take my call, but they'll step on my guts, too. Several years ago, a world-famous star solicited me, gave me an important piece of information that I wasn't to attribute to him. I checked it out. His information was correct and I used it on the evening television show I was doing at the time. That particular night, this famous star had eighteen people to dinner, and he turned on my program. 'What a bitch that Rona Barrett is,' he told them. 'What a loudmouthed bitch. You'd think she'd have had the decency to call me to confirm that information.' "

Rona gives her trust only to her audience, who, she says without a trace of humor, consider her "a messiah." And she works diligently to please those viewers. At seven sharp each Sunday, Monday, and Tuesday night, she tapes her news and interviews for the following day's "Good Morning, America"; on Wednesday evening, she tapes her Friday film reviews. She speaks of herself as "an ordinary movie fan" and adds that what she likes is most often successful at the box office, while what she hates usually flops. Yet her reviews are surprisingly tough and perceptive. She is proud of having "spoon-fed my audience *Network*. I wanted them to know it was a brilliantly unique film, so I did three or four different reports on it before I hit them with my big review. MGM told me that, more than any other reviewer, I helped make the film a success."

Although Rona considers herself "a commentator, a hard-working reporter," it is an image that would be disputed by many of the studio executives and press agents whose secrets she reveals. "She's simply a glorified gossip columnist," says one Barrett detractor. Another adds tersely, "She's a joke." Still, the executives who laugh at her prefer not to be identified, because, whatever they may think of Rona's intellect and reporting skills, they do not deny her rough and wicked tongue. And many, however grudgingly, respect her. "She's always accurate," says John Friedkin, a former vice president at 20th Century-Fox before moving over to Warner Bros. "When I was at Fox, it once took me ten days to verify an item she'd run about a star being cast in one of their new movies. Turned out she was right." Phil Kriegler, ABC's West Coast public relations vice president, echoes half a dozen other public relations men when he admits that "Rona gives me problems. I'm ready to break a story tomorrow and she announces it today, either because she's a good reporter or has good contacts or both." She recently embarrassed Columbia Pictures by leaking the resignation of its president some sixty days before the intended release date, forcing the red-faced studio to rush out an announcement two months prematurely.

At the moment, Rona is screaming into the telephone because her good contacts have, as happens at least once a week, panicked someone. This time, the warfare is internal. ABC has had several negative phone calls about a Barrett item on Margaret Trudeau delivered on "Good Morning, America," and the producers are worried.

"I'm tired of being called a liar when I'm a good reporter. That story was totally verified and I read it to them. If they back down on it, I'll take them to the cleaners. I never go on the air with a lie. I do my homework, and I won't take the brunt from all those stupid idiots in New York who don't know what they're

doing. . . . What should you tell them? Tell them whatever Rona Barrett says is the truth."

Now it is Rona who slams down the receiver. "They hire you to dig up the news. You dig up the news, and then you get it right up your kazoo. Very sweet. When Farrah Fawcett-Majors left 'Charlie's Angels,' I had the exclusive story that there'd be a fourth Angel and the role would probably go to Cheryl Ladd. That morning, several station owners got up at an affiliates meeting and asked Freddie Silverman [ABC's entertainment *Wunderkind,* who became president of NBC and now runs his own production company] if it was true. Silverman said, 'No. Definitely not.' The head of programming at my own network said a story I had verified was untrue. When I saw him at a banquet that night, I said, 'Would you do that to Barbara Walters? Goddamned right you wouldn't.' He said, 'Well, gee, Rona, I'm sorry, but I didn't get up to watch your broadcast this morning.' "

Being taken lightly rankles Rona. It festers beneath the professionally teased and tinted and shag-cut golden hair, aches behind the eye shadow and lipstick painted on at eight this morning, as every morning, by a Hollywood make-up artist. She reaches up to touch the gold-and-diamond R hanging as a permanent talisman around her neck, a tangible reminder that she is no longer five-year-old Rona Burstein of Queens, New York, wearing a nine-pound brace and limping from a muscle disease that would eventually be misdiagnosed as fatal.

Rona has other talismans: a salary in excess of \$250,000 a year, 27 acres of Los Angeles mountaintop she plans to subdivide, a black-and-tan 1967 Rolls-Royce Silver Shadow with the license plate MS RONA. But none of these can quite erase the memory she harbors of the sausage-shaped Jewish child sprawled helplessly on the sidewalk while half a dozen boys poked and jabbed at her with long sticks. Rona's only defense then was rage. "Someday I'll be so important and so famous none of you will ever be able to touch me again." Now the same acid rage spews out. "When I came to ABC for 'Good Morning, America' four years ago, they had no one like me on the tube. I hoped they'd let me be a female Edward R. Murrow, capable of handling every story. Just a few months later, the network made that deal with Barbara Walters. I got put on the back burner. It was a very, very crushing blow."

By the time Rona Barrett reached "Good Morning, America" in 1975, she had pushed her way from a fan-magazine column (for which she was paid $25 a month) to syndicated columnist for 100 small-town newspapers to a succession of regular spots on local Los Angeles TV news shows to a stint on the nightly news televised by Metromedia stations across the country. "I met her in 1958 when she first came to Hollywood," says Shelly Davis, a press agent turned independent TV packager and probably Rona's best friend. "She was young and eager and unattractive, dumpy and abrasive and pushy. She was a celebrity freak, a girl with a limited outlook who hung like a wart around all those young singers [Bobby Darin, Fabian, Frankie Avalon, Tommy Sands] she pushed in her column. Yet I knew she was special. She's always been tenacious, a stubborn mule, and everything she's done in the last twenty years has been a step up. Physically, she got her nose fixed and restructured her body. Intellectually, she grew. Professionally, she quit the local ABC station because the anchormen didn't show her respect and found herself a better slot with Metromedia. When she resigned from Metromedia, along came 'Good Morning, America.' She always had the mission to make personality news a vital part of journalism. Today, her kind of journalism is copied by *People* and *Us* magazines, and you can't turn on a local news show without seeing a Rona Barrett copycat."

Still, the fan-magazine beginnings cling like tar to Rona's

open-toed shoes and bright red toenails. "I've been called 'Rona Big Mouth,' 'Rona Blabbermouth,' 'ABC's hired gossip,' " she says with a sigh. "But I'm not a gossip columnist. Do I get on television and say Hamilton Jordan doesn't wear underwear? The Washington *Post* reported that, not me. I don't give my audience gossip about underwear. I tell them, exclusively, that Henry Kissinger and Betty Ford signed contracts with NBC.

"For five days during Jimmy Carter's inauguration, I worked so hard in Washington I didn't sleep. I'd go to my hotel from the studio at 5:00 a.m., take a bath, put on my make-up, and go back to broadcast live at seven. But ABC's Washington news bureau treated me like dirt. They wouldn't let me edit my material even when the machines were free. They were angry that the President's son and daughter-in-law preferred to talk to me rather than to them."

To be sure, a few days of watching her staccato performance on "Good Morning, America" makes clear the social distance that separates Rona from the gossip columnists of Hollywood's golden age. They dealt in sexual innuendo: spying on elopements to Las Vegas, announcing—with real or feigned sorrow —that lovely Lana Turner and her second or third or fourth husband had separated, confirming (most shocking of rumors!) that Hedy Lamarr was *enceinte,* and occasionally hinting at which starlet was more than a friend to which male star. Rona rarely peers into anyone's bedroom. Instead, she deals in money, death, and power. She delivers obituaries, reports on foreign funds surreptitiously buying gambling licenses in Las Vegas, covers the bitter lawsuits and countersuits in which Dustin Hoffman has embroiled himself, tells of studios bought and sold and executives made and broken, scoops reporters who were taken in by an announcement saying 13-year-old Brooke Shields was to get $400,000 for her next movie when she makes

her own announcement that in fact a Columbia memo showed
Brooke was to be paid only $250,000.

Much of Rona's material has simply to do with casting and
fiscal news that will appear in the Hollywood trade papers a few
days later. ("One wonders what a farmer in Kansas must think
of her stories about industry finances," says press agent Mike
Maslansky.) Yet even the driest item is delivered in a nervy,
flamboyant, headlong style reminiscent of the late Walter Win-
chell, perhaps the most powerful columnist of the forties (he
was well known for his exposés of show-business and political
figures) and the man after whom Rona has patterned her professional self. It is the style, not the content, that tricks Hollywood into dismissing her as a gossip columnist.

The Barrett style is evident in yet another raging telephone
confrontation with the New York office of "Good Morning,
America" (the topic is still Margaret Trudeau). *"If you call me
a liar, I'll punch you out when I see you. I present you with stories
you say don't click. But you'll do twenty-seven interviews with
Muhammad Ali which all say nothing. Then, when* People *magazine runs my stories, you tell me, 'We have to have them right
away.' The honest thing for you to say is, 'I don't care about
journalism. I'm only in the business of getting ratings.' "*

It is almost 1:00 p.m. and the telephone has left Rona Barrett's ear for no more than 15 minutes since her arrival at the
office three and a half hours earlier. In all that time, she has not
stood up, stretched, or even slumped in her green vinyl desk
chair. She sits rigidly upright, waiting for the phone to ring, her
fierce concentration much like a sprinter's while awaiting the
starter's gun.

"Hello . . . Who am I?" The press agent at the other end
of the line apparently is not sure whom his secretary has dialed.
*"This is Cybill Shepherd. Did you maybe call Rona Barrett?
Here I am in living"*—she looks down at her two-piece dress
—*"blue."* Rona brusquely dismisses the press agent's offer of

an item about his actress client by saying, *"Oh, shoot. You ask her and she'll double-cross me and give that item to the trades first. No thank you!"*

Whatever pride Rona has centers around her being an accurate, tough reporter. "Nobody feeds me press releases the way they feed the trade papers. I find my own news." Even back in high school she was stringing for several Long Island newspapers at $8 per story. "If I were *Ronald* Barrett, people would see me as a hard-hitting reporter. Because I'm a woman, they dismiss me as a gossip columnist. When I broke the story that Princess Margaret was living separately from Anthony Armstrong-Jones and there might be a royal divorce, my bosses said, 'Oh.' When Walter Cronkite reported the same thing eight weeks later, the wire services gave the item banner headlines."

Rona picks up the phone again and dials. This time her voice is soft and wheedling. *"Have you and your lady client split? Is Miss X her alleged new manager? . . . You're relieved? You're thrilled to pieces? I was shocked that she'd leave after seventeen years. You've been her arms, her legs. I love you, but are you going to continue to defend a sad, sick girl? Isn't there anybody in the world who can get her off this crap? Why does she have to be dependent on drugs? One day, one of those suicide attempts of hers is going to be successful."* The woman under discussion is a major television star who has, indeed, left her manager. But Rona decides not to write the whole story. Too many unsavory and hurtful things would have to be said. Each week, she is offered half a dozen tidbits about one star's homosexuality, another's drug habit, a third's 18-year-old mistress. "But I feel what's done in the privacy of a star's home is his business, just as what's done in your home is your business. If they do it in public, that's a whole different ball game."

Swiveling her chair to face the electric typewriter, Rona quickly bangs out an item. There is, she says, "a Rona Barrett rhythm—three lines of passiveness and a fourth line of punch."

And the stories always come out of the typewriter precisely to measure, give or take four seconds of air time. "You know, people imagine me running from set to set and having lunch with Robert Redford and cocktails with Warren Beatty," Rona says, staring down at the Saran-wrapped salad and Styrofoam cup of black coffee her secretary has just placed on her desk. "But I spend eighteen hours a day—mostly in the office—gathering and writing maybe four pieces of information."

It is three o'clock in the afternoon before Rona pushes herself out of her chair for the first time. She gets up awkwardly, her right leg at a peculiar angle, the biceps in her arms compensating for the atrophied leg and thigh muscles. She diverts attention with a choice anecdote about a female reporter known for sleeping with the actors she interviews. The reporter's negative story on director Robert Altman, Rona says, is because "he wouldn't touch her with a ten-foot pole, including his own."

Rona Barrett uses sleight of tongue to brush aside her miserable legacy from Rona Burstein. When she was five, she could climb a staircase only by crawling. When she was nine, she repeated a graceless lurch from sitting to standing position again and again for two noted doctors, then overheard them tell her mother she would be dead in three years. Her problem, they said, was a congenital deteriorating muscle disease. Little Rona screamed that she was not going to die, because "famous people don't die young." At 13, Rona the survivor dragged herself up three flights of subway steps to brazen her way into the job of organizing fan clubs for a singer she had seen at a hotel in the Catskills the summer before—Eddie Fisher. When the receptionist asked her name, she answered, "Rona Barrett," shedding Burstein like a cobra sheds its skin. *Burstein* belonged to the mismated man and woman who had conceived her—the fastidious, nagging mother with the mouth of a fishwife and the passive father who owned a grocery store and longed to make a killing in the stock market.

The dream back then was to marry Eddie Fisher and live happily ever after. Nearly 29 years later, now sitting in dappled sunlight in her Beverly Hills mansion, Rona Barrett smiles at the absurdity of her adolescent fantasy. She doubts there are many happy marriages in Hollywood. "A lot of marriages of older actors seem stable because their wives have nothing to live for except to be Mrs. Movie Star. There's one happy wife of one of our biggest superstars whose whole happy life is a fraud. She and her husband are probably the most unhappy married people I know."

The house in which Rona lives with husband Bill Trowbridge, a land developer who has been married twice before, is in strange contrast to her crude public flamboyance. Here, everything is muted and gentle. The gray wood is bleached and pickled cane. The fabrics are soft—velvets and satins in shades of beige. Pale-apricot flowers accent the sofas. Abstract trees of pale-green moiré climb the walls. "Deep down, Rona *is* gentle," says Trowbridge. "She's a pussycat." Yet he remembers being embarrassed by his relationship with her during the months between June 1973, when they met, and their marriage in September of that same year. "She had this reputation for being a hard, conniving gossip. I kept feeling I had to justify her to my friends. I'd say, 'She's really sweet. You'll really like her.' "

Still, Trowbridge does not deny that part of the Barrett reputation is accurate. "The entertainment business is dog eat dog. You can't succeed by being Ms. Milquetoast. For Rona, the nature of the beast is honesty. She wouldn't compromise herself to the President of the United States. I'm producing my first movie. If Rona doesn't like it, she'll be Miss Negativity to me and lambaste it on 'Good Morning, America.' " That said,

Trowbridge, tall and distinguished-looking, with black mustache and a mane of gray hair, throws his wife a kiss. "I love you, sweetheart."

Rona met Bill Trowbridge after an intensive psychoanalysis enabled her, she says, to discard the sadistic man with whom she had been having a humiliating affair for 11 years. Her 1975 autobiography, *Ms. Rona,* details the sick passion for "an emotional, sexual cannibal" who was being groomed "to become a senator from California . . . he drank the guts of my soul like a vampire drinks blood or a computer drinks information. Then, in the wee hours of the morning, leaving me almost empty, he would take my psychic guts back with him wherever he went." An overwhelming depression brought on by that relationship and a nasty libel suit instituted by a financier, which Metromedia—her employer at the time—forced Rona to settle, culminated in an overdose of pills seven years ago. A month later, with almost unendurable self-contempt for her weakness, she made an appointment to see a psychiatrist.

Rona had always thought that by fighting harder she could overpower every obstacle—from the boys who prodded her with sticks to the high school classmate who beat her out for valedictorian by two tenths of a gradepoint to Eddie Fisher's presumed contempt for her fat body. With the first money she made writing fan-magazine articles, Rona had her nose bobbed and her torso reshaped by massage. When told by a TV executive that she'd never get on national television because of her New York accent, she hired a speech teacher who helped her polish her diction. Yet that near-suicide convinced Rona Barrett that she no longer knew how to fight off the crippled Rona Burstein she had been dragging behind her for 36 years.

However much six months of intensive therapy may have changed the private person, it has not changed the public image. Rona Barrett is still, professionally, the woman of whom Johnny Carson once said, "She doesn't need a steak knife. She cuts her food with her tongue." During the taping of her "Good Morning" segment one Wednesday night, Rona was compulsively and exhibitionistically needling the crew. She carped at a delay by saying, in a poisonously sweet southern accent, "I nevah get a chance to see my husband. He could have died in the Civil War." When a crew member made a mistake, she startled him with a bitchy "Have you impregnated your wife lately?" He muttered, "I get home too late." "I get home too late, too," she said icily. "Have you noticed the pimples on my face?" Yet when one of her staff was seriously injured in an automobile accident, Rona kept the woman on the payroll during the six months it took her to recover. In turn, members of the staff are fanatically loyal to their boss, even though she fires them repeatedly.

Rona is still a self-proclaimed "manic depressive." She is also, says Shelly Davis, who telephones her almost every day, "a lonely person. I think she's more affected by loneliness than anyone I've ever known." She is not, however, lonely in her marriage. "This man has worked out just as good as I thought he would," Rona says of Bill Trowbridge. "Whenever a woman steps out to be bold and brave, she's told she has balls. A woman with balls is a threat to men, unfeminine. Bill gives me a great deal of latitude, a great deal of support." Trowbridge himself claims even to be "proud of the openness of *Ms. Rona.* I couldn't be that forthright," he says of his wife's autobiography.

It is Friday, her day off, but Rona has risen at 6:30 a.m. as usual and, after a cup of black coffee, spent the next hour on the telephone to her sources in London and New York. By nine o'clock, also as usual, she has brushed her teeth, taken her birth-control pill, read the Los Angeles *Times, Variety,* the Hollywood *Reporter, The New York Times,* and the *Wall Street Journal.* She has watched herself on television and eaten two pieces of Melba toast and half a grapefruit cut by her housekeeper to resemble an exotic flower. Now, trim, impeccably coiffed and bejeweled, Rona is sitting in the *lanai* of the Beverly Hills house she has only recently bought and already sold. (From the moment 13 years earlier that she could scrape together a down payment—by using a $2,500 settlement from an auto accident suit—she has bought, remodeled, sold, and bought yet another, and always bigger and more expensive, house.)

Rona is, by some standards, powerful, and, by most, famous. Fame and power have always been the two chief components of her American Dream. "If you became very powerful, no one would dare say a bad word about you. No one could pick on you if you were famous." Life, however, rarely measures up to fantasy. "It's a lot more fun climbing up than it is to be on top. I chose a profession where you can't win for losing. Even if I'm accurate, there's always someone who doesn't want the information out. Whatever I do, somebody will be angry with me. The classic statement about Hollywood success was one that Freddie Prinze's mother made to me. She said, 'Freddie always wanted to be famous, but when he got to be famous, he found it was everything he hated in life.' "

The telephone rings—an invitation to a party. Rona will probably not go. She does not drink, and her hatred of drugs borders on the fanatic. Having buried one of her few close friends—whose life ended in a despairing overdose of sleeping pills—on his fortieth birthday, she says, "Whatever the silliness of an old-time movie star like Mickey Rooney who's been married umpteen times and blown his money, it's wholesome compared to the self-destruction of the young actors today whose escapism is drugs. They're physically destroying their minds."

The telephone invitation reminds Rona of the first Hollywood party she ever attended. She was 23 years old and awed by the movie stars who clustered around the pool. "I learned my initial and most important show-business lesson, and it was taught to me by the late Mike Connolly [gossip columnist of the Hollywood *Reporter*]. The party was given by Louella Parsons and [songwriter] Jimmy McHugh at Louella's house, and everybody was there, including Marilyn Monroe. Louella walked up to one of the bars scattered around the yard, ordered two Scotches, and toddled off. For a minute it looked like she was going to fall in the swimming pool. Nobody laughed. There was a hush over the garden. At this point, Mike turned to me and, pointing to Louella, said, 'Sweetheart, you see that lady over here and you see those people over there. Those people come and go, but that lady and I stay forever.' "

Still driven and discomforted by people who refuse to take her seriously, Rona Barrett left "Good Morning, America" for NBC's "Today" show and found that the grass was equally prickly on the other side. She was, as always, a Hollywood gossip columnist to her new employers. As of September 1982, she is her own employer, the creator and proprietor of "The Barrett Report," a weekly newsletter that analyzes trends in the movie industry. Those studios, magazines, agencies, and Wall Street brokerage firms that want the benefit of her exclusive information must now pay her $1,200 a year for the privilege.

What Price Glory at Columbia

No industry that manufactures dreams can be entirely sane.

This is a Hollywood story—the dismantling of a movie studio through accident and ambition. There is, in this fable of Columbia, an analogy, perhaps, to the unstable land on which it takes place. In earthquake country, there is no margin for safety.

Brigands and buccaneers have always congregated here on this far end of the continent, where there is no place or reason left to hide. There are pirates buttoned into three-piece suits in corporate board rooms everywhere, but their knives are sheathed and their thieveries discreet. The men who successfully spin fantasies into gold and impose their choice of dreams on the world must, of necessity, be a different breed.

The catastrophe began, innocuously enough, with a $10,000 forged check. In an industry where your breakeven point expands, for bookkeeping purposes, with each dollar your movie makes, where one producer charged $60,000 worth of lumber

October 1980

and concrete to his production and built himself a house, $10,-000 is not a memorable sum.

The check, made out to actor Cliff Robertson, was forged by David Begelman, the 56-year-old president of Columbia Pictures. It became the nail for want of which shoe, horse, rider, battle, and war were lost. The power struggle for control of Columbia that followed Begelman's disgrace would sweep from the studio Alan J. Hirschfield, who was then president of Columbia's parent company and Begelman's boss; Daniel Melnick, Begelman's elegant head of production; Robert Cort, then a 30-year-old whiz kid in charge of advertising and publicity; Norman Levy, the sober head of sales who was responsible for getting Columbia movies into the right movie theaters; and Peter Guber, producer of two of the studio's biggest hits, *The Deep* and *Midnight Express*. When they were torn away from Columbia, a hemorrhage of lesser executives would follow, decimating the studio's advertising, publicity, and sales departments.

The pivotal figure in the power struggle was a short, witty, secretive, 64-year-old man—Ray Stark, Columbia's star producer. The head of an independent production company responsible for *Funny Girl, The Way We Were, Murder by Death, Smokey and the Bandit, California Suite,* and *The Electric Horseman,* Stark was unquestionably the winner. The debris of battle—canceled contracts, canceled movies—has been cleared away, and a new team that Stark selected is completely in control. This is the story of how Stark drove out his rivals only to find them crossing the mountains to take control of 20th Century-Fox.

The first question about a forged check came in a telephone call from a Los Angeles police detective to Alan J. Hirschfield, president of Columbia Pictures Industries, late in September 1977. "She said something about a forgery involved in a check issued by our advertising department," Hirschfield says. "No bells went off in my head. I'd had two or three such calls from the police during my years at Columbia. But it did ring a bell with Joe Fischer, our chief financial officer. He had had a discussion with Begelman in June, and Begelman had said a kid in the advertising department illegally issued a check and that it was being taken care of. I told Joe to call David. Then Joe came back into my office and said there was something 'funny' about the conversation. I remember telling him, 'Go to L.A. And you'd better get us a lawyer.' "

When David Begelman picked up the telephone to talk to Joe Fischer, he had already stolen more than $60,000 of company money. Although he admitted nothing to Fischer, he felt, inexplicably, "a sense of relief" when he hung up the phone. He had, he says today, "been living with the dread thing for too long."

At that moment in September 1977, Columbia was in perfect balance. Tottering on the edge of bankruptcy four years earlier, the studio was now poised on the edge of euphoria. The success that summer of *The Deep,* Peter Benchley's glossy potboiler, had kicked the wolf far enough away from the door to allow the studio to wait hopefully for *Close Encounters of the Third Kind* to be released.

Begelman—a charming, talented executive—had refused to sell off half of *Close Encounters,* even when the cost of the movie rose to $20 million and he was pressured by the Columbia board of directors to lay off half the risk. It was a gamble he was prepared to take.

A decade earlier he had been a heavy gambler; he still luxuriated in a high-stakes poker game on Friday afternoons, although he says that gambling had nothing to do with his forgeries and padded expense accounts. The thefts, he would insist, were caused by "emotional problems." Even Hirschfield, who was soon to become Begelman's bitterest antagonist, agrees. "I never thought he needed the money, because he never took enough," Hirschfield says.

Begelman's celluloid gamble paid off. *Close Encounters of the Third Kind* has brought Columbia nearly $150 million in worldwide film rentals.

Begelman, now president of MGM's film company at a salary of $500,000 a year plus perks, has for much of his life delighted in living on the edge. In 1977, on a salary of $300,000 a year, he spent wildly, extravagantly beyond his means. A fleshy, latter-day Jay Gatsby, Begelman invented himself and lived up to the invention. After the initial shock of the scandal, he adjusted sardonically to the pain with gallows humor. Daniel Melnick, who would briefly take his place as president of Columbia, says, "Once we were passing some prop police cars for one of our movies. David stopped and said, 'Oh, my car is here.' "

The balance that would be broken by what Begelman and his friends would forever after call his "aberration" was not financial. It was psychological. David Begelman was the fulcrum on which Columbia rested. On the New York side of him were Herbert A. Allen, the then 38-year-old investment banker who controlled Columbia's board of directors, and 42-year-old Alan Hirschfield. On the Hollywood side were his head of production, Dan Melnick; his head of distribution, Norman Levy; and Ray Stark. When Begelman was abruptly suspended for "unauthorized financial transactions" on October 3, 1977, the war began.

On the eve of Yom Kippur, Ray Stark was summoned by the board and told to come east immediately; he assumed the company was being sold. He met with Hirschfield and Herbert Allen in Allen's apartment at the Carlyle Hotel in New York, and he remembers saying, "You're kidding," when he was told that Begelman had forged a $10,000 check. He offered instantly to put his independent production company in trusteeship and take over the presidency for four or five months "until David is given a proper chance to defend himself." His offer was not accepted.

"I didn't take it as a serious suggestion," Hirschfield says. "The conflict of interest would have been horrendous. I had a life-sized picture of Ray telling our other independent producers what pictures they could or couldn't make. It would have caused complete chaos."

"When I offered to put my company into escrow," scoffs Stark, "Alan told me, 'I'll have to be involved in production.' I realized Alan wanted to be his own president involved in production decisions instead of confining his efforts to corporate and financial decisions."

Stark is one of Columbia's biggest stockholders. His close association with the studio started in 1968 with his production of *Funny Girl.* When Columbia appeared to be on its way to bankruptcy in 1973, he got his friend Herbert Allen of Allen & Company, investment bankers, to take control for $2 a share. "Columbia owed me $4 million or $5 million then," says Stark, who was afraid he would lose his money if the company went bankrupt. "Columbia was in terrible shape," Allen says. "We really came up through a vacuum. The company was not so much controlled by a new group as abandoned by its old group."

Allen describes Stark as "the most important Hollywood producer post–1948." The statement is hyperbole; nonetheless, Stark's record is impressive. In 1979, he was given the Thalberg Award, the highest honor the Academy of Motion Picture Arts and Sciences can bestow on a producer, for his body of work. His films stretch from *Night of the Iguana* and *Reflections in a Golden Eye* to *The Sunshine Boys* and *The Goodbye Girl.* The movies he makes are rarely daring or original, but they are usually intelligent and entertaining. Of the 24 films he has made in the last 12 years, the 18 he did for Columbia have earned that studio grosses close to $250 million.

According to Allen, Stark has never had any "corporate influence" at Columbia, though the company did defer to his judgments about the movie studio. "Ray never took a stand on acquisitions. He's not a king, although he's certainly not a servant," Allen says. It was at Stark's recommendation that the corporation hired his close friend David Begelman—then an extremely important and successful talent agent—as studio president.

Although one observer describes the situation as "Ray controls Herbie Allen and Allen controls the board," Ray Stark continues to insist that he has no power at Columbia. "I can do any picture I want there," he says, "but I can do any picture I want anywhere in town—except at Fox. I resent the word 'power.' There is no such thing as power. There is selling, salesmanship, and influence based on your record."

Stark is an intensely private man. While the marionettes dance on stage, he prefers to stand behind the canvas, pulling strings. He would have been happiest, perhaps, as general manager of a sports franchise, shrewdly wheeling and dealing players. A slight, sandy-haired man, he opens telephone conversations with a conspiratorial whisper: "Are you alone?" If the answer is yes, the litany continues:

"Are you sure?"

"Yes."

"This is just between us."

"Yes."

"Swearzy!"

Inside his immense house, once owned by Humphrey Bogart, individual recessed ceiling lights shine on each Monet, Renoir, Chagall. Outside, a massive, rolling backyard has been turned into a sculpture garden to rival the Museum of Modern

Art's. There are a Giacometti, a superb Magritte, and three
Henry Moores. Socially, he is lionized. His wife, Fran, is the
daughter of the late comedienne Fanny Brice. Even Stark's
detractors refer to her as "a terrific and stylish woman."

Stark now has all the money he will ever need and, periodically, he has gotten more by selling a piece of his Rastar production company to Columbia. One of the most astonishing facts
that surfaced during the Begelman scandal was the sale of
Stark's Rastar Productions Inc. to Columbia three years earlier.
The acquisition had been handled in a legal but highly unusual
manner. It had not been reported to the Securities and Ex-
change Commission or to the public, although Rastar's name
was listed—as the Government requires—among 84 subsidi-
aries of Columbia in the company's annual 10-K reports. Even
Metro-Goldwyn-Mayer, which co-financed and distributed Rastar's *The Goodbye Girl,* had no idea that Rastar was no longer
independent and that the producer's share of the movie's profits
would be going to a rival studio, Columbia. At the time of the
Begelman scandal, Stark said that he owned 100,000 shares of
Columbia stock. In January 1980, he was given another 300,000
or so shares when he sold his Rastar Films Inc. to Columbia.
He now owns approximately 4 percent of Columbia's stock.

His wit is legendary and he is a master of practical jokes.
On the telephone, he impersonates other producers and executives, and he once convinced a reporter that he was Martin
Ransohoff, producer of *Nightwing,* and that all the problems of
that movie were due to a sulky bat. James Bridges, director of
The China Syndrome, says he was called into Begelman's office
one day and berated. But it was Stark playing president from
the depths of Begelman's high-backed swivel chair, while the
real studio president hid in a corner and watched.

Even his enemies describe Stark as "brilliant" and "charming," but the word most often attached to his name is "Byzan-
tine." "If crying is the technique that seems most likely to be

successful, Ray will cry," says one associate. "If being your best friend is the right technique, he'll be your best friend." He giggles a lot and is never quite as happy with a hit movie as he is with a problem picture he can try to save.

His relationships with the artists he hires to direct and act in his movies are rarely smooth. Before Sydney Pollack and Robert Redford would make *The Electric Horseman* for Stark, they insisted on contracts that would keep him from taking away their creative control. Both men felt so battered after *The Way We Were* that they never wanted to work for him again.

"My two experiences with him were quite crazed," says James Bridges, who worked with Stark on two projects that never became movies. "We had such a fight over *Houdini* [one of those projects] that I thought I could never work with him again. But I'm tempted because he gets his hands on the best material, and he's a superb producer."

His relationships with his employees are equally explosive. "No one who's ever worked for him has escaped his generosity," says one ex-employee. But he is also demanding and controlling, and few of his executives stay with him more than two years.

His gifts are compulsive and imaginative. He gives two or three $75 baskets of Italian sausages, lasagne, wine, Italian candy, and homemade pasta a day. After Pauline Kael wrote a particularly nasty review about the Richard Pryor–Bill Cosby segment of *California Suite,* he sent Pryor a chocolate torso with the card saying, "I wanted to give Pauline a bust in the mouth but am giving you one instead." The gifts are a way of communicating, a final period to any conversation. "Every time we had a fight, he'd send me a chocolate heart with 'I love you, Jim' written on it," says Bridges. People who cross his path often, like Neil Simon, with whom he has done half a dozen movies, find themselves drowning in chocolate legs, chocolate hearts, and chocolate telegrams.

Stark himself cannot gracefully accept a gift. When a young actress sent him a token present of figs and dried apricots, he insisted on retaliating with a bigger basket.

His need for secrecy is so all-consuming that flushed into the light he stiffens, like a rabbit paralyzed by the sight of a hunter's gun. Thus, it was tremendously difficult for Stark to offer to become Columbia's president "until David can come back." When Alan Hirschfield refused his offer, it was the beginning of the end between them.

Hirschfield, now chairman of 20th Century-Fox, sits in his office at the studio, alternating between huge cigars and handfuls of nut-and-raisin trail mix and remembering the moment the first psychological wedge was driven between himself and Begelman. "David had assured me there was just one forged check. I discovered there were two more. There was a whole series of deceptions. He played fast and loose with expenses. How do you trust him after that? In a public company, how do you justify it?"

In retrospect, Hirschfield thinks that his "key mistake" was not to fire Begelman immediately. "I suspended him instead because it was the most charitable, human thing to do. I thought if what he'd done wasn't *that* bad we could give him a consulting job. In my wildest dreams, it never occurred to me that he'd come back as an executive. But the suspension gave Stark time to politicize the situation."

When Hirschfield refused to take Begelman back as president, Herbert Allen and Ray Stark were astounded. Hirschfield had been a dutiful Allen & Company employee for nearly 20 years. His father and Charles Allen, Herbie Allen's uncle, had been friends since the 1920s when both were struggling for success on Wall Street. When he graduated from Harvard Business School, Hirschfield had been taken in by the Allens as an investment banker. At first he had been grateful for the opportunities he was given to make money and help run the corporations the Allens purchased. Gradually, however, he had come to feel unappreciated. In particular, he began to chafe at being subordinate to Herbie Allen, who was four years younger, immensely wealthy, and, Hirschfield felt, not nearly as clever or talented in business as he himself was. By February 1978, Herbert Allen would be publicly calling Hirschfield "a man with a reasonable reputation as a hireable $700,000-a-year executive with his own home screening room in Scarsdale." And Hirschfield would retaliate with, "I simply could not buy putting an admitted embezzler back in charge of the two divisions of Columbia which produce more than 60 percent of the company's revenues. The whole business showed a lack of respect for authority, for values, for the company. It was 'public be damned, shareholders be damned, SEC be damned.' It was the Ray Stark version of history."

Why was it so important to Stark to have Begelman back? "Like Richelieu," says Dan Melnick, "Ray doesn't like change. Everything was structured comfortably. David was not Ray's handmaiden; Ray didn't control Columbia. But he did have constant access to the president and he controlled his own destiny there. More significantly, David was his friend."

That friendship was already in the process of breaking up. "Ray cared so much for me," Begelman says today, "that he felt like a member of a family might feel towards someone he loves who has done something god-awful."

Even so, the situation gave Stark a reason to indulge in what Melnick calls "his favorite avocation—vendetta and rapprochement."

Hirschfield reinstated Begelman as president in mid-December. "The board, behind my back, had continued to consult him on every decision," says Hirschfield. "The stock phrase at board meetings was, 'What does David think?' It became a no-win situation. If I didn't take him back, I'd lose my ability to run the company. If I did, I'd lose my morality.

I hoped I could preserve a semblance of order, but, either way, I felt I was a loser."

Hirschfield says that one of his embarrassments was the fact that Stark, although not a Columbia board member, sat in on several board meetings where "fairly confidential information was discussed." Stark also kept reassuring the board that any trouble over the reinstatement "will go away in two weeks."

It didn't. When Begelman was reinstated, Cliff Robertson, whose name had been forged on the $10,000 check, talked to the press. The day after the first article was printed, in the Washington *Post,* Robertson had what he calls "a bizarre forty-minute telephone conversation with Ray Stark in which I doubt if I said five words. Ray asked me to take back my accusation. He asked me if I wanted to be responsible for the man putting the barrel of a gun in his mouth." Robertson recalls that when he was able to break into Stark's torrent of words, he said, "I will not be an accessory."

Six weeks later, on February 6, 1978, Begelman resigned and a new figure took center stage. "The only thing Ray, Herbie, and Alan could agree on was that I was the solution to all their problems," says Melnick. But Melnick—the former head of production at MGM—is adept at swimming in a sea of sharks, and he had no intention of getting his toes bitten off. He refused the Columbia presidency three times and accepted only after being given a contract that, he says, "allowed me to leave virtually at whim"—which meant that if he left, he could convert his presidency into a lucrative independent production deal.

Melnick has always ridden the cutting edge of new Hollywood trends without ever losing his balance or getting blood on his feet. When big dogs became fashionable a few years ago, there was a Great Dane at the end of his leash; an Earl Reibach kinetica pulses on the wall of his living room. *All That Jazz,* his last succès d'estime, is a typical Melnick choice of picture—

glittering, original, far out. So was *Network,* his prestige picture at MGM. But his taste for originality can sour into pretentiousness, as it did in *Nightwing,* an affected horror story about bats, which he initiated at Columbia.

The wallpaper in his bathroom is a geometric design of gold-and-silver foil, and there is a Jacuzzi in his dazzling black projection room. His house, like Ray Stark's, is an art gallery, but his art is modern and restrained—drawings, lithographs, prints of tortured faces. And *his* sculpture garden is primitive, a hillside of Indian totem poles, pre-Colombian statues, and Eskimo carvings.

Melnick's taste in art may be different from Stark's, but there is not so much difference between the two men as either pretends. Both are clever, smart, witty, intelligent, elegant, and manipulative.

What Melnick may not have known is that Columbia's board of directors did not have the confidence in his ability that he thought they did. According to Herbert Allen, "I sent up a list of twenty-five people. In discussions, Melnick was clearly eliminated."

Later, when Melnick was selected, the board looked for someone to bring in over him. The chief candidate was Sy Weintraub, a personal friend of David Begelman's, who had lent Begelman the money to clear up his embezzlement and had then negotiated Begelman's resignation. Options to buy stock were sold to Weintraub.

All spring, while Melnick debated and negotiated becoming president, Hirschfield was in difficulties over the Weintraub appointment. "I felt to put Weintraub on the board was the worst possible move they could make," Hirschfield says. "He was Begelman's surrogate. They couldn't have thought of anything to inflame the situation more. I won that battle, but it was clear I was losing the war. From the end of January through June, every day was a fight. They were pecking away at me; they had decided to get rid of me. They were paranoid that I was trying to mount an attack and take over the company." By the middle of the spring, Hirschfield's only ally on the board was chairman Leo Jaffe, who had been with Columbia for nearly 50 years.

According to Herbert Allen, Hirschfield's explanation is much too simplistic. "Alan had a lack of confidence in the board that was reciprocated," Allen says. "He didn't tell the board he was trying to sell the company."

In mid-December, Hirschfield had had a secret meeting with Sir James Goldsmith, the European food and newspaper tycoon, in an attempt to get Goldsmith to make an offer for the Allens' approximately 1.5 million shares of Columbia stock. The meeting didn't stay secret very long.

"Within five minutes of his meeting with Goldsmith, I was informed," says Herbert Allen. "Then, early in 1978, there were two purely business disagreements between Alan and the board," Allen continues. "Alan wanted to merge with Mattel on a share-for-share basis or to merge with Filmways, giving nine-tenths of a share of Columbia for every share of Filmways. We disagreed with his judgment."

And there were two additional disputes. "After Begelman's departure, salaries jumped astronomically," says Allen. "That disturbed the board." And as finding a replacement for Begelman dragged on for ten weeks, "some of the directors felt an inability on Alan's part to make the key management decisions. Some felt he was simply wavering. Others felt he didn't want to hire anybody to run it because he wanted to run the studio himself."

Melnick accepted the presidency in May. The ax fell on Hirschfield during the Fourth of July weekend. Melnick, who has something of a reputation as a rake, was roused out of bed in St. Tropez with the news that the board had called a meeting to fire Hirschfield. "I left my girlfriend and flew back on the

Concorde to plead for Alan," Melnick says. He was joined at 711 Fifth Avenue, Columbia's corporate headquarters, by 14 or 15 heads of the company's other operating divisions.

The board, says Hirschfield, "threw them a bone." But the reprieve was temporary. He was fired three weeks later. His first reaction, like Begelman's, was "relief to be out of the nightmare."

Hirschfield crushes out his cigar and sighs. "The rumor that I wanted to run a movie studio myself was so ridiculous that I just ignored it. But it wouldn't go away. Ray Stark created that 'Hirschfield-going-Hollywood' myth. He's the kind of person who does take delight in playing with people's lives. This is like a game to him; he gets his kicks from it."

When Dennis Stanfill, Fox's chairman, was in the process of hiring Hirschfield as vice chairman in October 1979, Stark called to protest. Hirschfield lights another cigar and smiles. "Ray should have known that such a call would only have stiffened Dennis's resolve, not discouraged him."

At Columbia, Hirschfield was replaced by Francis T. Vincent, Jr., a buddy of Herbert Allen. "He was a medium-level lawyer at the SEC who had never managed anything and who didn't know the movie business," says one former Columbia executive contemptuously.

Vincent immediately made Begelman's pal Sy Weintraub, who was best known in the industry for having once produced a Tarzan television series, the chairman of a newly invented "Film Entertainment Group," a title that made him Melnick's boss.

Even people who consider Ray Stark responsible for almost everything that has happened at Columbia concede that bringing in Weintraub was not his idea. And, in fact, he helped to ease Weintraub out several months later. But by that time Melnick had resigned.

Melnick had been continually assured by key members of

the board that Weintraub was not going to be brought in as his superior. He reacted to the appointment with rage. He recalls his exact words as, "I won't report to him. I don't respect him, like him, or trust him." He agreed not to resign on the condition that the board "keep Weintraub out of my hair." When Weintraub began to assert his authority, Melnick simply quit and retreated to the profitable independent production deal he had had the foresight to arrange for himself.

It is Melnick, after all, who once defined a Hollywood contract as a document that "lays out the terms by which the parties get a divorce." Looking back, he sums up those months of turmoil by quipping, "I do extraordinarily well under pressure. It's everyday normal life I have trouble with."

Melnick's resignation had two effects. It created an interregnum during which Stark was able to consolidate power. And it made Melnick the focus of Stark's hatred.

"Ray never forgave me for leaving the presidency," Melnick says. "He turned on me for a complex variety of reasons. Leaving was a betrayal of him, of Herbert Allen, of Columbia—since all three are merged in his mind. Ray loves Herbie. His affection for Herbie is genuine. He sees him as a son."

Melnick, who knows the uses of flattery, had knighted three heirs apparent by giving his three top executives the title of president. Pat Williamson was the president of Columbia's international operations, Norman Levy the president of domestic marketing, and Frank Price the president of production. For the first few months after Melnick left the stage, each of the three men ran his own area and reported to corporation president Vincent.

Norman Levy insists that he was comfortable with that arrangement. "It was a wonderful system of checks and balances," he says. "Because the president of a company is usually production-oriented and spends 90 percent of his time in that area, people involved in marketing often have to say and do things to accommodate to certain production requirements. If you report to a man, you must support his deals, even when you think they are wrong. I only got uncomfortable when I learned that Mr. Price was campaigning to sit at the top of the pyramid."

Frank Price had always been campaigning to sit at the top of the pyramid. An extraordinarily successful head of television at Universal, he had given up $3 million in not yet vested stock in order to come to Columbia as Melnick's head of production a few months earlier.

"I was Mr. Clean," he says, "the head of the most successful television outfit in the industry, on the Universal board of directors. I was the image Columbia needed. When I left Universal, I didn't know if I could ever become president of Columbia. But I didn't want to wake up at the age of sixty-five and not have taken that chance to run a movie studio."

A 50-year-old, ruddy-cheeked, steak-and-potatoes man from the Middle West, Price seems out of place in the company he keeps. Dressed in an open-collared, checked sport shirt, he gives an impression of stolidity and ingenuousness. It is hard to imagine him swimming with sharks. Yet it is Frank Price who is the current president of Columbia Pictures.

Early in his Columbia career, Price had started paying Ray Stark the attention smart Columbia executives had always paid Stark. Other executives talk frankly about what was expected. "When I came to Columbia, I was repeatedly told that it was a good idea to call Ray at home, ask his advice, and drop by his office a lot," says Bob Cort, the bright young man Begelman and Hirschfield had hired as head of advertising and publicity. In addition, Price was definitely not a Hirschfield man. He was one of the few Columbia division presidents who had not flown to New York to plead for Hirschfield in July.

Norman Levy did not court Ray Stark. Serious, conservatively dressed, precise, and almost courtly in manner, the 45-

year-old Levy is not a man who likes a lot of fuss. He speaks softly but seems almost to writhe in pain as he whispers, "Mr. Stark expected our relationship to extend beyond the business day. He felt he was entitled to that kind of attention."

Close observers of the intrigues at Columbia believe that Norman Levy would be president of the studio today if he had been willing to curry Stark's favor, which would have meant asking Stark's advice about how to handle other producers' movies. And although Levy doesn't admit to it, most of his associates contend that he would have liked to be president. But he was unable to play the Hollywood game of lining up with the power. Alan Hirschfield had brought him into Columbia; when Hirschfield was thrown out, his loyalty never changed.

"Norman never courted Ray," says Bob Cort. "He simply beautifully distributed Ray's movies."

If Norman Levy is vain about anything, it is about his reputation as a distributor of movies. He has a combination of stubbornness and arrogance about the way he does his job. When the studio was on the verge of bankruptcy in 1974, he held the distribution apparatus together with the chewing gum and baling wire of "picking up" finished pictures for release by Columbia. His choices of *The Lords of Flatbush, Aloha Bobby and Rose, Obsession,* and *You Light Up My Life* helped to keep Columbia afloat for two years. Hardly a penny of Columbia money was invested in those films except the cost of prints and advertising.

"Levy's vaunted reputation for pick-ups is nonsense," Price has said. "Norman even told me that you don't make money on pick-ups. At best, you break even."

"I invite Columbia to allow me to return all my salary and bonuses and take as my share just what the company netted on [the pick-up] *You Light Up My Life,*" Levy retorts.

Producers are always squabbling with studio advertising and sales executives, but the quarrels between Levy and Stark eventually took on a darker tone. In 1977, Stark had disapproved of the Levy-Cort advertising campaign for his hard-edged family film about quarter-horse racing, *Casey's Shadow*. The picture got good reviews but was—unusual for Ray Stark—a failure at the box office. After Stark's complaints, Levy and Cort rereleased the movie with a campaign Stark had chosen. The film was still a failure.

Then, at Christmas 1978, came the great Crest Theater debate. Stark, like many producers, prefers to have his movies play Westwood, the Los Angeles equivalent of New York's East Side in terms of status. As part of a multiple release of *California Suite,* Levy insisted that the movie play just outside Westwood at the Crest. The movie made more than $1 million in the 25 Los Angeles area theaters it played during the holidays, but Stark continued to be angry.

"I felt a lot of my pictures were being used by Norman as locomotives to carry a lot of freight trains," Stark says. "The Crest will play all those pick-ups. Columbia needed that; Rastar didn't. I didn't get the play dates I wanted."

What is important, according to someone close to Stark, is that the squabble over the Crest Theater triggered Stark's feeling that it was intolerable for him not to be able to appeal Levy's decisions. He was particularly nettled because Levy was head of both advertising and distribution, a dual responsibility that is now a common practice in movie studios. "Mr. Stark," says Levy, "felt his position would be stronger if he dealt with two separate entities."

With Ray Stark's backing, Frank Price was named president of Columbia Pictures in March 1979.

"After my initial disappointment," says Levy, "I had no problem reporting to Mr. Price. I didn't imagine I would ever want to leave the company. I was assured that my operation would not be impaired, that my authority would not be undermined. Within three months, it was."

Levy's first suspicion that something was wrong came when he tried to renew Bob Cort's contract in April 1979. "I thought it would be a formality," Levy says. "I literally had to beg to get Bob's option picked up."

Bob Cort is a generation younger than most of the other men in this story. He has curly black hair, large blue eyes, and a Hollywood manner, despite the fact that he was trained at the Wharton School of Business and came late to Hollywood. Cort is a new-style advertising man; he believes in doing sophisticated research on both movies and movie audiences. Stark, on the other hand, is an old-style showman. He responded to Cort's questions about "target audience" and "media plan" with, "Show me an ad, kid." Cocky and abrasive and much too quick-tempered for his own good, Cort didn't even consider deferring to the older man. Their collision was inevitable.

"I was instructed to replace Bob Cort," says Levy. "There was no doubt in my mind his dismissal was prompted by Ray Stark, despite the fact that Bob had contributed heavily to the two best years Columbia ever had. He had just finished the most brilliant campaign of last year—for *The China Syndrome.* I was told that *some* of our producers couldn't 'relate' to him."

Ray Stark denies having any hand in the dismissal of Cort. "He's not really worth talking about because from my standpoint he was never any great help to me since I had my own marketing division. I don't think I had a dozen conversations with him."

"I enjoyed working with Bob Cort," says Michael Douglas, producer of *The China Syndrome.* "The campaign, a difficult one, was done with style and taste."

"I wasn't entirely happy about the campaign for my picture," says Norman Jewison, director and co-producer of . . . *And Justice For All.*

Frank Price has said that he decided to get rid of Cort

because of disappointment over inferior advertising campaigns for . . . *And Justice For All* and *Nightwing.*

To Levy, firing Cort marked the complete ascendancy of Ray Stark at Columbia. "As close as David Begelman was to Ray Stark, that never would have happened," Levy says.

Nonsense, says Stark. "Frank Price is a man who makes his own decisions. I talk with Frank on the same level I talk with David Begelman or any other head of a studio."

Despite Stark's denials, Hollywood reporter Rona Barrett spoke on national television of Ray Stark's "shadow government." Even David Begelman casually defined Columbia as "Ray's barony." Later, when Dan Melnick's protégé, Sherry Lansing, became president of Fox, the wits announced that Alan Hirschfield had appointed Melnick the Ray Stark of 20th Century-Fox.

Stark soon had the power to decide when he would send his films to market, no matter what effect his decisions had on other Columbia movies.

Levy had picked up *When a Stranger Calls,* a low-budget horror movie, from Melvin Simon Productions with a promise to release the movie at Halloween 1979. Stark insisted that his *Skatetown U.S.A.* be moved into that good playing time at the end of October. Levy was unable to honor his promise and had to shift *When a Stranger Calls* to early October.

Stark decided that his *Chapter Two* was good enough to contend for the Academy Awards. The movie was scheduled to be released in February 1980. He had it released at Christmas 1979 instead. But Columbia already had two Christmas pictures, *Kramer vs. Kramer* and *All That Jazz,* which were expected to compete for Academy nominations. Their producers, Stanley Jaffe and Dan Melnick, were furious. Jaffe, whose father, Leo, was chairman of the Columbia board, threatened to quit the studio. (In the summer of 1980, after a ferocious series of fights with Price, he finally did quit, taking his independent production company to Fox.)

"It reached a point," says Levy, "where Mr. Stark was calling the shots on his films. He had carte blanche. He had the right to create his own advertising campaigns and could spend what he wanted. I felt my responsibility was to the company. I had a lot of pictures to release, not just Ray Stark movies."

Stark shakes his head. "I couldn't care less if Norman Levy was at Columbia or not," he says, "although I prefer him at Fox."

Levy, however, felt that Stark was trying to get rid of him. The fact that he had to ask five times before the studio would renew the contract of his other vice president, Ray McCafferty, only reinforced that feeling. Then, after soliciting Levy's recommendations, Price hired a man of whom Levy did not approve to replace Bob Cort. Finally, Levy's power to pick up films for release by Columbia was taken away.

"At that point I knew I didn't want to be part of the continuing Columbia story," Levy says. "I just wanted it to be over as soon as possible, but it had to linger for four or five months. Never having been divorced, I imagine it was much like going through a divorce. You look at the beautiful house you've built and realize you won't live there any more and that you're leaving the kids behind."

There are other people who felt Stark was trying to get rid of them. One of them was the producer Peter Guber.

"I was the Columbia baby," Guber says. "I was twenty-six years old, a punk kid from the East, the first day I walked into Columbia. My pictures—*The Deep, Midnight Express, Thank God It's Friday*—did $130 million in revenue for Columbia. I had never lost a penny for the studio. I enjoyed a good relationship with the management. I thought Ray was my papa. He can be the sweetest man, the most charming to be with. But his involvement with Columbia at the time of my departure was so all-encompassing that it caused one of the most incredible, bizarre episodes of my life. I was run out. The offer I made Columbia would have given me less than what every other studio offered me. They turned it down. Then I had to see if I was being run out, so I offered them *no pictures* for *no money.* They said, 'Well, we have a problem with that.' "

Guber took his Casablanca FilmWorks to an eager Universal. Now, at the age of 36, the chairman of Polygram Pictures, he paces his office in an old football jersey, pouring out the lessons he says Ray Stark taught him.

"I learned you're not in control of anything except yourself. Now, when I'm riding along on the freeway with a trailer truck behind me doing fifty-five and a van in front and two cars going sixty on each side, I think, 'All it takes is one driver to drop a cigarette, fumble for an aspirin, have a heart attack, and it's all over.'

"Ray didn't dislike any of us, you know," he says, with an almost childish bewilderment in his voice. "He was like my father. He sponsored me. He didn't want any other *presence* on the lot, but that doesn't mean he wanted me to be hurt. If I had called the day after I left and said, 'Ray, I'm desperate,' he'd have done almost anything for me, including giving me a couple of hundred thousand dollars."

If Guber is bewildered, he is not bitter. He doubts that he would ever have left Columbia on his own. Being pushed out was "the greatest thing" that ever happened to him financially and emotionally. "I truly love Ray," he says. "I'd do anything he asked me to do. It's just that I can't live with him any more."

Dan Melnick is considerably less emotional about Ray Stark. "Ray turned on me because he didn't want another strong independent producer on the lot, but he's still a charming man with a wonderful sense of humor," he says.

"Danny and I have been friends for a long time," says Stark. "I disagree with a lot of his taste, and he disagrees with a lot of my taste. At Fox, Danny is going to do what he thinks I do, what people accuse me of doing. He wants to be the force there."

Another of Ray Stark's surrogate sons, David Chasman, former vice president at Columbia, adds, "There is more warmth in the rivalry between Stark and Melnick than there is in the friendships they have with other people."

There is, however, no warmth in the relationship between Melnick and Frank Price. The two men live a few blocks away from each other, but Price's house—a two-story Beverly Hills mansion with imposing swimming pool and tennis court—is worth considerably more money. From Melnick's lean, sardonic face, black velour pullover, and the immense abstract painted on the wall of his bedroom to Price's square jaw, plaid shirt, and the immense mural of family photographs sprawled across the wall of his den, nothing about the two men's style or taste is similar.

"Danny is whipped cream, chi-chi," Price says of Melnick. "He likes whatever is in at the moment. Our tastes were completely different. I liked *Kramer vs. Kramer.* He liked *All That Jazz.* He thought *Kramer* was too sentimental."

"When I make a mistake, it's a beaut," Melnick says of his decision to bring Price in as his head of production. "I felt he had no creative abilities, but he did have a reputation for being a good administrator. I thought he would free me to work with the film makers on such movies as *The China Syndrome* and *Kramer.* Price set out to destroy me. He did what he did in order to convince Ray he was Ray's man, not my man. He sat in a booth at Chasen's and told me, 'I think [the psychological horror film] *Altered States* is terrific, but I have to prove to them I'm tough.' "

Whatever strings may have been pulled by Stark, it is Frank Price who made the decisions to abort two of Melnick's pictures

—*All That Jazz* and *Altered States.* Price also turned down a third Melnick movie, *First Family,* and refused to buy him an expensive first novel, *The Four Hundred,* by Stephen Sheppard.

The Four Hundred did not sell even moderately well as a book and was undoubtedly not worth $1 million. *All That Jazz* was nominated for an Academy Award as best picture of the year and has done quite well at the box office. *First Family,* a spoof of life at the White House, was both a critical and box-office disaster. And *Altered States,* about a scientist's obsession with altering his consciousness, got some excellent reviews but was only marginally successful commercially.

Whether Price was right or wrong in his decisions is hardly the question. What is important is that Melnick perceived Price's actions as an attempt to humiliate him.

Humiliation, of course, is relative. In the fall of 1979, Alan Hirschfield was consulting for Warner Communications. Bob Cort had a Columbia independent production deal. Melnick was selling his rejected Columbia packages to Warner Bros. Norman Levy still had the title of head of Columbia distribution. All of them were making lots of money, even if Ray Stark had contained them where they could exert little power.

Ironically, containment was an illusion. Stark won Columbia, but this is a Hollywood story and Hollywood stories have happy endings. In June 1979, Alan Ladd, Jr., had resigned as president of 20th Century-Fox, and in October, Hirschfield took over that studio.* Now Hirschfield had a power base as strong as Stark's. Levy, Cort, Melnick, and Sherry Lansing, formerly a senior vice president at Columbia, followed him. Then—in a surprising show of loyalty—most of Columbia's publicity and advertising executives and half of the sales executives followed Levy to Fox.

*See page 62.

A dozen other top executives left in the turmoil, including Norman Horowitz, president of syndication, and David Chasman.

The people who left have been replaced. And the first fruits of Frank Price's presidency found eager purchasers. There were failures, of course, including *Used Cars, The Competition,* and *Mountain Men.* But his *Blue Lagoon,* a sexy film about teenagers stranded on a desert island, was one of the surprise box-office hits of summer 1980. And in 1981 his *Stir Crazy,* with Richard Pryor and Gene Wilder as two con men who dress up like chickens, sold over $100 million worth of tickets and was the third most successful movie of the year. Columbia's army comedy *Stripes* was in fifth place, and *Seems Like Old Times,* a Ray Stark movie, almost made the top ten box-office successes of the year.

Four years after the telephone rang in David Begelman's Columbia office, most of the players, including Begelman, have new titles and are making more money.

"I keep looking back and telling myself that it wasn't a cure for cancer, it wasn't the hostages in Iran, it was only the movie business," Peter Guber says. "All of us are little boys with big toys. We traded in our electric trains for a changed arena and upped the odds."

"You're looking at a group of men who, for various reasons, have achieved a great deal," says Dan Melnick. "We may be neurotic overachievers, but—God knows—Ray, Alan, Norman, David, and I are very smart. We just have varying values and ethical systems."

Norman Levy laments the destruction of the sales organization he built at Columbia. "It was," he says, "like breaking up a team that just won the pennant. And there was no reason for any of it to happen."

People who know him well have always spoken of Ray Stark's "enormous need for power, enormous need to control."

But Bob Cort puzzles further. "None of the substantive issues between Rastar and Norman Levy were any greater than the normal complexities that arise between partners. Perhaps the conflict itself was, in some way, satisfying to Ray."

Another ex-Columbia executive goes another step down the same road. "Whatever money Ray gained wasn't the object. I don't even think power was the object. Ray genuinely enjoys tumult. So these last years have probably been the happiest years of his life."

In Hollywood, alliances and allegiances are written in sand. Suspicion and envy are the bedrock of an industry that must decide in the summer of 1983 what movies the public will be willing to pay money to see in the summer of 1985. As Alan Ladd, Jr., then president of 20th Century-Fox, once said, "It takes a long time for a movie to go through your system." The novel Kramer vs. Kramer —the story of a child custody fight which was turned into a movie that won the Academy Award as best picture of 1979—was first brought to Columbia by Stanley Jaffe when David Begelman was president of the studio. The scripts were prepared and the movie went into production under Dan Melnick. The movie was edited and marketed under Frank Price.

When people in Hollywood sigh over how very few "good pieces of manpower" there are in the industry, they are lamenting the lack of wizards who can unerringly say No to the wrong—i.e., uncommercial—projects and Yes to the right ones. As president of MGM, David Begelman, whose correct choices had brought Columbia back from the edge of bankruptcy, made a string of disastrous box-office failures. He was fired in July 1982. It is interesting to note that when Begelman embezzled money from Columbia, he was allowed to resign. When his movies didn't make money at MGM, he was fired.

The friendship of Dan Melnick and Alan Hirschfield ended even sooner. When Marvin Davis, the Denver oil magnate, bought 20th Century-Fox in 1981, he was appalled by the lavish amounts of money to which Melnick was entitled. Melnick had signed a contract to bring his independent production company to Fox in 1980. By 1985 he would get $5 million just to cover his overhead. Hirschfield was told to renegotiate Melnick's contract. After months of savage fighting, Melnick left Fox with a $2.5 million settlement.

When Hirschfield came to Fox as vice chairman in the fall of 1979, he was given options on a large number of shares of Fox stock. After Marvin Davis purchased the studio 18 months later, that stock would be worth $2.9 million. In July 1981, Hirschfield won a year-long power struggle with Dennis Stanfill and replaced Stanfill as Fox's chairman. A year later he was fighting to keep his balance against two cronies of Marvin Davis and against Norman Levy. At Fox, Levy—the president of Fox distribution and now vice chairman of the corporation—reversed his situation at Columbia. His power far surpassed the power of the president of production, Sherry Lansing. In December 1982 Miss Lansing resigned to form an independent production company at Paramount with Stanley Jaffe. She was impelled to resign partly because Levy blocked pictures she wanted to make.

Frank Price has also done well. Columbia was so pleased with Price's record of box-office winners that, in the summer of 1981, he was given a new four-year contract worth $10 million. The new contract included 100,000 shares of Columbia stock. When Columbia was sold to Coca-Cola early in 1982 for $750 million, Price's stock brought him another $6 million. Success in Hollywood tends to be cyclical, and 1982 was a mediocre year for Columbia movies. It was Universal—with On Golden Pond and E.T. The Extra-Terrestrial—that topped Hollywood's wheel of fortune in 1982. But Columbia climbed back at Christmas with Tootsie and a Ray Stark movie, The Toy.

As to Ray Stark, his 4 percent of Columbia stock brought him more unnecessary millions when the studio was sold. However, the purchase of Columbia by Coca-Cola diluted his influence. And 1982 was a bitter year for Stark. He had lavished all his energy, all his love, and $50 million making a movie from the Broadway musical comedy Annie. The movie would, he insisted, take in $200 million in film rentals. He wanted, he said, "the producer of Annie" carved on his tombstone. The movie actually did well. Partly as a result of millions of dollars of unrefundable guarantees put up by theater owners, Annie's box-office gross was well over $60 million. But it was perceived as a failure by Hollywood. Because Annie cost so much, Columbia will probably be lucky to break even, without considering the psychological cost. More recently, Gandhi won the 1982 Academy Award as Best Picture for Columbia, and was a surprising box-office success.

As 1982 ended, Melnick had reconciled with Price and was talking deals at Columbia. And David Begelman was president of a small production company that would be releasing its movies through Alan Hirschfield and Norman Levy at Fox.

Two years after *Star Wars* became the most successful movie of all time and brought 20th Century-Fox more than $200 million in film rentals, Alan Ladd, Jr., resigned the studio presidency after a bitter six-month stalemate with the studio's chairman, Dennis Stanfill.

As a result of *Star Wars*—a movie he had convinced the Fox board of directors to allow him to make after Universal and United Artists had turned it down—Ladd became the highest-paid executive in Hollywood history; he earned $1,944,384.92 in salary and incentive bonus in 1978. He resigned in the end because Stanfill refused to allow him to share his bonus with members of his production team. But it was really a contest between the way things are done in Hollywood and the way they are done in more serious corporate worlds.

Ladd is a pleasant but taciturn and emotionally reserved man. He is a stocky, dark-haired version of his lean, blond movie-star father. Called "Laddie," even by the newest of office boys, he is, perhaps more than any other current top executive, in love with movies. "There are only three things in Laddie's life," says Gareth Wigan, his production vice president both at Fox and at his new Ladd Company. "His family, films, and—four months of the year—football. He's seen nearly every film that was ever made. When his cable television went out a year ago because of the floods, in desperation he watched a cassette of *Cleopatra*. He lives with films twenty-four hours a day, I think, because I'm sure he dreams them."

In an industry where nearly everyone is glib—writers must sell the wonders of their scripts to producers, producers must sell the commercial possibilities of their packages to studios, studio executives must sell the artistic advantages of those same projects to stars and directors—Ladd's whisper-soft speech studded with pauses has given him an unearned reputation for being stupid. What sometimes seems almost a childlike groping for words is an emotional, not an intellectual, hesitation.

Dennis Stanfill is an Annapolis graduate, a spit-and-polish financial man who delights in command and believes in lists of regulations. Silver-tongued, with a practiced charm, he was at his imposing best each year when he commanded Fox's annual stockholder meeting. Although he eventually lost a power struggle to Alan Hirschfield and resigned, he can assuage his pain with the $7.5 million he received for his Fox stock when the company was bought by Marvin Davis. Since he left Fox, Stanfill has taken on the job of reorganizing KCET, Los Angeles's badly mismanaged public television station. As chairman of the board, he is accepting no money.

The irrevocable trouble between Ladd and Stanfill began in December 1978, but, says Ladd, "There was always trouble when it came time to set raises. In 1978, the film division had contributed over 70 percent of company revenue and our people weren't getting bonuses equivalent to the money-losing divisions. Every year the television people, who had accomplished nothing except keeping 'M*A*S*H' on the air, got double bonuses. I was supposed to sign a contract for the next three years every December 31. In 1978, I refused to sign."

"Dennis is a businessman-manager in the tradition of the business schools," says Ashley Boone, vice president of marketing under Ladd at Fox. "He feels most comfortable with figures, charts, and graphs. Management by objective—sitting down with your boss and seeing whether you've met your six-month goals—doesn't fit a business that is predicated on human taste. You can't make pictures to fit a formula of 25 percent return of invested capital. If you think a movie will bring you back only 20 percent profit, you shouldn't make it? That's crazy."

When the corporation refused to give what Ladd felt were proper raises and bonuses to fit the magnitude of *Star Wars'* success, Ladd and his two lieutenants—Gareth Wigan and Jay Kanter, who had also profited from *Star Wars*—put their 7 percent raises into a pool for the top members of their production team. Stanfill refused to allow such a challenge to his orderly system.

"The method of reward at Fox as it applied to bonuses was very complex," says Wigan. "Under the system of bonuses in effect in 1977 and 1978 if we had gone home on Labor Day and done no more work for the year, we'd have gotten exactly the same bonus we did. Very few people understood the system, but they felt they didn't have to understand it because they trusted Alan Ladd. So Laddie felt more pressure. A stand had to be made, not the least because the three of us had been very generously rewarded."

Both Stanfill and Ladd expected that the other man would eventually give in. "With hindsight, I can see the egos involved on both sides," says Wigan. "In any quarrel or protracted disagreement, inevitably both protagonists harden their positions. In the end, Fox was prepared to agree to everything on a sort of checklist, but after six months in an atmosphere of total confrontation, it was too late."

"Some people can negotiate forever," says Ladd softly. "But at a certain point I said it was all over. All the rage was going on inside. Two years previously I had gotten so angry at Dennis over a different matter he saw as petty that I put my hand through a wall and was in a cast for eight weeks. To Dennis, it's like people are in his army and he's saying, 'O.K., this platoon go out, and we know you won't come back.' "

Although their contracts still had 18 months to run, Ladd, Wigan, and Kanter were thrown off the Fox lot on June 26, 1979, a little more than two years after *Star Wars* reached movie theaters. "On Tuesday, June 25," says Ladd, "in Stanfill's office, he read off a piece of paper that I must leave by 6:00 p.m. I begged for more time because I had things to do on one of our movies. He said, 'All right, I'll give you until 11:00 a.m. tomorrow.' The date sticks in my memory because it was so degrading. I came in at my usual time, 8:45, and left at 11:00, with nothing but my briefcase."

"I don't know if the decision to order us to leave the lot was a legal concept or deliberate humiliation," says Wigan. "I was in tears. Laddie is more restrained in his emotions, so he suffers more."

"The studio transportation department used to take our cars to be serviced," says Jay Kanter. "I went outside at 11:00 and my car was gone. It spoiled my grand exit."

"I must say I thought I would be back," says Ladd more than two years later. "It was so absurd I thought the board of directors would step in. My fury turned to sadness after I left. You leave a family; you're being abandoned."

More than 22 high-level executives, most of them vice presidents, would leave Fox in Ladd's wake. He arouses fierce feelings of loyalty that are almost unique for a Hollywood executive. A dozen or more former Fox employees, including secretaries, are now at his Ladd Company, which makes some five or six movies a year and releases them through Warner Bros. Ladd Company movies have included *Nightshift, Outland, Blade Runner,* and *Five Days One Summer.* A movie The Ladd Company sponsored, *Chariots of Fire,* won an Academy Award as the best picture of 1981.

"As the weeks go by, you become involved in new things and the pain fades," says Ladd. "But it doesn't completely go away. Any time something happens to a film you left behind—an award, a reissue—the pain comes back."

Jack Nicholson—Odd Man Out

Jack Nicholson is wearing a red terrycloth bathrobe and one red slipper. It is past noon, and he has been up for an hour, but he is not yet really awake. Actor Bruce Dern once told him that he had "only one real weakness as an actor. A lot of days you fake it until 11:oo a.m." Dern's criticism, says Nicholson, is "absolutely true. I beg for the late call."

Rumpled, half-asleep, Nicholson defends against the day and the lost slipper by reaching for a cigarette. On the screen he projects a dangerousness that is surprisingly absent now. The latent hostility of the swordsman in *Carnal Knowledge,* the blatant hostility of Petty Officer Buddusky in *The Last Detail,* the acid angers of Bobby Dupea in *Five Easy Pieces* are nowhere visible. Nicholson's dark brown hair stands up in stiff peaks like well-beaten egg whites, and his ears are slightly pointed. He is more handsome than his screen image and simultaneously less solid, all charm and antic good humor. And, when he smiles, his face seems row upon row of dazzling shark's teeth.

March 1974

He flicks his cigarette ashes into a chrome ashtray, rising like a tulip on its thin chrome stem. All the things in the living room of his hilltop house—from the ashtray to the aluminum-and-smoked-glass Museum of Modern Art coffee table to the massive armchairs of rust and dark blue leather to the hot yellow and bright red Strombotne paintings on the walls—were chosen by Nicholson. Even the two pounds of candy in the heart-shaped box were carefully selected by Nicholson. Offering the box, he names each piece.

What is unexpected is his kindly helpfulness, his grandmotherly air of concern. But this visible Nicholson may be, if not quite an illusion, at least an ephemeral model. "I'm like a linebacker," he says. "I see a hole and I plug it." What he means is that he is quite willing to be a chameleon. "If they want me aggressive, I'll be aggressive."

The house is huge and multifaceted. Nicholson is proud that he "bought it before I could afford it." Beneath the plain, rectangular swimming pool, the canyons plunge away, three mountains melting into a tangle of chaparral and scrub oak and orange vines. Far below is the concrete ribbon surrounding the reservoir where he runs a measured three miles three or four days a week.

Although he started running at the suggestion of Dern—a former, almost Olympic class runner—in order to force himself into alertness early in the day, he is most inclined to do his running at sunset. A night person, he stumbles out to the swimming pool at 8:00 a.m. to throw rocks at the helicopters that, flying over the mountains, disturb his rest. But evenings, when his energy level is high, he puts on a record and dances by himself for half an hour or more, doing the tango to Bach or Beethoven. Now he basks in the midday sun, his feet planted on the cobblestone edge of his dazzling mountains, his face expanding with pleasure like a helium-filled balloon.

In the last five years, Nicholson has been nominated for

three Academy Awards. "The first time [for *Easy Rider*] I thought I would win it, but . . ." He slows down, drawls the words, forcing the naïve, rural undertone that is always latent to the surface. The tone is a comment on his previous state of innocence. "But I didn't have as sharp a view as I do now." The second time, for *Five Easy Pieces,* he expected to lose— "and deservedly lose," he adds—to George C. Scott's *Patton.* His comment on his third nomination, for *The Last Detail*, is that "A nomination for the Academy Award still blows my mind."

Though he is obviously serious, one finds it hard to take the statement at face value. On screen, he is the archetypal alienated hero—the southern lawyer drowning his liberalism in booze and the friendship of two stoned hippies, the musical son of desiccated musical parents who is now shacking up with a waitress and doing manual labor, the womanizer impaling the women with whom he sleeps.

Yet the alienation seems firmly limited to celluloid. A melon-colored felt pig with six piglets sucking at her belly lies on the tan leather couch. There is a pig matchholder, a pig needlepoint, carved baby pigs tumbling at the teats of a wooden mother pig. "When pigs became the symbol of all evil," says Nicholson, "I tended to adopt them."

Active in the McGovern campaign, he was given "a huge book" contrasting the current and past positions of McGovern and Nixon on each issue. "Very methodical," he read and digested the entire book before embarking on his political journey. His voice cracks with anger when he speaks of Nixon's "Operation Intercept," which closed the U.S.A.–Mexican border to the flow of marijuana.

"At that time I said the use of hard measures would skyrocket the use of hard drugs. Almost $50,000 worth of cocaine can go in your pocketbook; $50,000 worth of marijuana goes in a truck. I never saw cocaine before two years ago. Now the

washrooms of the racy urban complexes of our time are filled
with the sounds of harried people sniffing cocaine."

His own drug usage—he once admitted to using marijuana
every day for 15 years—is, he says, "very square. I guess I'd be
called an old pothead. Quite unglamorous. Not into anything
else." He tries, he says, "to be pro-life. All the statistics now say
cigarette smoking is more addicting than heroin, but I'm not
really an authority on anything but my own habits. But I know
it's not good to have laws that make criminals out of a large
proportion of the population."

Right now he is trying to quit smoking. "Two weeks ago I
was down to two cigarettes a day," he says, reaching for his fifth
or sixth cigarette of the morning. "Not being able to eliminate
those last two did me in." He had stopped smoking for ten years
before a role as a private detective in Paramount's *Chinatown*
started him smoking again. He is struggling to stop, "not because cigarettes are going to kill me eventually but because they
eliminate 30 percent of my physical effectiveness at every level
every minute of every day."

As he speaks, he moves closer and closer, demanding eye
contact, defying the territorial imperative, until his face is
barely two inches away. His point made, he recedes, sits back,
his cat on his lap, his black Labrador puppy lying at his feet.

The cat, doglike, licks his face. The puppy wets the rug and
is carried, squealing, from the room. Anjelica Huston, daughter
of director John Huston—the woman who has been sharing
Nicholson's house for nearly a year—kneels on the floor and
rubs at the spot with paper towels and water from a copper
teakettle. Whether Nicholson and "Toots" will someday marry
is, he says, a moot question. He has learned that it doesn't pay
to make pronouncements, "to have policies toward that sort of
thing." He was married once, briefly, to actress Sandra Knight,
and has a ten-year-old daughter, Jennifer, who owns the mother
of the black puppy.

In the bedroom that he now shares with Anjelica, there is a closed leather album containing a photograph of Michelle Phillips, from whom he fled in February 1973 after being painfully involved for nearly two years. He opens the album and looks at the pretty girl in the picture. "For the first time I stayed friends with someone afterwards. We didn't end angry or bored."

He bought the house next door—one of the two houses that share his private canyon—for Michelle to live in "when we wanted to live together but couldn't *live* together." Now the house is occupied by an elderly Spanish housekeeper and by actress Helena Kallianiotes, with whom he has had "a fifteen-year platonic friendship." Kallianiotes, so impressive as the hitchhiker in *Five Easy Pieces* and as Raquel Welch's nemesis in *Kansas City Bomber,* considers Nicholson "one of the three kind men I have ever met."

She has been living in one of Nicholson's guest houses for the last three and a half years, the most permanent but by no means the only guest. (No month passes without three or four houseguests because "I have lots of friends and I like to see lots of them.") "If Jack likes something," says Kallianiotes, "whether it's a person or a lampshade, he'll bring it back."

The people who throng his house tumble from all the cupboards of his past. There are actors met in Italy or France; Millie Perkins, with whom he shared *Ride in the Whirlwind,* the sparse, existential Western he wrote for Roger Corman and Monte Hellman in 1965; his railroad brakeman brother-in-law, Shorty. It was Shorty's wife, his nearly a generation older sister, Lorraine, who shooed him out of the shore town—Neptune, New Jersey—in which he was born and raised. "She told me, 'If you go somewhere and do something, it'll be to your credit. If you stay here, no matter what you do, you'll be little Jackie Nicholson.' "

So he left the back bedroom of the house that served both as his mother's beauty shop and as home, saying goodby to his mother and to the "mysterious, pleasant, snappy dresser, smiley Irishman" alcoholic father who had deserted the family within a year of Nicholson's birth, but who reappeared periodically throughout Nicholson's childhood. In Hollywood but with seemingly no acting ambitions, he worked briefly in the cartoon department at MGM. He drifted equally casually into acting. He did not drift out again.

Kallianiotes calls him "a peasant with aristocratic feet." He smiles that open, amiable, slightly tigerish smile and insists that "the best of the amenities of being a movie star is picking up the checks." There is a Mercedes in the garage but it is there only because "I couldn't keep putting people in the back of the Volkswagen."

The Volkswagen is still there, too, yellow and battered. The Mercedes is "an investment. I was going to get a Chevy. But if I sold the Mercedes now, I would have a profit on all the cars I've bought in my entire life. One must, I guess, understand certain things about the material world." (Nicholson is lucky that other things about the material world no longer need concern him—since he has just lost his wallet for the tenth time in the last six months.)

At the age of 36, he has "total options." Six years ago his horizon was no higher than Hollywood's lower depths—the make-them-in-ten-days-and-shove-them-into-the-theaters-two-months-later world of motorcycle gangs and monsters and current headlines exploited on film. Says producer Roger Corman, for whom Nicholson did nearly a dozen of those exploitation films, "I always did think Jack was a potential star. I used him in leads. But I eventually moved him to smaller parts because nobody else seemed to see him as a star. So I thought maybe my faith was misplaced."

Now he commands up to $500,000 a picture. In return, he gives as much artistic integrity as he can muster. His view of acting is "to please the peer group. If I'm a navy man, I want navy men to say, 'That's the way it is.' " He is "very, very good at changing the way I look." He has become a star despite being willing to burrow deeply enough into his roles to change both his physical appearance and his personality.

"It was an act of integrity for me," he says, his tone both mocking and serious, "to allow those two guys to be cast with me in *The Last Detail.*" He is speaking of 6-foot 2-inch Otis Young and 6-foot 4-inch Randy Quaid, whom he and Young are escorting to naval prison in the film. Nicholson—a moderately broad, 164-pound, 5-foot 10-inch—looked extremely short and rather frail beside the other two men.

In 1973 he casually, without regret, turned down *The Sting,* even though "I liked the project, I liked the period, and I knew it would be commercial. But I wanted to put my energies into a movie that really needed them." The picture into which he chose to put his energies, *The Passenger,* was directed by Michelangelo Antonioni and is filled with Antonioni's despairing sense of loss and pain and uncertain identities.

In the years since he began to have "options," Nicholson has used them to shore up delicate or needy films. He starred in Mike Nichols's black and bitter *Carnal Knowledge,* directed *Drive, He Said,* an interesting commercial and artistic failure, and starred in Bob Rafelson's *The King of Marvin Gardens,* another commercial failure but a fascinating and weirdly unique—although overly talky—film.

For his three months' work on *The King of Marvin Gardens,* he made "nothing, absolutely nothing" except the minimum the Screen Actors' Guild demands that an actor accept. When he asks for large amounts of money, the money usually comes from "a primary up-front gross position. I get paid from the first dollar that comes into the studio. That's the only way anyone involved in a film *should* make a lot of money—by taking a certain risk."

With options has come complexity. There was a recent

moment, caught by Helena Kallianiotes, when "not a drinker, Jack drank a bottle of wine one night and got to feeling silly. As I watched, I saw him eat that day's mail."

Much of his energy is spent "trying to simplify my responses —not to be guilty if I'm late or mad if someone else is late." He holds up a pad thick with telephone messages. He will make sure that he returns every call, gives a reasoned answer to every request. There are few guideposts on the wind-buffeted plateau of stardom. He makes do with one from Thoreau's *Walden.* "There is a story about an Indian making baskets simply because it is worth his while to have made them. That's good enough. You can say a lot of things about my work since I've had options. Not everyone may like the films, but they're not a waste of two hours of your time. Watching them is not having your twine jerked for a couple of hours."

After five nominations, Jack Nicholson finally won his Academy Award, in 1975 for One Flew Over the Cuckoo's Nest. Since then, his career has been almost all downhill, although he was nominated for another Academy Award in 1981 for his portrayal of a brilliant, angry drunkard: Eugene O'Neill, in Reds.

The Missouri Breaks, The Last Tycoon, Goin' South, The Shining, The Postman Always Rings Twice, and The Border were either critical or commercial failures and, most often, both. There are fashions in movie heroes, and Nicholson's shark's grin and implacable hostility—his eternal outsider thumbing his nose at authority—matched the cynicism and hedonism of the Vietnam years. Longevity among movie stars has less to do with talent than with style, and Nicholson's style is now at odds with his audience's desire for safety.

Hollywood's Hot New Screen Writer

A screen writer's tools are simple ones, which may be why Hollywood—intoxicated from the beginning with huge machinery—treats screen writers with an uneven mixture of envy and contempt. A script is the necessary evil, the 125-page, Xeroxed platform on which can be erected those fragmented, triplicated, spliced-together images that are so much more fun.

Lawrence Kasdan's tools are even simpler than most—a pot of sharpened pencils and 15 yellow pads. Lawrence Kasdan is this year's *hot* new screen writer. Sixteen months ago, he was unknown. He burst into Hollywood's consciousness in much the same way and at the same time he moved into public view —with crisp, clever scripts for *The Empire Strikes Back, Raiders of the Lost Ark, Continental Divide,* and especially the sultry, sweaty *Body Heat,* a movie he also directed.

"Half the executives in Hollywood get their news from the media," he says. "There's no research or development. It's a crazy way to do business. The industry works with a small list of writers, a small list of directors, a small list of actors. The fact I've gotten onto that list doesn't make the list less crazy."

He is short and stocky, and his rimless glasses, curly black hair, and thick beard make him look like an overweight rabbinical student. There is something of the seminarian, too, in the way he inches, slowly and with painstaking care, into a conversation. His appearance belies the crackling, slightly askew dialogue that makes his scripts so appealing.

At 33, he is an overnight sensation. Studio heads take meetings with him. Fawning producers invite him to lunch and send him other people's scripts to direct. The only way to "stay sane," he says, is to "divorce" himself from their flattery just as he had to divorce himself from their careless rejections during the seven years before he sold his first script and the 11 years before he became an overnight success.

That Larry Kasdan was talented has been clear for 20 years. In Morgantown, West Virginia, he would "enlighten and liven leaden English classes" according to John Racine, a high school friend whose name Kasdan borrowed for the seedy lawyer led by his lust into murder in *Body Heat.* He chose the University of Michigan, he says, because of the rich undergraduate writing awards it offered—awards previously won by Arthur Miller, David Newman, and John Ciardi. He helped pay for college by winning such awards three years in a row, one year taking first place in both fiction and drama. Two years later, with equal ease, working for an advertising agency, he won a Clio, the equivalent of an Academy Award, for the first television commercial he wrote. (It was a 60-second comedy for West Virginia brand bacon about what to name a new state, the solemn decision being "Bacon.")

What is less clear is why he had the stamina to keep hammering on the seamless wall of indifference with which Hollywood surrounds itself. "I had no alternate plan," he says simply. "There was nothing else I wanted to do except direct movies. To direct, I had to write first. Hollywood was a double-layered fortress. To sell something was hard. To get the script you sold produced was harder. To have a script produced in a way which allowed you to direct the next movie was hardest. I was making good money in advertising. If I hadn't hated it so much, it might have been seductive. I tell young writers to park cars for a living, because they'll never settle for being a car park."

He winds a chain of paper clips around his fingers like a string of prayer beads. Writing was "in the air" during his childhood, "like some families all play tennis." Both his parents had planned to be writers. His mother had even been accepted into Sinclair Lewis's writing program at the University of Wisconsin. But life intervened. His mother raised four children. His father sold television antennas in his brother-in-law's store. He died, a bitter and defeated man, one month after President Kennedy was assassinated. "I was fourteen," says Kasdan. "It was a big jolt to me how little notice the world seemed to take of this second death."

The story of how Kasdan wrote *Continental Divide* in two lunch hours on the grass in front of the Los Angeles County Museum of Art and had 20th Century-Fox, Columbia, MGM, and Universal fighting one another for it is now being elevated into myth. That was in the spring of 1977. It had taken him six scripts and five years even to acquire an agent. The script that finally interested an agent in 1975, "The Bodyguard," was submitted 67 times without selling. An expensive-to-make, historical script about early California had followed "The Bodyguard" into the studio void before he sat down to write a cheap, "makable" contemporary comedy "about two people who love their work and can't reconcile their environments."

It is true, he says, that in two lunch hours he had written and rewritten the entire story about an overweight Chicago columnist and a spunky female ornithologist who fall in love. "It was never that easy before, has never been that easy again. But the story was lacking all the scenes, all the mood of the piece, all the characters except the two main ones, all the dialogue and all the images. A good screenplay has hundreds of images written into it. It was an *idea*. When you have an *idea* for a movie, you have *nothing*. Six months later I had a script."

Sitting in a borrowed office at The Ladd Company, where he wrote "The Return of the Jedi," the third in George Lucas's *Star Wars* trilogy, Kasdan tries to define the essence of writing movie scripts. "I loved all my early scripts and I expected everybody else to love them," he says. "It wasn't until I wrote 'The Bodyguard' and sensed it was different that I realized I was writing an increased level of density. A good script has levels of action going on, unexpected turns. Movies are an economical form. Your script must communicate in the tersest possible way an emotional feeling, imply it in a mosaic of tiny scenes. An unknown screen writer selling a speculative script must deliver a delight. An established writer gets a lot of rope. The producer reads his script and says, 'I don't feel any delight, but he must know what he's doing.' A lot of times he doesn't, and you have a lousy movie."

Another object lesson in screen writing occurred a few months later when Steven Spielberg, who had gotten *Continental Divide* purchased by Universal, and George Lucas commissioned Kasdan to write their *Raiders of the Lost Ark.* The three men sat in a room for two weeks and talked. "We wound up with a one-hundred-page transcript, and I felt the work was pretty well done. Then I read the transcript and realized once more that an outline is not a movie. I had to create order out of chaos, take all the possibilities and choose."

As in any good Hollywood movie, Kasdan's break, when it finally came, tripped on the heels of his moment of deepest despair. "My agent had begun to lose faith in me," he says. "He suggested I write for television. I had a flip answer: 'I already have a job I hate.' At the end of two years, I gave in and said O.K. He took 'The Bodyguard' to 'Starsky and Hutch'; they wouldn't hire me. My agent told me maybe I'd be better off at another agency."

Two weeks later, "The Bodyguard" was optioned by Warner Bros. for $13,000. Kasdan asked for an office. The only one available belonged to Robert Towne, the Academy Award–winning screen writer of *Chinatown*. "That bungalow had originally belonged to Jack Warner," Kasdan says. "The bathroom was done in pink-and-black tile; it had a sauna and a bathtub big enough for six; and all the mirrors were tinted so you had a perpetual deep tan."

He had promised himself that when he sold his first script he would never again write at night or on weekends. "A writing career is like having homework your whole life," he says. "If I wasn't writing, I felt guilty. I had a marriage that worked, a son I loved, and a job that paid good money. Being utterly miserable and constantly depressed began to seem tinny even to me. But when you do something you despise for five years, you get contemptuous of yourself. Who's making you? You're killing time you'll never get back." The measure of his despair is that "I refused to bring a second child into a world in which I was working in advertising."

On a sun-drenched Sunday afternoon, beneath two immense eucalyptus trees at the edge of his 40-foot swimming pool, he is no longer the shaggy writer in a shapeless pullover. He seems thinner, neatly trimmed, basking in his two sons and the pleasures of suburbia, the "kind and gentle husband and father" that Meg, his wife of 11 years, calls "perfect."

What has astonished most critics—even those who felt that *Body Heat* simply recycled the 1940s film noir—was Kasdan's assurance as a director. Why be surprised, he wonders. "Screen writers make their movies in their heads. They visualize every scene. By the time you begin to direct the film, you've already done it once. Another director can shoot the movie you wrote word for word, but if the tone is different, the whole movie is not what you intended." *Continental Divide,* with John Belushi and an English director, Michael Apted, was faithful to Kasdan's script but an entirely different movie from the one in his head.

Body Heat is so carefully written that by the time the film is over there are no loose ends, no unanswered questions. "Larry thinks things through," says George Lucas, who hired him to finish the script for *The Empire Strikes Back* after the death of Leigh Brackett, the original screen writer, even though he had not yet read Kasdan's screenplay for *Raiders of the Lost Ark.* "It's amazing how many scripts aren't plausible. I could tell about Larry because of his sensitivity toward things, the alternatives he suggested in story conferences. But his real strengths as a writer are his characters, his ability to develop satisfying human relationships."

In *Body Heat,* Kasdan says, he used the conventions of film noir to scrutinize a spoiled generation "who believed that the world was ours" and then petulantly discovered it wasn't. The bravest thing he did, Kasdan feels, was "having the nerve to make an extremely stylized picture. I was willing to sacrifice realism for mood."

Kasdan has been accused by some critics of being a facile writer who spews out old movie genres—retreading *Double Indemnity* and *The Postman Always Rings Twice* in *Body Heat* and Tracy and Hepburn in *Continental Divide.* "The irony," says his friend, the producer Michael Shamberg, "is that people see Larry's work and think he's the most meretricious guy in the world. But he took the film noir form and put in contemporary characters. He doesn't have any obsession about old movies."

What he does have, according to all the people who know

him well, is what John Racine calls "an insatiable curiosity about other people's lives. He'll know you better in half an hour than you'll know him in a month," says Racine. He also has, says Shamberg, "a tension between ambition and integrity. He knew he would get recognition from *Body Heat* and he wanted it, but he had already responded to it in his head before the movie came out so he wouldn't be changed by it."

"Integrity is a luxury not available to the poor," says Daniel Melnick, the producer of *All That Jazz* and the current and third owner of "The Bodyguard." "If their producer says of a scene, 'I want it blue,' most writers say, 'Blue's my favorite color.' Larry doesn't give in like that."

Kasdan is mildly amused and mildly annoyed that he has also already been accused of copying himself in *Continental Divide* because the sexually tinged scene where Blair Brown kisses John Belushi's wounds duplicates the shipboard scene where Karen Allen kisses Harrison Ford's wounds in *Raiders of the Lost Ark.* "But I didn't write the scene in *Raiders,*" he says. "Spielberg took the idea from the *Continental Divide* script."

Kasdan was an English major, not a film school student. He even got a B.A. in education before discovering there were no jobs for high school English teachers in Michigan. Although he overdosed on *The Great Escape, The Seven Samurai,* and *Gunfight at the O.K. Corral* during his West Virginia childhood, he thinks that Roberto Clemente, "the greatest right fielder who ever lived," was a far greater influence on him. "Clemente's grace and confidence and approach to life shaped my attitudes. Working in Hollywood, because the stakes are so high, you can get involved in deals, career moves, and projects and forget the real world, never remember to ask yourself, 'What is the environment my kids are growing up in? What is the state of their nation?'

"Lots and lots of people in Hollywood are simply trying to

impose their fantasies on everyone else, prove that they are great artists or producers or know what will make money. Whoever's fantasy is strongest wins. So you'll see a producer control one meeting and then go into another meeting and completely deflate in the face of a stronger fantasy."

What is "adding confusion to his already confused life," Kasdan says, "is deciding what I want to give my time to now. For so many years I was simply striving to get in." With *Jedi* as with *The Empire Strikes Back,* he was simply "at the service of George Lucas, trying to fulfill George's grand design." After *Jedi* came an attempt to fulfill his own design. He is directing *The Big Chill,* a "biting comedy" he co-wrote which stars William Hurt and Kevin Kline. The title refers to the difficulties of being grownup.

Holding his two-year-old son in one arm and a plastic bag of garbage in the other, he has one last thought. "If your work is going to draw from life, you'd better work very hard to keep up with reality."

Jessica Lange—Film Star Whose Future Is Here

The Christmas tree is small and temporary, decorated with only a half-dozen white angels with golden wings. Jessica Lange will be going home for Christmas, and this red rented house in a California canyon is temporary, too.

What is not temporary is Jessica Lange's career as a movie star. Directors and producers who ridiculed Jessica Lange four years ago are "developing projects" for her now, the result of two extraordinary performances that have just reached movie theaters—her wayward, headstrong, doomed movie actress Frances Farmer in *Frances* and her soft, submissive, casually sensual foil to Dustin Hoffman in *Tootsie.*

At the age of 33, she is near the top of the movie industry's short list of female stars; probably her only competition for roles now, as well as for the 1982 Academy Award as best actress, is Meryl Streep.

At Christmas six years ago, things were different. In December 1976, she was the plaything of *King Kong,* as disposable

December 1982

a bauble as any of the angels on her tree. Pretty models with golden hair who can squeal on cue are plentiful in Southern California.

"I was so incredibly naïve about what was business and what was caring in Hollywood," she recalls. "It turns out it was all business. *King Kong* took one year, including a six-week publicity tour around the world. I was doing twelve or fourteen interviews a day. And then it was over, and I was all alone at the Pierre Hotel in New York, and everybody had gone and left me. It was finished. I got my lesson in the expendability of the human spirit in Hollywood."

Her hair, damp from a 90-minute workout at a gym, curls into ringlets; her ski sweater is smeared with banana. She is extraordinarily luminous, as cherry-red and milk-white as an illustration in a fairy tale. If she doesn't have it all now, she certainly has quite a lot—beauty, talent, fame, and a 21-month-old daughter. The baby climbs the mountain of her lap. A kitten, rescued from the pound a few days earlier, burrows into the pillows at her shoulder.

"I didn't get another part for two years after *King Kong,*" Miss Lange says. "I decided to go back to New York and pick up where Hollywood had interrupted me. I had a contract with Dino De Laurentiis, and he paid me a salary so I didn't have to support myself as a waitress any more."

Two years before *King Kong* she had sat in an acting class and watched fellow students do a scene between a mother and a daughter set in an insane asylum. After a search of movie bookstores, she found the book from which they had excerpted their scene, Frances Farmer's autobiography, *Will There Really Be a Morning?* From then on she talked about the tragedy of a rebellious actress railroaded into a madhouse to any director who would listen. But Bob Fosse, the director friend who revived her career by giving her a small part as the Angel of Death in *All That Jazz* in 1979, wasn't interested in a woman sliding down a self-destructive path she had greased herself. Nor was Bob Rafelson, even after he had cast Miss Lange as the slatternly murderess in his *The Postman Always Rings Twice* in 1981. But Graeme Clifford, the film editor on *Postman* and a man looking for his first picture to direct, was extremely interested.

The real Frances Farmer spent seven years in insane asylums, but Miss Lange's Frances Farmer is totally sane. "She was very high-strung and had overpowering elements in her personality of self-destruction, but she was a real warrior," says Miss Lange admiringly. "It was misguided heroics. There are certain battles that aren't worth fighting, but Frances never let anything slide.

"I was," she adds, "raised with women—a mother, an aunt —who let things slide by. My fear of unpleasant things when I was a child, avoidance at all costs, was so great that if I anticipated an embarrassing moment coming up for a character on a television show, I had to leave the room. That kind of 'I won't say anything' settles in your heart and fills the well of rage. I don't let it happen any more."

What was most amazing about Miss Lange's *Frances* was the extraordinary intelligence with which she endowed her character. Nothing in her previous roles as a voluptuous mannequin, sex-starved or satiated, had prepared for it. In Hollywood, particularly, beauty is expected to be shallow. In real life, languid on an overstuffed couch, she projects the same unexpected tough-mindedness so at odds with her yielding body.

Miss Lange doesn't find the docile young woman she plays in *Tootsie* nearly so admirable as Frances Farmer. "It angers me when I run into women who are totally submissive, completely dependent," she says. "What angers me more are men who like that kind of woman. I'm one hundred eighty degrees opposite. I don't have an ounce of masochism in my pioneer upbringing."

The differences between 1938, when Frances Farmer defied

Hollywood, and 1982, are instructive. Jessica Lange's life-style would not have been tolerated for a minute 40 years ago. She did not, in fact, start divorce proceedings against her husband until she was pregnant with Alexandra, Mikhail Baryshnikov's daughter. Although she and Baryshnikov have been together for six years, they are not married, and they zealously protect their privacy. "We have been physically separated a lot," she says of the dancer. "But we are still together. I'll join him in New York in January."

She and her former husband separated six years ago and were divorced last July. "Northern Minnesota is homogeneous, and I was swept off my feet by this handsome Spaniard I met during my first year of college" is all she says of her marriage.

When Jessica Lange was in high school, she sat on the porch of her parents' home in the smallest of small towns in Minnesota "and saw lawn mowers and heard dogs barking and felt if I had to live there any more it would kill me.

"When I lived in Paris for two years and came back for Christmas, there was a band around my heart, and I prayed, 'Don't make me have to stay here.'" Now she can hardly wait to get home. "The other day I reread my final thesis for high school English, an extensive autobiography I wrote at the height of my rebellion. At the bottom the instructor had written, 'Not all traditions in life should be disregarded.' My most powerful connection is to Minnesota, to that part of the land. I have a certain love for it I have for nothing else. I feel better there than anywhere else in the world. I walked outside today into a warm wind. It reminded me of all those springs, of the winters they followed and the summers that would follow after; and all those yearnings bordered on a sadness."

She realizes it is Alexandra—mouth stuffed with banana, fist reaching for the reluctant cat—who is the bridge. "I've built a log cabin there. I want to give my daughter my same small-town upbringing. How does it work, this thing of mates, partners, male and female? I want a strong marriage, a partnership, more kids, a family, generations caring for generations. I still have my grandparents. At ninety-three and eighty-nine years old, they're still the hub of the family. You know if a car comes down the road it will be family, my aunt bringing vegetables from her garden or my cousin bringing venison."

There is, she says a little ruefully, "a long history of marriage in my family." Her grandparents just celebrated their 71st wedding anniversary. It is only her own casual generation that has brought the first divorces and the first abandonment of the land. None of her parents' brothers or sisters "strayed more than thirty miles."

She has strayed much farther, an interior as well as exterior journey. Today—or tomorrow—she will tuck Alexandra under her arm and go back once more.

Jessica Lange was nominated for two Academy Awards—as Best Actress, for Frances, and Best Supporting Actress, for Tootsie. She was the first performer to be nominated in both acting categories the same year for performances in two different movies since Teresa Wright, in 1942. She won as Best Supporting Actress.

Rating the Ratings

Medium Cool, A Clockwork Orange, Last Tango in Paris, and the Academy Award–winning best picture of 1969, *Midnight Cowboy,* have two things in common. All are serious movies by serious film makers, and all were originally rated X—no one under 17 admitted—by the Classification and Rating Administration.

Times change. "And the rating system moves with the mores of the public," said Jack Valenti, president of the Motion Picture Association of America, the Hollywood trade association that oversees the rating board.

A Clockwork Orange with its mindlessly violent youth gang and *Midnight Cowboy* with its male hustler hero/victim have since been rerated to the less forbidding R (Restricted: children under 17 must be accompanied by parent or guardian). *Medium Cool,* a politically disquieting appraisal of the Democratic National Convention in Chicago in 1968, would probably get a PG (anyone admitted but Parental Guidance suggested) if it was resubmitted today.

Even the X for the erotic *Last Tango in Paris* with its scene of implied sodomy between Marlon Brando and Maria Schneider was challenged. In 1978, *Last Tango in Paris* was resubmitted to the seven-member rating board in Hollywood.

The X rating was upheld, both by the rating board and by a 22-member appeals board in New York.

Hollywood's alphabet soup—G, PG, R, and X—is a 14-year-old, self-imposed rating system designed to stave off any outside censorship of movies. The system's stated goal—"its only job," according to Richard Heffner, rating board chairman —is to serve as "an early warning system for parents. The board is designed to reflect what parents feel is appropriate for their children to see. How do we distinguish between PG and an R? We make an educated guess as to what most parents would feel."

That educated guess gets the ratings administration into hot water at least once a year. In 1980, when *Cruising*—an Al Pacino movie about a psychopathic killer of homosexuals who has sadomasochistic sex with his victims before mutilating them with a bread knife—was rated R, several theater chains refused to play the movie. "If this is an R, then the only X left is hard core," wrote one critic.

At first, Heffner defended *Cruising*'s R rating with, "The question we had to answer was whether every parent of a seventeen-year-old in New York City had to be prohibited from bringing his child to the movie. We didn't think so." A few weeks later, the rating board revoked the rating. In a welter of charges and countercharges between the rating board and Jerry Weintraub and William Friedkin, producer and director of *Cruising,* Heffner alleged that at least three of the crucial changes the rating board had demanded in order to give *Cruising* an R had, in fact, never been made.

In 1981, the furor was over the PG rating for Steven Spielberg's *Raiders of the Lost Ark.* Full of melting skulls, red-hot pokers, a pit teeming with hundreds of writhing asps and cobras, and more than 60 deaths by gun, poison dart, propeller blade, knife, and the wrath of God, *Raiders of the Lost Ark* took in nearly $200 million at American box offices.

"I had a lot of problems with *Raiders,* as did my colleagues," said Heffner. "But we're not here to judge whether a
picture is moral or immoral, pretty or ugly. We ask only one
question: Would most parents feel that kids should not be
allowed to see a particular film unless they are accompanied by
an adult?"

Despite being deliberately bland and nonjudgmental, the
ratings system continually runs into trouble with theater owners and theater patrons who feel it is too lenient—or too restrictive. Two Michigan mothers sued in 1979 because the R rating
of *Animal House* did not allow them to drop their children off
to see the movie. Suing under Michigan's age-discrimination
law, they lost. They appealed and lost again.

The inflexibility of the code's four ratings has come under
attack many times in the last half-dozen years. One often
suggested remedy is to divide the R rating into R–13, no one
under the age of 13 allowed without a parent or adult guardian,
and R–17. Splitting the R rating would allow teen-agers 13 and
over free access to such films as *Animal House* and *Raiders of
the Lost Ark* but would require younger children to come with
their parents.

In 1978 the system was scrutinized because of complaints to
a government committee that the rating board favors major
studios with its PG rating, while dealing the less powerful
independent film makers a harsher R. (Most producers feel that
the less restrictive PG means more money at the box office.
Many don't care because theater owners in big cities tend to
close their eyes when teen-agers buy tickets to R films.)

The House Subcommittee on Special Small Business Problems called such claims groundless but added that the public
was not getting enough information. In particular, the subcommittee felt the rating board should explain to the public the
reasons for its PG's and R's, the two categories that blur into
each other.

"While we found no evidence of discrimination," said Representative Marty Russo, Democrat of Illinois, "we did find that there was a great deal of confusion about how the system works. The big question remains—Why can't the raters explain their ratings?"

"It seems so simple to do," responded Jack Valenti, who left his job as special assistant to President Johnson to become president of the MPAA in 1966. "We could make it R–V for violence, R–S for sex, R–L for language. But how much more would that tell you? What kind of violence? How much sex? Are there a few unacceptable words or is the picture full of them? Or perhaps we could give a one-line description. We did take one hundred pictures and tried to devise one-line reasons for each rating. But describing why becomes pejorative. That scene where a cop hits someone in the stomach with a nightstick may only take up thirty seconds in the film."

Mr. Valenti's solution was to leave such descriptions to the press. Publicly at least, employees and former employees of both the association and the rating board echoed Valenti. Privately, some hint that giving more information would not be as complicated as Valenti thought.

In 1978, when the House subcommittee made its suggestion, theater owners were generally in favor. Motion picture executives were, in general, cautiously unfavorable. Daniel Melnick, then head of production at Columbia, said he was "basically opposed to anything that reinforces any bureaucracy and the rating board is a bureaucracy." Richard Zanuck, head of Zanuck/Brown, was "all for disseminating information" and "yet my instinct tells me that keeping it general is better." Mike Medavoy, head of production at Orion, favored "some form of public knowledge as to what R means—in simple terms."

By August 1982, when the subject was again discussed, at an MPAA meeting, movie studio presidents were still cautious but a bit more inclined to give ratings explanations a try. But there is still the residual caution of someone who has already been burned. To understand this "don't rock the boat" attitude, one must see Hollywood as it has always seen itself—a fragile maiden with the slavering wolf of government censorship chained only a few feet away.

Hollywood has been combating outside censorship for more than 70 years. Because movies started as cheap and not quite respectable entertainment for the lower classes, the Establishment was critical of them as early as 1907, when Chicago passed a censorship ordinance. By the mid-1930s, the Catholic Legion of Decency was able to boycott successfully theaters that played pictures of which it disapproved.

In self-defense, Hollywood in 1930 instituted its own production code, which required movie makers to submit books before they became scripts, scripts before they became films, and films before they were released. Among other things, the Production Code proscribed lustful and open-mouthed kissing, drug addiction, the use of impure love as a subject for comedy, law enforcement officers dying at the hands of criminals on screen, any identification of a brothel, and the use of the words "chippie," "pansy," "S.O.B.," "alley cat," "abortion," "nerts," "hell," "damn," "fanny," and "tomcat."

The system worked well until Otto Preminger refused to remove the words "professional virgin" from his comedy *The Moon Is Blue* in 1953. The movie went out without a production code seal and made money.

"Cardinal Spellman made it an occasion of sin to see the picture," said Arthur Krim, who was chairman of United Artists when that studio released *The Moon Is Blue.* Referring to the then archbishop of New York, Francis Cardinal Spellman, Krim added, "He stood in front of theaters in New York. Unfortunately, he didn't stand in front of theaters in Europe, so the picture didn't do very well there."

Krim's joke is part of the basic truth that American morals

had begun to loosen up. At about the same time, the studios were forced to sell off their theaters by the Justice Department. They no longer had any way of keeping movies out of the marketplace. The Production Code was amended, stretched, reinterpreted, and, finally, abandoned. It is ironic that today, under the new rating system, the inoffensive G awarded to a film suitable for everyone in the family is considered nearly as devastating to a movie's box-office chances as an X rating. *Star Wars* is only one of many films whose producers fought to get a PG in order to entice teen-agers. Several film makers have put a single "Oh, shit" in the mouth of a character to ensure against a G rating.

Although the current rating system tries very hard to be noncontroversial—"We are not censors; we are not concerned with what adults see; we only give guidelines to parents"—it is perceived as heir to many of the sins of its father.

Robert Radnitz, an independent producer *(Sounder),* calls it "an unacceptable form of censorship," while a group of middle-western theater owners censured Heffner for giving a PG rating rather than an R to Radnitz's movie *A Hero Ain't Nothin' but a Sandwich.* The theater owners felt that any film with a four-letter synonym for sexual intercourse should be restricted.

A California film critic, Stephen Farber, who spent six months as a member of the rating board, worries that the board offers pre-censorship because, during his tenure, it often looked at scripts and gave guidance as to possible ratings. Others in Hollywood are unhappy because the board refuses to look at scripts. When *Convoy,* a movie about a war between truckers and police directed by Sam Peckinpah, received an R rating, Ed Sands, president of E.M.I. Films, said, "For independent producers, what rating you get is crucial in an economic sense. The rating administration used to be more free with their advice. Our deal with United Artists said that *Convoy* must bear a PG rating."

Convoy's R was based on the only strict rule followed by the board—that certain harsh sexual expletives get an automatic R rating. The board has no X or R themes. A movie's theme is considered only in the case of a G rating. Certain themes are, by their nature, not considered G.

The automatic R can be reversed on appeal. *All the President's Men* was the first film to have its automatic R repealed. Since then, numerous others, including *The Front, Small Change, The Last Tycoon, A Bridge Too Far, A Hero Ain't Nothin' but a Sandwich, The Grateful Dead,* and *The Last Waltz* have been reclassified on appeal. Since *Convoy's* R was based on one joking expletive, E.M.I. cut the offending word rather than go through the appeals process.

Beyond the automatic language rule, there is only the subjective judgment of the two young men, two middle-aged men, and three women who constitute the current rating board. Heffner, who became chairman in 1974, has shaken up the board, getting rid of elderly men who had served for more than six years and replacing them with younger men and women. In order to keep the board from getting stodgy, he has made three of the positions short term. Among the three members who serve less than two years is one nominated by the Parent-Teacher Association.

In the board's early years, under the chairmanship of psychiatrist Aaron Stern, the board tended to count nipples. There is a perhaps apocryphal story attributed to actor Jack Nicholson that "if you see a nipple, then it's an X. But if someone comes along and cuts it off, then it's an R." Under Heffner, violence is treated harshly.

"Violence that was once comfortably ensconced in a PG is now an R," says Heffner. He speaks of a new climate of opinion, of a sensitization to violence on the part of parents. But the philosophy and sophistication of the members of the rating board also play a part in the ratings, and it is obvious that

Heffner, a Rutgers University professor who was trained as a historian, has little fear of nudity and a relatively low tolerance for violence. "*Barry Lyndon* and *Lies My Father Told Me* had the kind of nudity that had always gotten an R," Heffner said. "But we felt that, in the context of those pictures, parents wouldn't feel their brief nudity deserved an R."

The board rates an average of 400 pictures a year. For the rating service, the maker of each film pays a fee based on the cost of his film and the size of his company. The fee ranges from $800 to $8,000, but it is occasionally waived if a film maker has run out of money. In 1977, 378 films were rated. The G rating was given to 45, PG to 149, R to 160, and X to 24. That year, the PG was applied to, among others, Brigitte Bardot's *And God Created Woman*—considered a steamingly sexy movie when it was first released in 1956.

The 1981 ratings show clear differences. The X category remained essentially the same, 27 of the 336 films rated. But R clearly overpowered PG, 198 to 104. And G movies were almost nonexistent. Only 7 movies got that rating.

If any changes come in the rating system, they will come slowly and softly, creeping in the back door. After all, when the boat is rocked, somebody tumbles into the cold water.

Astaire at 80

On Thursday (May 10, 1979) Fred Astaire will be 80 years old. Although he will still "occasionally get up and move around with some music I hear on television," he has not really danced for almost eight years.

"I don't want to be the oldest performer in captivity. I don't know why anybody should expect a dancer to go on forever. No athletic career goes on forever." His tone is a mixture of irritation at the insult of being 80 and exasperation at a world that chooses to make a fuss about such things.

"I don't want to be a professional octogenarian. I feel very much the same as I have always felt, but I couldn't attempt to do the physical exertion now without being a damn fool. At this age, it's ridiculous. I don't want to look like a little old man dancing out there."

Through 35 years and 30 motion pictures, he looked like what he was—an inimitable artist whom George Balanchine has called "the greatest dancer in the world." He was absolute elegance moving in intricate and surprising ways, with more wit in his feet than most people have in their heads.

May 1979

None of the elegance has been lost to age. With his paisley handkerchief, his matching paisley cravat pinned to the open throat of his yellow shirt, and his yellow cardigan beneath a gray tweed jacket, he looks spiffy. His 5-foot 9-inch frame is slim and natty, with no hint of a potbelly under the belt buckle that matches the buckles on his suede shoes.

He got on so many best-dressed lists, he says, "because I wore a dress suit in so many movies." Yet, he added, "I hated dress suits. I had to change the collar five times an hour because it wilted like a piece of lettuce. Now I only have to wear one at the White House." He made his last visit to the White House in December 1978, to receive a medal. He became— along with Marian Anderson, George Balanchine, Richard Rodgers, and Arthur Rubinstein—a recipient of the first annual Kennedy Center Honors in the Performing Arts. But he is wrong about all those best-dressed lists. No matter what he was wearing, the stylishness with which he wore it would have put him on.

He sits in the massive library of the house he carved out of a Beverly Hills canyon in 1960. The house is a bowl scooped out of the hillside; three weeks ago coyotes killed a fawn in his rose garden. There are six Emmys crowded into a bookshelf on one side of the enormous room. They were won for the Fred Astaire television specials he did in the 1960s. Now he is more likely to watch television than perform on it. He has become addicted to "As the World Turns" and "The Guiding Light." If he misses either of these soap operas, he will telephone his housekeeper to find out what happened.

But he is by no means retired. He wakes, as he always has, at 5:00 a.m. After working a few crossword puzzles, he is likely to spend half the morning writing songs. The task is more difficult since his partner, Tommy Wolf, died. He appears occasionally on television, most notably last spring opposite Helen

Hayes in "The Family Upside Down," as an elderly housepainter trundled off to a convalescent home after he has a heart attack.

To please one of his six grandchildren, he even played a role in "Battlestar Galactica." He turned down a role in *The Hurricane,* because he didn't want to spend three months in Bora-Bora, but he is in negotiation for a possible movie to be made in 1980. He did dance a little in *That's Entertainment, Part 2* in 1976. "Gene Kelly and I were hosts in that movie. I told Gene we can't just stand around and talk or it will look like we have fallen arches and can't move any more. It worked well but it was so very, very strenuous."

He remembers his career as "all foreground." It moves inside his head like a panorama without depth. "It's like it all happened at once," he says. "It must be the same for football players, all the years blending into one big tackle and run. I was always planning or rehearsing or doing new numbers and there was nothing I didn't enjoy when I was doing it. Afterward, when I saw it on the screen and it didn't quite work, I was disappointed with the failure. *Finian's Rainbow* was the biggest disappointment."

The quiet life he lives now is little changed from the quiet life he has always led. He breakfasts on a single boiled egg, keeps his weight at a perpetual 134 pounds, is most often asleep by 10:30. His first and only wife died in 1954, after a marriage of 21 years. When he takes a young lady out, "she kindly drives," he says, joking about his own distaste for driving. He has been forced to drive himself, however, "since my chauffeur died on me, too."

He considers moving to a ranch where he can keep his brood mares. Where the library is crammed with statues and plaques he has won for his dancing, the bar is covered with the bowls and cups such race horses as Triplicate and Don's Music have won for him. On the opposite wall are dozens of aging photographs—Noël Coward, Cole Porter, Jerome Kern, George Gershwin. He throws up his hands in a gesture of anger. "All those people gone!"

His own health has been remarkably good. Except for breaking his wrist when he fell off a skateboard two years ago, "nothing seems to go wrong with me," he says. His mother died two summers ago at the age of 96, her wits intact.

There will be a small party at his house to mark his eightieth birthday—his son, daughter, and stepson and their families, and his older sister, Adele, his first dancing partner. Someone, he suspects, will bring him a cake. There is, in his voice, a warning that he will manage to keep this celebration private, as he has managed to keep most of his life private.

A thin trace of exasperation still in his voice, he says: "All I can really say about it all is that I swear to you I have no regrets. I'm not trying to be modest, but I never thought of myself as number one. I'm cold-blooded about dancing. I wanted to make it good, then make it better. In the end, I didn't want to hear people say, 'He doesn't get around like he used to. Why doesn't he quit?' So I thought, I'll quit when I feel like it, not when someone else tells me to."

Although he has been unfailingly courteous, unwaveringly a gentleman, he is obviously relieved when a reporter is about to leave. He throws back his head and trots beside the car down the steep driveway toward the street below. Or, rather, he dances beside the car, elegantly, impeccably dances.

Since he turned 80 nearly four years ago, Fred Astaire's life has been surprisingly public. He has made another movie, Universal's Ghost Story. He was awarded the American Film Institute's 1981

Life Achievement Medal. *And in June 1980 he married again. His new wife is 38-year-old Robyn Smith, one of the first female jockeys.* "We were friends for ten years before we married," he says. "I married a delightful girl, and I'm a lucky fellow."

The $110,000 Blunder, or The Man Who Couldn't Work Movie Miracles

Barry Jagoda arrived in Hollywood on December 1, 1980, with the screen rights to a novel, $110,000 to spend, and a jaunty confidence that by the end of a year he would be a movie producer.

When the moving vans came on November 30, 1981, to take his furniture back to Washington, he was sadder but wiser. His option on *The Man Who Brought the Dodgers Back to Brooklyn* would expire the next day, along with his year's lease on the wrong house in the wrong neighborhood. The $110,000 was gone, and he was as far from producing a movie as ever.

"This is a story of mistakes," he said.

The intense, 37-year-old Jagoda is not a hayseed with a dream. A 1967 graduate of the Columbia School of Journalism, a former CBS News producer and media adviser to former President Jimmy Carter, he is the proprietor of a small consulting concern in Washington. When he decided to put more than $100,000 of his own money into becoming a movie producer, he had a few friends in Hollywood and the expectation that his White House background would enable him to get his phone calls returned. Before leaving Washington, he called Jack Valenti, president of the Motion Picture Association of America, for advice.

"Get an agent," Valenti said.

"I never understood 'the Culture' of Hollywood," Jagoda said in retrospect. "I never understood the importance of relationships and neighborhoods and agents. There are so many newcomers here, and every one of them has so many Hollywood dreams. How do you discriminate among the dreamers? By the kind of car you drive and the neighborhood you live in and who your agent is."

His first mistake was leasing a four-bedroom house in Oxford Square, an aging neighborhood on the fringes of downtown Los Angeles. "The first question anyone asked me was 'Who's your agent?' The second question was 'Where do you live?' " said Jagoda. "Then they always said, 'Oh.' My lawyer added that he never drove east of La Cienega except to the Music Center, and that was on the freeway. I hadn't realized the importance of living in West Hollywood or Beverly Hills. It was a large house, and David Ritz, the author of *The Man Who Brought the Dodgers Back to Brooklyn,* lived nearby."

His choice of car was luckier. "I leased a Volkswagen convertible, and everybody seemed to admire it, maybe because there aren't too many of them around."

His second mistake was "not really realizing the importance of an agent. For a newcomer, an agent is everything."

He had sent a copy of *The Man Who Brought the Dodgers Back to Brooklyn* to Michael Black, a moderately important agent at ICM, a large and successful talent agency. When he phoned, he got turned down by a secretary with a curt, "We're not interested, Barry."

"In Washington and even New York, when you call somebody on the phone, you're treated with respect," he said. "But the culture here is all first names and rude secretaries. For the first four or five months, I didn't even get in to see anybody. It was all done on the telephone. A few people treated me courteously, and in retrospect I see that as an aberration. Frank Rosenfelt, the chairman of MGM, was a gentleman. Norman Lear called back immediately. Director Dick Donner was polite enough to call us back after reading the screenplay to say that it was a 'charming story' but not for him. While the middle-level people were always rude, the top-level people were often civilized."

Thinking back on the year, he realizes that he wasted the first several months learning elementary things. "We started sending the book around. It wasn't until February that we learned everything in Hollywood works off a screenplay and that we shouldn't have approached anybody before the screenplay was finished."

For $25,000, he had optioned the unpublished *The Man Who Brought the Dodgers Back to Brooklyn,* about two friends who restore Ebbets Field brick by brick. The book was to be published in the spring of 1981, with Simon and Schuster printing 20,000 copies and spending $35,000 on promotion. David Ritz was a former college roommate—and is still a friend, although the relationship has been somewhat strained. His next mistake, Jagoda said ruefully, was hiring Ritz to do the screenplay. "He'd had no experience writing scripts. As an amateur, I needed a well-known screen writer."

He freely admits that Ritz's first screenplay was awful. "I saw the script as a good presentation of the book, but I had no idea what a screenplay was supposed to be. We had fifteen people hot to read it, including Universal and MGM, and all their responses were similar. The script didn't grab you in the first ten minutes, it didn't have three acts, and the characters didn't develop."

He was stuck with Ritz because he had given him the Writers Guild minimum fee of $26,250 for two drafts and a polish; he couldn't afford to hire another writer. Ritz's second draft was, according to everyone who saw it, a "vast improvement." But the property was now somewhat stale and overexposed. Jagoda had shown it to too many people too early. By this time, it was September. The novel had been published without the supposedly promised $35,000 for promotion. It didn't sell well, although it got excellent reviews. Christopher Lehmann-Haupt praised it in *The New York Times* as a "charming novelty."

Jagoda was also in the process of learning that, by Hollywood standards, the novel was not a "commercial" subject. "It's a love story and a story of male bonding," he said, "but, to Hollywood, none of that mattered. To Hollywood, it was 'a sports story.' "

During his early months in Hollywood, he had thought if he could just get the novel and a script to Dustin Hoffman, his hoped-for star, and George Roy Hill, his hoped-for director, everything would be fine. A cynical producer had laughed at him. "If old George is interested, he'll eat you up alive," the producer said. "He'll take over the project. As a matter of fact, anybody will. You have no track record, so I don't know how you expect to get the picture made."

George Roy Hill was not interested, but Jagoda was, he said, strung along by a number of other people: "Jennings Lang at Universal encouraged us to death for six months." Such encouragement didn't translate into a development deal—in which a studio puts up seed money to get a new script written.

Someone influential at Johnny Carson Productions was interested, but he left the company, and the new head of production told Jagoda to make his script for television.

By November, a lot of other people were telling him to make his movie for television, a polite brush-off. But he couldn't. "I had paid too much for the book and the script," he said in frustration, "so the numbers wouldn't work out for television.

"One looks around for a happy ending," Jagoda added, on his way out of town. "But, then, this isn't a movie."

ReCooping: The Rise and Fall and Rise of a Child Star

At the age of eight, Jackie Cooper was nominated for an Academy Award as best actor for *The Champ,* and his salary was $1,300 a week. At 18, he was Joan Crawford's lover. At 28, twice-divorced and washed up in Hollywood, he was trying to carve out a new life on Broadway. At 38, he was a television star. At 48, he had spent five years as a television mogul and was trying to earn his living as a director. At 58, as a successful television director—"I am having fun," he says, "more fun than I've ever had in my life."

His childhood as a movie star, he has made abundantly clear in the autobiography he published in April 1981, was *not* fun. Written with Dick Kleiner, the book, *Please Don't Shoot My Dog,* gets its title from the trick played on him by his grandmother and by Norman Taurog, the director of *Skippy,* the movie that made him a star in 1931. In order to force him to cry for a scene, his dog was dragged off the set by his grandmother and then "shot" by a security guard. Even though the dog was miraculously restored to life after the scene, the boy remained hysterical—vomiting and crying for hours until a doctor was summoned to give him a sedative.

On the screen, Jackie Cooper was "America's Boy," a sturdy little Anglo-Saxon tyke with a pug nose, a firm chin, and tousled blond hair. There was nothing of the sissy in the way he climbed fences, used tough slang, or slugged it out with such screen fathers as Wallace Beery in *The Champ*. In real life, he was the probably illegitimate son of a frail Italian mother and a Jewish father who went out to get cigarettes one day when Jackie was two and never returned. From the time he was three years old, his grandmother, whom he remembers with loathing, pinched, slapped, and pulled him down to the studio gates, where a director might give the two of them $2 and a box lunch for a day's work as an extra. Then, when Jackie became famous, he was too valuable to roller skate, ride a bicycle, or cross the street by himself.

"Later, people tried to rationalize to me that I had gained more than I lost by being a child star," he wrote in the most moving passage in his book. "They talked to me about the money I had made. They cited the exciting things I had done, the people I had met, the career training I had had, all that and much more.

"But no amount of rationalization, no excuses, can make up for what a kid loses—what I lost—when a normal childhood is abandoned for an early movie career. Everybody knows horror stories about stage mothers. I'm talking now about the nonhorror story that, in a sense, is even more horrible. I'm talking about the child who grows up empty and doesn't realize it until it's too late."

The 58-year-old Jackie Cooper has the same square face, the same almost painfully firm handshake, as the little boy who used to spend his weekends on Louis B. Mayer's yacht. But the little-boy face is lined and creased, and perched on the pug nose are gold-rimmed glasses. He has kept his own four children, he says, as far away from the movie business as is possible when you grow up in Beverly Hills:

"The parents of almost every child they knew are divorced and the father is living with a girl twenty-five years his junior or the mother with a man ten years her junior. Barbara and I have been married for twenty-seven years and we lived in the same house for twenty-one years. I didn't want my kids to get a soft job in my business at an early age. I know a lot of drunken doctors and lawyers who are doctors and lawyers because Daddy was one. When my kids graduated from high school, I put a down payment on a car for each of them. Then they took over the payments. They've made their own way, and three of the four are rich in self-esteem."

His own self-esteem came slowly and with pain. "When I was a child, the business ran me. I did whatever Momma, the agent, or Mr. Mayer said. At the same time, adults did what I wanted to do. They spoiled me. To me, 'sharing' and 'friendship' were when people did what I wanted. When I was thirteen, I was having sex two or three times before 9:00 a.m. with the twenty-year-old girl across the street. Joan Crawford wasn't the only older woman I had an affair with. There were half a dozen friends of my mother, bored with their husbands. Before I was eighteen, I was having experiences a man doesn't get in his whole life. It's not good for a child—and an eighteen-year-old is a child—to look around the room and say, 'Not a man in this room knows what I know or has done what I've done.' I made sure it didn't happen to my kids, made sure none of my sons were having sexual intercourse with my wife's friends or my daughters with mine.

"Too much too soon," he says, with measured solemnity, "impedes the growing-up process. Growing up didn't start for me until I was thirty-one and met Barbara. If I hadn't met Barbara, maybe I would have turned to booze or drugs."

Even now, he seems almost pathetically grateful to Barbara Kraus for having married him 27 years ago. Except for one desperate middle-aged fling a few years ago, he has remained contentedly at home and, for their twenty-fifth anniversary, bought a full-page ad in the *Racing Form*—they are both inveterate $20 horse players—to express his love. A compact man in faded jeans, a Levi shirt around his 16 1/2-inch neck, and an authoritarian manner, Jackie Cooper has used his book to rake up old quarrels—with Alan Alda, whom he calls cold and ungenerous; with Merle Miller, who made a fool of him in *Only You, Dick Daring!,* a kiss-and-tell book about an ill-fated television pilot they worked on together; with Norman Taurog, who he always suspected was his real father. Taurog, once married to his mother's sister, was, after his mother's death, the guardian of his person, his money, and his career. Cooper still bears a grudge against his uncle for not preparing him for such tasks of adulthood as handling money. Taurog, who refused to be interviewed for *Please Don't Shoot My Dog,* died April 8, two days before the book was published.

Despite the bitterness of his book, Cooper is rather well liked in Hollywood. "He's an aggressive go-getter who keeps his word," says one of his colleagues. "If he says he'll be there at eleven, he'll be there at eleven. His problem is that, because he was a child actor, a lot of people still don't take him seriously."

Cooper's first attempt to break away from being a child movie star was to plunge into the more real 1950ish Broadway world of such friends as Eli Wallach, Anne Jackson, and Eva Marie Saint. His reviews were good in such plays as *King of Hearts* in 1954, but, he says, there "was still no sense of self. Because acting was something that had always been done to me. What could I turn to that was my own?"

The answer was auto racing. "I'm a mechanic. I loaded Mitchell Cameras at twelve, fixed my own car at fourteen. Even today, I repair our washing machine. I started racing automobiles very, very seriously. Winning silver-plated little bowls, beating professionals, gave me a sense of self because it was something I chose for myself. But I was always close to the wire, close to the extent of my talent, and, a couple of times, beyond my talent, and, luckily, the car landed right-side-up. I never had anything in reserve and it finally became clear that, one day, I was going to kill myself. In the middle of one race, I was ten seconds late on a lap and I looked up to see Barbara sobbing and two friends holding her up and I knew that the three of them thought I was dead. The race was only three-fourths over, but I drove in and stopped and I never raced again."

After auto racing came directing. "No one encouraged me to be a director—not my wife, my agent, or my managers. But the sheer joy of acting—of putting on the make-up and holding in my stomach—left me a long time ago." Although he still occasionally acts and was seen on movie screens as Clark Kent's newspaper editor in *Superman II,* he has won an Emmy for directing "M*A*S*H" and gets all the fun, all the satisfaction, from directing television movies. He was head of a television studio, Screen Gems, for four years and would not like to repeat the experience. Having made and lost and made several fortunes, he is, he says, comfortable for the rest of his life; directing—though it pays less well—is more fun.

He looks down at his well-manicured nails and then up again, shyly, and the scrunched-up face of the tow-headed little boy is somehow superimposed on the man's face, as he says, "I'm a lousy director of children, however. I can't wring out of a kid what I should for the good of my films because I won't lie to them or deceive them or shake the bejeezus out of them. I suffer enough because I think they should be out playing, and so I find ways not to make them unhappy."

Peckinpah: "Man Was a Killer Long Before He Served a God"

"The noble savage?"

The voice is a stream bed eroded by rivers of whiskey. The face is a road map of the high country—nights cold enough to freeze your butt off, chunks of venison tossed in the fire while the dead buck hangs high, covered with a web of snow.

"The myth of the noble savage is horseshit, lady. Law and order and grace and understanding are things that have to be taught."

Sam Peckinpah sits in his Warner Bros.–7 Arts office dreaming of Hawaii. His four children, the salvage of his first marriage, are on the beach at Kuhio waiting for him. He will join them tomorrow, when a pause in the editing of his new film allows him to flee Los Angeles. After Hawaii, there is a woman, somewhere in Mexico. He wears around his neck the gold Spanish cross with its tortured Christ that she gave to him. For added insurance he wears a less agonized cross of Mexican silver. Occasionally, the gold and silver chains get tangled in his patriarchal beard.

In white Levi's and gray tennis shoes, he sits stiffly, as though to move would jar his bones. He has directed two pictures back to back—*The Wild Bunch* and *The Ballad of Cable Hogue*—and he is exhausted from 22 months of hacking at his guts and pasting them artistically on celluloid. Although the outer office is littered with empty bottles of club soda from some gargantuan revel, Peckinpah sips spartanly at a vodka. He is on the wagon—somewhat—"until I hit Shipwreck Kelly's tomorrow afternoon."

Forty-four-year-old Sam Peckinpah made his reputation—as a "genius" and a "bastard"—on just four motion pictures spaced out over seven years: *The Deadly Companions, Ride the High Country, Major Dundee,* and *The Wild Bunch.* There is no question that the last three films are his, even *Major Dundee,* which was sewn together with a meathook by a producer who wanted to make it commercial and only succeeded in making it grotesque. Peckinpah's spurs are dug into every frame, twisting the films toward the moral ambivalences that make them so annoying and so powerful.

In a Peckinpah film, a good man is incapable of doing good, and a noble action ends by destroying its maker. Yet it is not a question of being "beyond good and evil," as one critic said of *The Wild Bunch,* but of being *before* good and evil. Peckinpah hands out copies of Robert Ardrey's *African Genesis* by the dozens. He came across the book after he had finished *The Wild Bunch,* and he is "astounded" that Ardrey's theories are a scientific statement of his own theme.

"I have a twenty-year-old daughter who is a very strong pacifist and who believes that people are born without sin and without anger, which is not necessarily the same, and without violence. I totally disagree with her. People are born to survive.

They have instincts that go back millions of years. Unfortunately, some of those instincts are based on violence. There is a great streak of violence in every human being. If it is not channeled and understood, it will break out in war or in madness."

In *The Wild Bunch,* judgments of good and evil are irrelevant. Morality is irrelevant. Children play "an ugly game" with scorpions and ants, "but it's a game children play—unless they're taught different." The children were not taught to play the torturer's game by the brutality around them. "They would have had to be taught *not* to play that game." And man was a killer millions of years before he served a God.

"The point of the film," says Peckinpah, "is to take this façade of movie violence, open it up, get people involved in it so that they are starting to go in the Hollywood-television predictable reaction syndrome, and then twist it so that it's not fun any more, just a wave of sickness in the gut."

"The kids who came up to us at our first preview, in Kansas City, understood," says *The Wild Bunch*'s film editor, Lou Lombardo. "There was one nineteen-year-old kid on his way to Vietnam. He told Sam, 'I found myself shouting for more when William Holden was on the machine gun and saying *Go, baby, get them all,* and now I feel ashamed of myself for having felt that way.' Then he said, very politely, 'Thank you, Mr. Peckinpah.' "

At least 20 minutes of that Kansas City version are lying on various Hollywood cutting room floors because middle-aged members of the audience were so revulsed by the violence that they bolted from the theater, one or two of them to vomit in the alley.

Peckinpah, an uncompromising man, accepts that judgment with surprising equanimity. He is less polite about more recent cuts that drained ten minutes of humanity from the film, while leaving all the finger-licking violence. He is particularly angry about the elimination of a human moment between the Mexican general Malpache and a young Mexican boy. "Possibly one of the best moments in the entire film. It made the point that I tried to make with the entire film, that the Mexicans were no worse than William Holden's bunch. Removing that scene was an absolute disgrace." It is this boy who kills Holden at the end of the film. Without the earlier scene, the later one seems just an added senseless piece of violence.

One searches *The Wild Bunch,* as one does all of Peckinpah's films, desperately, for innocence. A few people escape the massacre at the end of the film, but Peckinpah denies their claim to being higher on the moral scale than those who have died. Of the least violent character, the head man of the Mexican village, Peckinpah says softly, "Instead of fighting, that old man ran away when the general's army raided his village. We are all guilty to some extent."

"Sam is the one person in American films who has truly caught the idea of ambivalence," says Gill Dennis, an open-faced, young American Film Institute intern who chose to work with Peckinpah when he was allowed to apprentice himself to any American director. "Sam respects his characters. He doesn't judge them, and that annoys people. They keep asking, 'Where does he stand?' Even in *Bonnie and Clyde,* you've got your villain in 'society.' Sam won't make it that easy, not ever."

Perhaps he *can't* make it that easy. Like the strained ground in earthquake country, slipping and shearing to adjust to an ever-shifting core, the ambivalences in Sam Peckinpah run deep.

Although he mocks his daughter's pacifism, he carries a pocketful of Another Mother for Peace medallions bearing the legend "War is not healthy for children and other living things." He hands them out as casually as he does Robert Ardrey's book. He skins the deer he kills and proudly boasts that "I've fed my family," but he is contemptuous of men who kill for sport. He is a Catholic convert who prays only at his own convenience, a booted westerner in a $250 custom-tailored suit.

He has a favorite Nevada bordello and a favorite Parisian restaurant where dinner for two costs $75. On his $90,000 lot at Malibu, he is planning to rebuild a 108-year-old mountain cabin that he bought for $500 in the high Sierras and took to Nevada for *The Ballad of Cable Hogue.* During the filming of *Cable Hogue,* he slept in the cabin, alone in the desert, "sometimes, just to get out of the motel."

Since the end of his brief second marriage, he considers himself unencumbered, but he clings to his past. He still wears the signet ring given to him by his father on his graduation from grammar school, and he has in storage a pair of torn blue denim pants that he could not bear to give away because "I had some good times in Nevada in these pants." His tastes are simple: eggs drowned in chili sauce, liquor—any kind, straight from the bottle—but his fantasies are complex.

He revels in having 200 crew members and actors under his thumb, but he hates it with equal passion. People who care too little about his film are "put on the bus" and sent back to Hollywood. Those who are cashiered from his sets speak of him as "a dictatorial bastard," "a weird son of a bitch." Those who stay become a family that travels together from picture to picture. He has formed a stock company that echoes the early John Ford. R. G. Armstrong, Strother Martin, Warren Oates, L. Q. Jones have appeared in all or almost all of his films. "They're all crazy, dedicated, lascivious bastards," Peckinpah says. "Basically they're all country people, like me."

Yet those who stay in his rough, masculine world with its sweat-stained longjohns and unprintable nicknames, also speak of him as "weird." He is, says Gary Weis, a barefoot young photographer whose buccaneer-length hair is tied back with a black ribbon, "a charming, strange, kind, weird man with a deep and primitive kind of insight." (The "weirdness" that both friends and enemies refer to is partly a strange intensity that seems to eat him up from the inside while he is making a film.) "He is a generous, gentle, and very angry man," says Gill Dennis. "It's a childlike anger. As a child, you're told the world is one way and you believe it. Then you grow up and it isn't that way at all and you still believe it should be and you hate the people who fooled you."

The world that Sam Peckinpah believes in has not existed during his own lifetime except for a few wilting fragments, stalks of dry wheat in a long unplowed field. ("That tent city of Coarse Gold in *Ride the High Country,* that was what the gold-mining camp Fine Gold looked like in 1930 when I was five years old, riding down from the mountains on my father's horse.") It is a world of tin hammered on salvaged wood to make a house where there was nothing but desert in *Cable Hogue;* of a country moving into the 20th century ("They're going to use flying machines in the war, they say," William Holden tells his gang in *The Wild Bunch*) without moving out of savagery; of old men with frayed cuffs and clean pistols selling their memories for ten cents a chance in *Ride the High Country* or not selling them, it doesn't much matter.

When he ended *The Ballad of Cable Hogue,* Peckinpah felt he had ended for a while his obsession with the moment of change when the West turned in a man's hand like a key in a lock and the horseless carriage collided with the man on horseback. The last, most beautiful evocation of that moment is in the final frames of *Cable Hogue.* A yellow motor car and a stagecoach move together for a moment, then turn and take their separate paths across the desert.

"I can't live it," Peckinpah says. "So I remake it."

His great-grandparents came to central California in covered wagons—the Churches in 1848, the Peckinpahs in 1851. At 14, his grandfather, Denver S. Church, was a professional deer-slayer and a tent-master for the Seventh Day Adventists. His father was born on Peckinpah Mountain. His grandmother came down from the high mountains to meet Calamity Jane.

The complexities started when they rode down from the high country into the valley. In 1917, Denver Church was one of three congressmen to vote against America's entrance into the First World War. His grandfather, father, uncle, and brother became Superior Court judges. The dinner-table conversation balanced between two worlds. "It was about the meaning of law and the price of cotton cake." Peckinpah describes cotton cake as "a winter food for cattle."

Sam Peckinpah's moral training was crude but effective. When he was in high school, his father forced him to sit through the trial of a 17-year-old boy arrested for statutory rape. At home and at military school, things were right or wrong, guilty or innocent, true or false—and so were people. The absolutes drove him crazy. "Things are always mixed. We're all guilty to some extent." His films, and his life, would become, in some part, a denial of the absolutes of his childhood.

He became a Republican in a family of Democrats (a phase which lasted "until I saw the Goldwater campaign on television"). A storyteller in a family of men who were solely concerned with truth. A year as a private on the fringes of World War II ("I was shot at in China and it meant nothing, absolutely nothing, just a sound heard through the window of a train") was followed by Fresno State College and an M.A. in drama from the University of Southern California. He became a screen writer with *Invasion of the Body Snatchers* in 1956. He created "The Rifleman" and "The Westerner" on television, directed half a dozen notable television plays including an adaptation of Katherine Anne Porter's "Noon Wine." In 1962, his 15-year first marriage broke up after the birth of his fourth child and only son, Matthew, and he got a chance to direct a movie.

After five movies, he sat in his office, bone-tired and bewildered. He is, as one friend says, "confused by this sudden recognition as a genius." He derides those who call him an intellectual. His strength as a director is both simpler and more complicated than that. His statements come from the guts of his heroes, who are obsessed in their own ways with morality, each "seeking a way to enter his house justified."

Will he make another movie as violent as *The Wild Bunch?* "Never. If I didn't say it in that one, then I'll never be able to say it." His next movie, *The Ballad of Cable Hogue,* starring Jason Robards, Stella Stevens, and David Warner, was a surprisingly gentle Western in which only two men were shot.

Ironically, he has never come very close to the death that he shows so graphically in his films. There was, of course, one fight in a Mexican bar, but he was not aware of his dangerously smashed kidney until after it had been mended. He shrugs at the thought of death. "I suspect it's inevitable. I'm not afraid of it. What I am afraid of is stupid, useless, horrible death. An automobile accident. A violent death for no purpose." For a moment the room is silent, and he leans forward wearily.

Twenty-four hours later, the office is empty except for remnants. A pair of skis and a tennis racket are left and a rosary hung across the desk lamp, but the skin diving equipment has gone with Peckinpah to Hawaii. There are enormous photographs of Pancho Villa and Zapata and a smaller—yet more real—one of his father, taken at the end of a brilliant trial. Smaller still, there is one photograph of himself, holding the horns of the first eight-point buck he ever killed. In the photograph, his white pants are splattered with blood.

But the man in the photograph is elsewhere, 20 years and

2,500 miles away, his white beard buried in the warm sand, far, far from the high country.

Throughout the fall of 1982, Sam Peckinpah was making The Osterman Weekend on the streets of Los Angeles. Before he was hired to turn Robert Ludlum's thriller into a film, he had not directed a movie for four years.

In 1971, Pauline Kael called Peckinpah's Straw Dogs "the first American film that is a fascist work of art." A number of major critics have been supportive of Peckinpah during the last decade, admiring the force with which he flings his personal vision onto the screen in such movies as The Killer Elite while recoiling from the obsessive cruelty of the vision. American audiences have found his movies both too violent and too misogynistic. Abroad, the nihilistic violence of his last two movies, Cross of Iron (1977) and Convoy (1978), has been a box-office tonic.

It is not audiences but studio executives who hire directors, and many a compliant hack has had a long and fruitful Hollywood career. But so have a number of directors of major quality and skill. Hollywood executives are often quite tolerant of genius, and they expect an adversary relationship with directors. At lunch one day in the Universal commissary, Ned Tanen, then president of Universal Pictures, pointed at a director eating a hamburger three booths away and said, "After we made the deal for him to direct, we had a pleasant meeting in my office. Just before he left, he said —in the nicest voice imaginable—'You know you're going to end up hating me because I'm going to make you into the enemy. I need an enemy to get my creative juices going, and you're the best target.'"

But Peckinpah's wars with his studios and producers have become so vicious and vehement—fueled by booze and by his feeling of betrayal when his pictures are cut or re-edited to make them more palatable to audiences—that most studios find it easier *to pass. After all, it's not as though his films are blockbusters. Convoy, the most successful of them, only did $9.5 million in film rentals. In retrospect, that moment in 1969 when The Wild Bunch was inflaming the passions of intellectuals and The Ballad of Cable Hogue had not yet been sent to its box-office doom seems not the midpoint of a career but something close to the climax.*

The Dime-Store Way
to Make Movies

Samuel Z. Arkoff is not feeling well. Last night he tried acupuncture, allowing seven needles to be inserted into his face. "Shingles is such an awful name for a painful disease. I feel like Camille. She died of consumption—a passé disease. For the young people to identify with her or me, we should make it a social disease."

It is not beyond the realm of possibility that, in Arkoff's projected version of *Camille,* the lady of the camellias will have traded tuberculosis for syphilis. After all, in Arkoff's version of *Dr. Jekyll and Mr. Hyde,* Hyde was a woman.

Arkoff's movie company—American International Pictures—has roughly the same status in Hollywood as the man hired to sweep behind the elephants in the circus parade. There is a rich aroma to AIP pictures, from 1957's *I Was a Teen-age Werewolf,* which featured healthy high school athlete Michael Landon wolfing down a fellow student in the gym; to 1969's *Three in the Attic,* which demonstrated how college stud Chris-

topher Jones was undone by the three girls with whom he had
been carrying on simultaneous affairs; to 1971's *Bloody Mama,*
which showed a fat but indefatigable Shelley Winters hauling
herself into bed with one or another of her grown sons.

"Garbage!" sniffs a producer at a major studio. "Trash,"
adds the inheritor of a tastefully decorated executive suite at a
different studio. But there is *garbage* and *garbage,* and, if what
Sam Arkoff peddles is trash, it is trash that finds an eager
market. In the 20 years of its existence, AIP has never lost
money. Between 1954—when it was founded by Arkoff and the
late James Nicholson—and 1960, AIP never even made a picture that lost money. For the fiscal year ended March 2, 1974,
AIP had a profit of $931,400 on sales of $32.5 million. The
highest profits in its history thus coincided with its twentieth
anniversary.

"I will be condemned for saying this," says Arkoff with a
sigh, rubbing at his scalp. The sigh may be part pain, part
acknowledgment that the "arty" movie aristocrats regard him
as a barbarian. "I look upon my movies as being merchandise,
just as Woolworth's has a line of merchandise. The fact that
many of my acquaintances wouldn't buy Woolworth's merchandise doesn't keep it from being perfectly good merchandise. Many people in this business feel that merchandise not
aimed at them must be shoddy. They wouldn't feel that way
about overshoes."

Arkoff's merchandise has always been aimed at the pizza-
eating, acne-pitted, Coke-drinking 19-year-old inhabitant of the
drive-in theaters. As such, it has changed dramatically over the
last ten years to match a changing audience. In the early sixties,
Beach Party, Pajama Party, Ski Party were all tease and froth.
Frankie Avalon never did get to attain what Annette Funicello
so tantalizingly promised in bubble-gum songs. A few years
later, AIP was presenting teen-agers quite differently. Teen-age
President of the United States Christopher Jones put his mother

in a concentration camp in *Wild in the Streets* in 1968. Two years after that, Jones was triple-raped in *Three in the Attic.* (With a theatrical film rental of $5,500,000 in the United States, *Three in the Attic* was still AIP's highest-grossing film in 1974.)

"Our pictures in the sixties mirrored the teen-agers as they went from high-spirited to rebellious but not sullen to rebellious and sullen," says Arkoff. "Kent State was the turning point. It was no longer fun and games to call policemen pigs. You could get shot. The big body of teen-agers turned off into nothingness by 1970. That's why the nostalgia pictures are successful today. Because those who want to believe can only believe if a story is set in the forties or fifties. Today a sixteen-year-old boy doesn't believe in virgins. Plenty of sixteen-year-old boys *are* virgins, but it's not credible to them except in *Summer of '42* or *The Last Picture Show.*"

In 1974, AIP is, as usual, trying to fathom what its audience —no longer the archetypal 19-year-old boy or girl—will buy. "There's no way to sell the young today that's as clear-cut as in the past," Arkoff says. "I don't think our audience is the same audience any more for any two different pictures. Each picture must be attractive to some segment of youth, to some part of the audience under thirty. But you can't buckshot any more. You must aim dead center at what you consider your audience for a specific picture and hope what you have will also attract a peripheral audience. Falling between two stools is not my idea of comfort."

As an example, he offers one of AIP's two films for Christmas—*Cooley High,* a black *American Graffiti* about black writer Eric Monte's bittersweet high school experience. Arkoff is taking a $750,000 chance that he is correct in his estimate that the black teen-age audience is ready for more subtle reflections of itself, and that whites are ready for subtle reflections about blacks, and that "the hard-action black film is coming to an end. Not that anything was wrong with them. We did very well with *Slaughter, Black Caesar, Coffy.* But they're no novelty any more.

"What are kids looking for today? They'll buy everything and nothing. They will not buy the political picture at all. Kids are less idealists today, bigger pragmatists. They're no less innocent, but they are more jaundiced. You need to be first and good today, rather than second and better. A more fickle audience wants something to tickle their carnival spirit. *The Exorcist* is simply a super AIP horror picture."

It would be easier to mock Arkoff's dime-store approach to movie making if it were not for two facts: (1) Between 1969 and 1974, while AIP was basking in the sunshine of modest but respectable profits, the old-line movie companies were losing half a billion dollars. (2) Much of that $500 million was lost not on seriously intended movies that happened to be commercial failures but on attempts to turn a trendy buck. *The Strawberry Statement, The Magic Garden of Stanley Sweetheart, Pretty Maids All in a Row, Born to Win*, and Dennis Hopper's *The Last Movie* were among the two dozen major studio films that failed to capture the magic drug-cum-sex-cum-youth market captured by AIP's *The Trip, The Wild Angels,* and *Wild in the Streets.*

Arkoff cannot guess which of AIP's 24 or 30 pictures for 1974 will make money. *"Truck Turner* I'm pretty sure of, but I wouldn't want to be a one-picture producer because on one picture you can go wrong. I would never predict the success of one picture or despair if one is a failure." What he is absolutely confident of is that "flying by the seat of my pants on twenty pictures, I'll come out O.K." He is convinced that AIP's inelegant but shrewd blend of horror *(Madhouse, The Bat People)*, melodrama *(Truck Stop Women, Macon County Line)*, black supermen and women *(Truck Turner, Foxy Brown)*, and audacious animation *(Heavy Traffic* rereleased in an R version and *The 9 Lives of Fritz the Cat)* will be commercially viable.

And it *is* a shrewd blend. AIP has an almost dazzling record for guessing what will tickle the public's fancy in any given year (e.g., sandy teen-age romance, motorcycle gangs, classic horror tales), and for making new genres by mixing old ones (e.g., Black + Horror = *Blacula;* Teen-age + Horror = *I Was a Teen-age Frankenstein*). AIP was one of the few studios not to lose money on drug pictures because it didn't make any except one carefully constructed drug experience, *The Trip.* Says Arkoff, "*The Trip* didn't say drugs were morally wrong or criminally wrong. If you're making a picture for a certain audience, you can't insult them. The major studios had drug pictures where everybody came to a bad end. How the hell could they expect the marijuana fanatics to come? And the antidrug parents would never come to *any* drug picture, no matter how moral."

Although AIP has distributed a dozen or more Kung Fu movies *(Shanghai Killers, Bamboo Gods and Iron Men, Screaming Tiger, Deep Thrust)* during the last year, there are no Kung Fu movies on its summer and fall slate. "The standard Kung Fu feature will be dead by summer," says Arkoff. "To be successful, Kung Fu will have to be grafted on to other genres."

Sitting in his office on the fourth floor of the five-story building that his company owns in Beverly Hills—a roly-poly, 55-year-old man with a black eye patch over one eye—Arkoff is no accidental tycoon, no garment manufacturer or insurance salesman who stumbled into Hollywood gold. Nor is he a barbarian. Even with the eye patch (a temporary memento of the shingles), he looks less like a buccaneer than like the winged leprechaun Mr. O'Malley in the "Barnaby" comic strip—a comparison made more apt by the cigars that he chainsmokes.

He is, in paradoxical actuality, a ferociously intelligent man who has chosen to use his intelligence to anticipate what a youthful, unsophisticated audience will buy for an evening's pleasure. In this pursuit, he has given a toehold on the often unscalable Hollywood wall to actors Jack Nicholson, Peter Fonda, Dennis Hopper, Bruce Dern, Mike Connors, and Woody Allen; directors Richard Rush *(Freebie and the Bean)*, Monte Hellman *(Two-Lane Blacktop)*, Menahem Golan *(Kazablan)*, and Martin Scorsese *(Mean Streets)*; writers Bob Kaufman *(I Love My Wife)*, John Milius *(Jeremiah Johnson)*, and Willard Huyck *(American Graffiti)*, and a score of others.

Arkoff is frank to admit that nurturing talent is in AIP's self-interest. "But it's not a one-way street. We're not exploiting anybody. When these young people come to us, they have a lot to learn."

John Milius worked for two years for $75 a week doing odd jobs at AIP before he became a high-priced writer with an itch to be a director. "Milius got $300,000 from First Artists for *The Life and Times of Judge Roy Bean,*" says Arkoff. "*Because* they wouldn't let him direct it. He would have taken $150,000 if they had let him direct. So we came to him with the idea for *Dillinger* and got him—as writer and director—for a fraction of his usual price."

Arkoff rubs his head again. Besides adding 20 pounds to his already ample figure, the shingles has slowed him down to an eight-hour working day. He usually works a 9:30 a.m. to 8:00 p.m. day, including lunch. ("This is a business of communication. You have to talk to people, reach for the hints they may not even realize they're giving.") Each Friday, Saturday, and Sunday evening, he sees movies. On no weekend does he see fewer than six movies, and he may see as many as nine.

His 24-year-old son, his 22-year-old daughter (wife of Mike Pinder of the Moody Blues), and 30 or 40 nieces and nephews ("My wife is one of ten children; I am the oldest of five") and their friends sprawl on the floor of the big living room of the San Fernando Valley house he built in 1957 and watch the movies with him. "I have always utilized the opinions of young people. No matter how good I think I am, after a certain age you don't react the same. One of the great fallacies in our business is exhibitors in their fifties and sixties telling distributors in their forties and fifties what audiences want to see." (If an evening's film comes from AIP, Arkoff's wife of 27 years usually watches one or two reels and then goes to bed. Hilda Arkoff, a sculptress, is proud of her husband as "a man, a human being, a successful father and husband," but she rarely likes his films. When she did like *Heavy Traffic* enough to see it four times, Arkoff was terrified. The last AIP film she had really liked was *Angel, Angel, Down We Go,* an unmitigated financial disaster starring Jennifer Jones.)

"How do you come to the conclusion the timing is right for something? If it's a subject the public is aware of, if it seems different, and if you can put it into an action vein—by that I don't mean gunplay, I mean dramatic—then you have to experiment. We made *Wild Angels* because three different people threw on my desk the *Life* magazine that had the Hell's Angels on the cover." With AIP's successful series of beach pictures, "I simply listened to my seventeen- and twenty-year-old nephews talking. Such-and-such, a friend, wasn't living at home any more. So-and-so had withdrawn from his parents. I sensed kids were ready for pictures totally about them as a tribe, unconnected to the adult generation."

Arkoff is equally attuned to poor timing. AIP's spring horror film, *The Bat People,* did poorly. And *Madhouse* is doing less business than is normal for an AIP Vincent Price film. To Arkoff, the figures augur the reality of something he has been half anticipating. "What we call 'horror' and they call 'suspense' is all over TV. You cannot sell what is being given away." The horror film, a staple of AIP since 1960, may soon vanish.

Arkoff freely admits his own errors of competence. "*De

Sade! An abortion. *Bunny O'Hare!* Bette Davis and Ernest Borgnine on a motorcycle. I knew it was a bad project. Too cutesy. And not inexpensive for us [$900,000]. But it was on our schedule, and the sales department had sold it. So we went ahead."

But nothing Arkoff says is to be misinterpreted as a complaint. Says Marge Carr, his secretary for the last 15 years, whose job includes (1) making duplicates of the car keys Arkoff loses "by the millions" and (2) reminding him whom he is telephoning since he often forgets between the time he dials and the time his call is answered, "Sam is a man who loves his business. Few people are that lucky." Even during the two and a half years Arkoff spent at Los Angeles's Loyola law school just after World War II, he never saw "less than one double feature a day."

It was as a lawyer that Arkoff first met James Nicholson in 1953. Nicholson—who left AIP in June 1972 to produce pictures on his own and died of a brain tumor six months later—often recalled admiringly how Arkoff managed to separate Nicholson's tightwad boss from $500 in an affair of title infringement when Nicholson was convinced Arkoff had absolutely no case. It was a moment in Hollywood history when the major studios were fighting the inroads of television with massive, widescreen, big-budget movies *(The Robe, Knights of the Round Table, Demetrius and the Gladiators).* Nicholson and Arkoff pooled $3,000 in 1954 (Arkoff's salary is now $106,000 per year) and went into business. They were convinced that there was money to be made supplying the country's 4,152 drive-in theaters (in 1946, there had been 100 drive-ins) with cheap, 70-minute features that could be changed twice a week.

Cheap, in those early years, meant cheap. Roger Corman made *The Beast with 1,000,000 Eyes* in eight days for $35,000. *I Was a Teen-age Werewolf* cost $123,000 and brought back

$2,000,000. *She Gods of Shark Reef, The Undead, Dragstrip Riot, Night of the Blood Beast, Sorority Girl,* and 50 others ranged in cost from $50,000 to $150,000.

If a picture threatened to go one day over its ten-day shooting schedule or $1,000 over its budget, Arkoff appeared on the set. "Jim loved being on the set," Arkoff recalls. "He was the nice guy, the guy in the white car. I was the guy in the black car. I only went on the set when there was trouble. I'd say, 'If you're not caught up by tomorrow night, I'm tearing five pages out of the script.' Generally that had a satisfactory effect. If not, I did it." (In real life, the black car–white car roles were more ambiguous. Says screen writer Robert Thom, "Sam was the Jewish papa who adored his kids and took every script home to them. Jim lived in high style. New yachts. New houses. He was always in debt and borrowing money from the company.")

The end of 1958 brought trouble. The cleverness of Arkoff and Nicholson lay in their ability to recognize that trouble was trouble and to recognize it immediately. "Our black-and-white, double-bill combinations were dead. Everyone was starting to imitate us. And the public was beginning to sense that if two pictures were advertised equally in splashy ads, both of them must be dogs." The decision was made "to go with bigger pictures. Color. Four-hundred-thousand-dollar budgets. Putting more into the one picture than we used to put into two."

Looking for cheap stories to make into salable color pictures, Arkoff and Nicholson chose Edgar Allan Poe. Poe was in the public domain. Equally important, the great Hollywood horror stars were *underpriced.* "There are actors in this town who haven't been in a successful picture for years who are grotesquely overpriced. Peter Lorre, Boris Karloff, Vincent Price, Lon Chaney, Jr., were underpriced." For *House of Usher* in 1960, AIP paid Vincent Price "more than he ever had been paid before, but we frugally deferred payment over years and years."

Seven more Poe pictures followed. The stylishly acted, stylishly directed (by Roger Corman) Poe pictures brought AIP a trifle closer to respectability. "At a cocktail party," says Arkoff, "a dozen people came up to me and said, 'You're so faithful to the book.' I hate pious talk and there's so much pious talk in our business. For God's sake, no Poe story is over six pages long!"

AIP's successful beach-party pictures of the early sixties started with the same sort of careful appraisal. Disney's exclusive contract with Mouseketeer Annette Funicello had lapsed. Why not jump in on a Disney star? The beach-party pictures (*Beach Blanket Bingo, Bikini Beach, How to Stuff a Wild Bikini,* etc.) were artistically dreadful but philosophically brilliant. "We never showed parents," says Arkoff. "The Peter Pan syndrome. No responsible adults. No school. No church. That's part of the success of *American Graffiti*. The only responsible adult was a teacher who was only in the film for five minutes. Someone slapped *For Those Who Think Young* on a picture once. As if any kid would go to see a movie with that title. That's a slogan for my generation. The kids know they're young and hate it."

A lot has changed at AIP since the bloody Poes and barefoot teen-agers of the 1960s. In the parking lot of Los Angeles's Ambassador Hotel in the spring of 1974, 30 members of the cast (Elizabeth Ashley, Joe Don Baker, Burgess Meredith, Ann Sothern) and crew of AIP's *Golden Needles* eat fried steak and apple pie. *Golden Needles* is an example of how much has changed at AIP in the last few years—and of how much has stayed the same.

In the early years, all of AIP's pictures were *house productions*. ("To make them topical, we had to make them ourselves," says Arkoff.) In 1974, approximately 10 pictures are house productions, 12 are co-productions, and 8 are pick-ups of finished pictures that lack a distributor. (AIP's pick-ups are

sometimes surprising. In 1973, AIP released Brian De Palma's
Sisters and Jane Fonda's anti–Vietnam war polemic *FTA.*)

Golden Needles—a cross pollination of the Kung Fu genre
with the Maltese Falcon genre—is a co-production. Financed
by AIP, it is being produced by Fred Weintraub and Paul
Heller, who produced the startling Kung Fu success, *Enter the
Dragon,* starring Bruce Lee. The deal was made over a two-
hour lunch. "At the end of an hour and a half, I told them I'd
go with the project despite the fact they had no written material," says Arkoff. "They were offering not only themselves but
Robert Clouse, who directed *Enter the Dragon,* and it was
obvious that that picture was very much helped by its director.
And while I was sure the standard Kung Fu would be dead by
summer, I had a hunch this blend of the Oriental martial arts
with a Maltese Falcon–type search might well be successful."
(Arkoff's *hunch* was partially based on his feeling that the
audience would like the protagonist of *Golden Needles:* "During the last several years there's been a style for the protagonists
to die or to be no more sympathetic than the so-called villains.
I think the public's had it. We have just too many antiheroes
in real life.")

Weintraub and Heller had been to another studio first. (AIP
is rarely the first choice of producers because of its ferocious
cost-consciousness.) The other studio would have given them a
larger budget for the film, but it offered only a development deal
—which meant the studio could back out after any of a number
of steps. Arkoff promised less money but a firm commitment.
Weintraub and Heller accepted. (AIP likes to go in lean, but,
according to producers who have made pictures there, it pays
off honestly on its profit percentages—"not like some major
studios.")

Golden Needles—which was penciled in on AIP's release
schedule to open before it was even finished—had a 34-day
shooting schedule and a budget slightly under $1,000,000. In

the past decade, AIP's budgets have crept up from $400,000 to $600,000 to $900,000.

"There was a change in philosophy a few years ago," says Arkoff, "just as we made a major step in 1959 based on the problems of 1958. The times call for different things." Chief among "the times" for AIP is "the greater and greater competition from television movies. There are more and more movies being made for television. TV mimics theatrical. Anything safe and successful TV apes. You hardly have time to follow up a successful picture before TV is there with a series or a movie of the week, with PG versions of R films. You cannot sell what is being given away. The industry's needs call for the expenditure of more money, and we have the money."

Arkoff hastily adds that he is speaking about "the judicious use of money," and launches into a long anecdote about the director of the sequel to *Dr. Phibes*, who spent good money to build sets so high that they would not even be seen on the screen. "If anybody tells you we've relaxed cost-consciousness, and they're right, then I ought to be deposed!"

"Every nickel we have up on the screen," as production manager Elliot Schick phrases it, is a litany at AIP. "I feed my crews good lunches on location," says Schick. "We give everybody the best single room the Holiday Inn has to offer. Blake Edwards's [*Darling Lili, The Wild Rovers*] lunches cost $1.50 per person more. In Boston in winter, he served fresh fruit. Feeding forty or sixty people a day for forty days, $1.50 per person becomes a lot of extra money."

Yet money-saving incident after money-saving incident pours from Schick's unending store. "We shot eighteen days in the mansion in *Frogs* for $1. The state of Florida gave it to us. We showed them it would be worth it because of the money we would spend in the area. For *Sugar Hill,* a restaurant owner allowed us to shoot free for three days and even use their voodoo dancers because we were willing to order dinner for the crew. The dinners cost $5 per person, and we had to feed the crew somewhere. We bought all our old cars for *Dillinger* as close to the Oklahoma location as possible. When the picture was finished, we sold them for a profit. People really paid extra to get the cars into which we'd put bullet holes."

Pennies are pinched in every conceivable way. AIP has no studio facilities of its own, and during the last five years none of the films it has made in the United States have been shot within studio walls. Says Robert Clouse, "The Ambassador Hotel is costing us $500. And it would take thousands to duplicate the fading elegance of the Ambassador on a set."

AIP's penuriousness starts before a film is made. "We made *Wuthering Heights* for $800,000," says Arkoff. "If the project had cost $1,200,000, we might have turned it down. At $1,600,000, we would definitely have turned it down. *Wuthering Heights* was a gamble because we were competing with a picture—the Olivier version—that had status."

Nor does AIP's penuriousness end when a movie is finished. "We never take a picture out of release," says Arkoff. "Even after they've been on television, we continue to play them, something most studios won't do. When the prints start to go, we cannibalize them—a reel salvaged here, another reel there."

A new feature is sent out with a slightly older second feature (e.g., *Dillinger* and *Boxcar Bertha*). "Ten years ago we began to realize you didn't need to give them a new second feature. We realized the average *successful* feature is seen by so few people we were better off to give a good two-month-old second feature rather than a new dog. So we bring back older pictures as second features and take advantage of the audience's subliminal memory of our advertising campaign."

Any film that does well is examined for possibilities of a sequel. "Out of a combination of cupidity and stupidity, we make a lot of sequels," says Arkoff. "Even though sequels generally do less well than the original. We did well with

Slaughter, so we made *Slaughter's Big Ripoff.* We were the only ones ripped off on that."

The sequels are a search for "a good vein" that can be made into a series. "A series, a genuine cycle like the beach or bike pictures, really does well. But sequels are also the path of least resistance. Exhibitors can be sold with them. In a business that has no signposts, exhibitors can only recognize what they just did well with. And we have to sell the exhibitors first in order to get into the theaters so we can try to sell the public."

AIP makes creative use of its sequels and series. Old films that have a central subject matter are arranged into four-film combinations that play from dusk to dawn in the drive-ins. There are two or three Poe combinations, one *Soul* combination. "When *American Graffiti* came out, we made a combination of four of our beach-party pictures. When some actor comes to notoriety, we'll make up a combination of his films. After *Easy Rider,* we had a 'Fonda Festival.' "

Unfortunately for AIP, Tom Laughlin only appeared in one AIP picture. But because of *Billy Jack,* that film, *Born Losers* (1967), was sent out with the advertising line, "The original Billy Jack is back again." In two weeks in 81 theaters around the Detroit area, *Born Losers* grossed $683,000, bringing AIP the awesome possibility of $3,000,000 on this single reissue.

"In the course of a usual year," says Arkoff, "we'll do a couple of million dollars on all our combinations. It's found money for a few dollars in advertising costs."

The hundreds and thousands of dollars AIP saves from never shooting inside a studio and never paying for anything it can get free, from combinations and cannibalizing of prints, are all penny-ante games to the major studios, just as the satisfying $1,000,000 profits from *Dr. Phibes* or *Frogs* are laughable when placed beside the profits from an *Exorcist* or *Poseidon Adven-*

ture or *French Connection.* AIP retaliates with disgust at the extravagances it does not allow.

Unprompted, employee after employee expresses outrage at the excesses of *Darling Lili* ("Blake Edwards used to wait days for the proper cloud formations") and at the $8,000,000 cost of Mike Nichols's *Day of the Dolphin.* "Nichols sent an airplane from the island on which they were shooting to Miami to pick up twenty-one copies of *The New York Times,*" says production manager Schick.

The heart of AIP's operation is not on the streets or parking lots of Los Angeles where most of its pictures are filmed but in the Beverly Hills building where the production and sales departments scream at each other across the halls.

In a once-a-week meeting in the fourth-floor conference room, the heads of the production, sales, legal, administrative, and advertising staffs get together with Arkoff. The session is not run politely. When Arkoff came in with a suggestion for a picture about the double standard recently, he was hooted down as hopelessly old hat.

"We are the only company that brings sales into a picture before production," says Arkoff. Bringing the sales department in is a necessary evil. "The sales people think like exhibitors. If I have a *new* idea, they're negative. What did business before? Make another *Exorcist.* But there's no sense making a picture if our sales department can't think how to merchandise it.

"The word 'exploitation' has an evil connotation, but *everything* has to be exploited. Even something presented with extreme dignity—*Summer Wishes, Winter Dreams*—must be exploited. You must be able to let people know about it, know why they should come to see it. We are a merchandising company. That may sound inelegant. But when you are not dependent on the geniuses—the Fellinis—you're dependent on competent people. Producers and directors with a big hit think of themselves as geniuses. They take on the trappings of royalty. In Hollywood, 90 percent of the people consider themselves geniuses. In actuality, 10 percent are brightly creative, and the other 90 percent do a competent, workmanlike job.

"To make money, you must *sell* your pictures. If you have a picture that's not based on a presold book and doesn't have big stars, you obviously need more and different exploitation in relation to its cost. We got Ray Milland for *Frogs* because *Love Story* had brought him back to public attention. His price was reasonable, and his name gave the picture a kind of solidity, took it out of the category of something which only had fifteen cents spent on it." (Respectable actors such as Milland, Bette Davis, Shelley Winters, Michael Caine, and Anthony Quinn have been showing up in AIP pictures recently with ever-increasing frequency.)

Some pictures have specific problems. Arkoff and his sales department went round and round over the title of *Golden Needles.* The golden needles refer to acupuncture needles. Will the public misinterpret and think the film is a dope picture? The decision was made to stick with the title and write extremely explicit advertising copy. "But," says Arkoff, "if we've guessed wrong, we can't undo it. You can change the style of an ad, but you can't change a title in midstream."

Almost of equal importance to selling is buying. Arkoff does his market research at the Cannes Film Festival. He sits "in the outside bar of the Carlton Hotel for hours." Listening. Talking to distributors from Greece to Thailand to find out what films do well and where. "At my hotel," he sighs, "there was also the president of a major American film company. He played tennis every day and went to parties."

Several years ago at Cannes, Arkoff came across the Fellini–

Louis Malle–Roger Vadim trilogy, *Spirits of the Dead.* "They were offering the U.S. rights for $1,000,000," Arkoff recalls. "And it wasn't really a very good film. A year later when I went back to Cannes, the film was still available. Nobody had wanted it. I got it for $200,000. Then I told them we'd have to cut the Fellini. There was a gasp. NO! Nobody cuts Fellini. I was supposed to meet with Fellini on my next trip to Rome. His interpreter called up the night before. 'Don't come. He is furious that you wish to cut one of his pictures.' I went. And Fellini ended up amused. I showed him that it would give him a new, non–art house audience. And he did the cutting himself. We sold the film as a Poe, and the picture did quite well for us. It wasn't artistic enough to be merchandised any other way. We grossed over a million dollars on a picture that really had no market in the United States."

Arkoff lights another cigar and ponders his company's twenty-first year. Although he is not willing to renege on his Woolworth's line, he is, he admits, "going to add a higher line." AIP has already picked up "a wildly artistic film," James Ivory's fictionalized version of the Fatty Arbuckle scandal, *The Wild Party,* starring Raquel Welch and James Coco. And the studio is involved with Warner Bros. in the $1,500,000 *The Destructors,* starring Michael Caine, Anthony Quinn, and James Mason.

But, still, the long hot summer will bring to the theater or drive-in of your choice: *Foxy Brown (Don't mess aroun' with FOXY BROWN. She's the meanest chick in town)* extracting a black superwoman's revenge from the white world; Isaac Hayes as a black skip-tracer in *Truck Turner (the last of the bounty hunters); Madhouse (If stark terror were ecstasy, living here would be sheer bliss).*

And *Golden Needles. (From the mansions of Beverly Hills to the teeming waters of the China Seas, she sought the forbidden golden needles of Pleasure or Pain. For the one who owns them rules the world.)*

Sam Arkoff's penuriousness was not enough to save AIP from the changes that infect the movie industry every decade or so. The costs of making and marketing movies skyrocketed at the end of the 1970s. AIP's low-budget exploitation films were no longer satisfying to teen-agers dazzled by the special effects of Star Wars. A high-budget attempt to cash in on the success of disaster films, Meteor, was no worse than any number of disaster films that had been successful a few years earlier, but Meteor had the misfortune to come at the end of the cycle. After agonizing for months, Arkoff, who was squeezed for cash, finally sold his company to Filmways in March 1979 for approximately $25 million. Ironically, if he had waited until the summer, he might not have had to sell. Love at First Bite, a spoof of vampire films, did well at the box office and earned AIP more than $18 million in film rentals, and The Amityville Horror was the fifth most successful movie of the year, returning $35 million in film rentals.

Richard Bloch, the proprietor of Filmways, quickly fell into the trap that Arkoff had avoided for 25 years. He tried to become an instant major studio. Among the unnecessary remnants of AIP's lower-class image that he threw out was Arkoff. When AIP became a subsidiary of Filmways, Arkoff had stayed as chairman and chief executive officer. He resigned in December 1979. Nearly every one of Filmways' "major" movies was a commercial disaster. Brian De Palma's Blow Out, which cost $18 million to make and another $9 million to market, returned only $8 million in film rentals. Filmways was in trouble. Its stock fell. It had to sell its successful insurance division and deal off several of its expensive movies to other companies, including Ridley Scott's Blade Runner and Dino De Laurentiis's $25 million Ragtime.

In February 1982 Bloch bailed out. Orion, a movie production company founded in 1978 by the former top management of United Artists, purchased Filmways for $26 million. Filmways was renamed Orion.

In the fall of 1982, one of Orion's first releases after swallowing Filmways, which had swallowed AIP, was Sylvester Stallone's First Blood. First Blood, a prototypical exploitation movie about a berserk ex-Vietnam veteran who outwits hundreds of policemen, tanks, and National Guard regiments, would have done AIP proud. It was a success at the box office.

How Hollywood Decides
If a Film Is a Hit

How can you tell if a movie is a hit? Why does the Hollywood grapevine insist that one film is a failure because it made $4 million its opening weekend, while another is a success because it also made $4 million that weekend?

Unlike a horse race, where 14 animals cover the same course at the same time, movies can be released in 42 theaters or 900 theaters, can be supported by $1 million in advertising or $10 million, can burn out in a week or play, as *Private Benjamin* did, for nine months.

The best way such apples and oranges can be compared is by using a per-theater average, comparing the average amount of money a movie takes in at each theater. Robert Cort, vice president of advertising at 20th Century-Fox, has a comparison system that ranges from "Wow" (over $15,000 a theater the first week) through "outstanding," "strong," "O.K.," "soft," and "disappointing" to "disastrous" (below $3,000 a theater).

Cort's system is accurate for movies that break nationally

in 600 to 800 theaters. The more theaters a film plays, the lower one can expect the per-theater average to be, because the additional theaters are small ones in small towns. Conversely, when a movie plays in only 200 or 300 theaters, they tend to be the bigger ones in larger towns, so the per-theater average should be higher.

Smokey and the Bandit II, which took in more money than any other movie its opening week, played in 1,201 theaters and averaged $15,000 a theater, while *The Empire Strikes Back* averaged nearly $25,000 a theater when it broke wide in 824 theaters its fifth week. The first signs that *Bustin' Loose* and *The Four Seasons* might be hits came because *Bustin' Loose* averaged an outstanding $10,000 its first week, while *The Four Seasons* averaged an even more outstanding $11,000.

While *Outland* averaged $11,688 the same week in approximately 350 theaters, it was actually perceived to be in possible trouble. Because it had opened in fewer than half the standard 700 to 800 theaters, it was expected to have a higher per-theater average. (In 126 theaters its first week, *The Empire Strikes Back* averaged $76,201, the highest average ever attained by a movie playing in more than 100 theaters.)

The next key sign to a movie's future comes in comparing what it did at the box office the first week with how it performs the second week. A drop of more than 20 percent usually means that a movie is in trouble, although exploitation films, which rarely have a life of more than two or three weeks, routinely drop 30 percent their second week. *Happy Birthday to Me,* a relatively successful horror movie, dropped 30 percent its second week, while *Take This Job and Shove It,* a surprisingly successful blue-collar comedy, also dropped 30 percent.

The portents for *The Four Seasons,* Alan Alda's comedy of middle age, were particularly good, as the movie was off only 2 percent its second weekend, while *Outland* was down 11 percent and *Bustin' Loose* was down 21 percent. Even *Bustin'*

Loose's minus 21 percent, however, was not too much of a cause for concern, because the second weekend had to be compared with the inflated box-office grosses of the Memorial Day holiday weekend when the movies opened. Another omen is that *The Four Seasons* received its box-office gross without the purchase of television time the second week, while *Outland*'s decline occurred despite television commercials.

What really makes a hit movie is staying power, referred to in the industry as "legs." A failure is often discernible by the second week; a success takes six weeks to appraise. In an industry in which the box-office appeal of themes, stars, and plots is now being tested before a studio agrees to finance a movie, that magical audience word-of-mouth that makes a hit is still unpredictable. *The Shining* opened to incredibly high ticket sales in May 1980; by the third week, sales had plummeted. *Brubaker* opened only moderately well around the same time but played solidly through the summer.

The Shining brought Warner Bros. $10 million more than *Brubaker* brought Fox, but it also cost $10 million more, and considerably more money was spent advertising it. Even gigantic box-office hits are not profitable if they cost more than they earn. Paramount's *Star Trek* earned money, approximately $56 million in film rentals in the United States and Canada. But the combined total of its cost and advertising was $52 million. Paramount's *Airplane,* which earned $38 million, cost $3.5 million, with approximately $6 million spent on advertising.

The last scene in the drama of how well a movie will ultimately do is played away from the spotlight of American moviegoers. Many a movie has crept into black ink because it has done well abroad. *1941,* a high-budget disaster at United States theaters, was salvaged by foreign theatergoers who responded to its anarchic clashes of tanks and airplanes. Other films have crawled to the profit side of the studio ledger because of a good sale to television.

Reap the Wilder Wind

Last Friday (June 22, 1979) was Billy Wilder's seventy-third birthday, and he had been making movies for exactly 50 years. The morning was punctuated with telephone calls praising him for having reached both milestones with his teeth, appetite, and biting wit intact.

"When you make your first picture, there's nothing to it," he said. "Little do you know the abyss beneath, how little chance there is of getting over the tightrope to the other side. With each picture, I get more frightened. You see how the percentages are against you for making a financially successful movie so they'll give you money to make another. As you get older, you're also gambling with time. There are fewer bullets in your gun. Unless you're a hack, you become reluctant to fire at a target."

Wilder, the first man to win three Academy Awards in a single night—as a writer, director, and producer of *The Apartment* in 1960—is not currently in fashion. "I'm the only man in town not thinking in terms of Dracula pictures, disco pictures, another Vietnam picture, or a monster extravaganza with gorgons made out of Gorgonzola," he said. "I kind of roll my own." His last movie, *Fedora,* based on a Tom Tryon novella, had a rudely unpleasant history: he would, he said, "start crying" if he were not able to deflect his memories with a joke.

Wilder sighed and rubbed his plump pink cheeks. He is a compact man, with pale skin, and when he talked about *Fedora,* he circled and recircled his office, as though the electricity in the subject made too painful a shock if he sat still. " 'Turnaround,' one of the ugly new words that sprang up in Hollywood," he said. "After I finished the script, I got a short little telephone call from Universal to tell me they were not going to continue the project. I folded my tent and started offering the script around town and got a unanimous NO. Nowadays, you have to go out and get the money to make your picture. By the time you're ready to direct, you're totally exhausted. In the olden, marvelous days, when those illiterate moguls were running the studios, we were spared all that."

Fedora is the melodramatic story of a mysterious movie star, played by Marthe Keller, who has managed to keep age at bay for 60 years; William Holden is a down-at-the-heels movie producer who discovers her bizarre secret. Vincent Canby called it "seasoned, elegant, funny and hugely entertaining" in *The New York Times.* Janet Maslin saw it four times and wrote of it as "A fabulous relic . . . old-fashioned with a vengeance, a proud, passionate remembrance of the way movies used to be . . . Rich, majestic, very close to ridiculous, and also a little bit mad."

After *Fedora* was rejected by Hollywood, it was made with German tax-shelter money. Then the negative sat on a shelf in Munich for a year and a half. "And," said Wilder, "unlike violins and wine, pictures don't get better with age. They don't improve when they're covered with cobwebs." Then a tangle among Lorimar, Allied Artists, and United Artists ended up, Wilder said, "with United Artists releasing it in a perfunctory and insulting way and spending about $625 on an advertising campaign."

Even so, the picture will, he said, make money. "It only cost $4 million, a B-movie price today; and it did extremely well in France and quite well in Germany. The thing that makes me miserable is that a picture that shows a small profit is regarded as a washout. A picture that makes its money back, keeps people employed, adds to the stature of the studio, is of no interest to them. In their eyes, it's a failure."

The "them" to whom he referred contemptuously are: "All those vice presidents you remember from when they were mail boys at William Morris or MCA or second-echelon lawyers; those worldy wise young men who ask for their quiche Lorraine al dente and have *The World According to Garp* on their coffee tables. But they've only read twelve pages, and they don't need to finish the book because another studio has already bought it. You may have had to drive at two miles per hour for Goldwyn, L. B. Mayer, or Harry Cohn to be able to read the Burma Shave signs, but I have great affection for those days when we made movies and didn't call it *cinema.*"

Among the movies of which Mr. Wilder is co-author (mostly with Charles Brackett or I. A. L. Diamond), and for which he was nominated for Academy Awards, are *Ninotchka, Hold Back the Dawn, Double Indemnity, A Foreign Affair, The Big Carnival* (also titled *Ace in the Hole*), *Sabrina, Some Like It Hot,* and *The Fortune Cookie.* As a director, he has been nominated eight times. In addition to *The Apartment,* he has won Oscars for writing and directing *The Lost Weekend* and for writing *Sunset Boulevard.*

It is *Sunset Boulevard* that *Fedora* most resembles, and the resemblances are not accidental. "I made *Sunset Boulevard* thirty-one years ago. A painter is allowed to paint in the same style. Surely, one is allowed variations on a theme, some added thoughts." Both movies star William Holden, and Mr. Wilder was pleased to have Mr. Holden in *Fedora,* as a link. "I didn't want audiences to forget *Sunset Boulevard.* But this variation is not just about the madness of a star. Fedora is a very rational and cunning woman who has written a scenario of her life and wants to bring it to the end she planned. *Fedora* was so much more difficult to do because it was almost uncastable. Not only did I have an authentic star in Gloria Swanson in *Sunset Boulevard,* I had Erich von Stroheim, H. B. Warner, Buster Keaton."

Wilder is well aware that the denouement of *Fedora,* the unraveling of the dreadful secret, comes midway through the film. "We worked with a big gimmick. We didn't think it would hold for two hours, and if it comes out at the very, very end, you never feel anything about that character trapped in a role. Should the story have been done at all? I'm only afraid if I do something bad, not something controversial."

When he was young, he used to torment himself "by directing last year's picture over and over."

"There's nothing I can do to change *Fedora* now," he went on. "It's last year's snow. It's melted; it's gone." Yet he would like to make changes, particularly in the placement of a dramatic scene between Michael York and Fedora's corpse, to which audiences respond by laughing. "But the negative was in a vault in Munich; I didn't have access to it; and then came the sheer exhaustion. I used to make a picture a year. This one took three and a half years." Although he doesn't "particularly cherish an audience laughing in the wrong place," there is nothing he can do.

He has considered leaving Hollywood, "getting the hell out of this Kafka atmosphere, like Elia Kazan, Joe Mankiewicz, Mike Nichols, Freddy Zinnemann, Stanley Kubrick," mailing his movies in from foreign addresses. But he has been in Hollywood since Adolf Hitler drove him into the arms of Adolph Zukor. "It is my métier," he said—not only of the movies but of the place.

He has compromised by leaving the studio lots, where, he said with a certain amount of frustration, "It is no longer even clear whose behind you should kiss." You realize, he asked, in speaking of the new Hollywood, "that Mr. Marlon Brando got, for an aggregate of twenty minutes on the screen in *Superman* and *Apocalypse Now*, more money than Clark Gable got for twenty years at MGM?" He described Universal, Warner Bros., and Columbia—three studios that huddle close together—as " 'The Bermuda Triangle.' People disappear there without even an oil slick." For the last two years, his office has been in the eccentric Writers and Artists Building in Beverly Hills. The day he moved in, he stopped reading the daily trade papers and, he said happily, "have no idea whether *Damian II* will outgross *Rocky II.*"

He is working on a farce, for which he dreams of Jack Lemmon and Walter Matthau, and a melodrama of social comment along the lines of his classic *Ace in the Hole.* He is, he conceded, "procrastinating, dreading the moment when I have to audition for all those vice presidents."

"I know," he said, "that to go from the ten Best Pictures to the one hundred Neediest Cases just takes one year. A fellow director in my age group was told to wear some old jeans and Adidas sneakers to his audition last week."

His office is bold, with walls of white pegboard, chairs of black leather, blistering graphics, a bleached cow skull. He is an accumulator of *things,* from Early American toys to Japanese dwarf trees. That birthday evening, his wife was to make him a special dinner—blini, Scotch salmon, petite marmite soup. He would open a bottle of his favorite champagne and listen to the Dodgers play St. Louis. He expected to spend the following afternoon at his beach house on the sand, flying one of his 30 kites. He has kites for every mood, from German stukas to Chinese dragons. "But my kite flying is brimming with self-doubt," he said.

He is jovial, clever, acerbic, peremptory, crafting his sentences with a sophisticated eye and a razor tongue; and he wants to be thought "adorable." But he is never, not ever, brimming with self-doubt.

He lighted a cigar. "Movies are all I know. I'll go to bat again here if they let me. If they don't let me, I'll latch on to a Japanese team, sit on the bench and wait for Kurosawa to break his leg."

When Billy Wilder came to America and American movies in the 1930s, he was working in a foreign language but not, in one sense, for a foreign audience. He was young, movies were young, and if his cynicism was a little extreme for cheerful Americans, his wit and mordant humor made it palatable. Now Wilder is nearly 80 and movies are made for teen-agers. Wilder has completed one movie since Fedora—Buddy Buddy, a dyspeptic farce about a man who is trying to commit suicide. Like another Viennese émigré, Fred Zinnemann—whose glacial treatment of a doomed love, Five Days One Summer, is much less shocking than it is meant to be —Wilder seems to have nothing to say to an audience young enough to be his great-grandchildren. But, like the man himself, his earlier work still delights and captivates. Some Like It Hot will, most likely, be enjoyed by his great-grandchildren's grandchildren, although both Zinnemann and Wilder are probably doomed to the retrospectives and honors that beribbon the chests of every major director who is lucky enough to live long enough to become dispensable.

Fonda at Forty

The kitchen is suffocatingly hot. Several years ago the hundred-year-old wood-frame house had no electricity. There is still no insulation, so Jane Fonda is sweating as she stands barefoot in front of her ancient white-enamel stove, eating the potato she has baked for her supper.

Most of the things in the house are cheap or damaged, purchased from thrift shops or borrowed from friends. There is no dishwasher, no garbage disposal, no set of enameled canisters, not even a double sink. Cereal, flour, sugar sit on open shelves in old quart jars; and her bed is a mattress on the floor that she shares with her second husband, political activist Tom Hayden.

Across the bedroom is an elegant English filing cabinet, cherry wood or walnut. "From my other life," she says, stroking the polished wood. In her 40 years, Jane Fonda has left a trail of other lives, like bread crumbs, behind her. She moved from a childhood of fine china and too many servants as the shy, awkward, tomboy daughter of movie star Henry Fonda to her own movie success as a coltish, long-legged ingenue in *Tall*

Story, The Chapman Report, Period of Adjustment, Any Wednesday. She leapt from those early simple-minded movies, which hardly required more of her than good cheekbones and liquid grace, to Paris and French movie director Roger Vadim. She was, says a friend who knew her in the late sixties, "for five years the perfect wife. She got up to make his breakfast, did the marketing, spent the day acting in his movies, made his dinner, entertained his friends." Whatever Vadim wanted, Jane was prepared to do, including turn herself into a wide-screen sex object as his *Barbarella.*

There are still a few mementos left from all those lives—an Early American dining-room table, a Queen Anne sideboard, and Vanessa Vadim, her nine-year-old daughter by her first husband. But the dining-room table is just a place to eat. The mental furniture from the past has been demolished during the past seven years.

Jane fries two eggs and dumps them into the baked potato. Then she fills a glass with organic apple juice for Troy, her four-year-old son by Hayden. She tilts her head back and takes two or three long gulps from the half-gallon plastic jug before returning it to the refrigerator. A few drops trickle unnoticed down her tie-dyed blouse. Troy is feverish and stalked by dreams. It is Jane who has zipped up his woolen sleepers against the ocean fog that will tie knots around the house by midnight. It is she who will sit and read from the picture books stored from her own childhood.

"We don't have people who work for us. There's no one who does laundry. There's no nanny. There's no cook. We do our own shopping. The laundry piles up because we both work long hours. If you want to be responsible for your life, it means you have to be responsible for your whole life, not just the pretty parts. I've always been ashamed of privilege. It began with my not ever understanding why it was that the people who have a lot are the ones other people are trying to give things to.

We didn't need anyone to give us a car or five cases of free beer or a free trip to New York. It didn't make any sense to me that I should eat all my food because there were children starving in Europe and yet we would accept all those freebies. I knew there were other people who needed them more, but no one offered gifts to them. I hated to feel different. I hated to feel set apart by privilege. And yet it's difficult to give up a way of life unless there's an alternative. I knew no alternative until I came back to the United States in 1970 and began to have contact with political activists. They worked harder than any people I had ever met, and they were trying to grapple with fundamental problems: how people should relate to each other, how women should be treated differently, how much is fair. They were putting themselves on the line, and I felt like—at last—I had come home."

In her faded blue jeans and faded blouse, pushing long strands of frizzy, tangled hair out of her eyes, Jane Fonda flaunts her age. There is no artifice—no lipstick, rouge, eye liner, mascara—to chisel off the years. Months too early she proclaims herself 40, embracing a destination "from which I used to run in terror. I was scared at turning thirty, terrified about growing old." She tells of dropping in, a few weeks ago, at the apartment of actor James Caan and finding a roomful of *"Playboy* pinups—young, sexy, exquisitely beautiful women. The anxiety I would have felt before, the competition, the desire to shrink into the wall—they were just gone from my life."

It is a constant motif—that she has given up competition for communality, exotic pleasures for simple ones, the decadence of buying for the decency of trying to exist on as little as possible. What makes it believable is not her considerable ability as an actress but the urgency with which she has plunged into this life, the ferocity with which she has stripped her closets and her pocketbook.

One cannot question the commitment, only its permanence.

She has always had a fierce single-mindedness that people con-
fuse with anger, although she is not, in most senses, an angry
person. Each of her past lives ended with an abrupt and abrasive cutting off, a sharp knife thrust at the cords that bound her
to ideas, places, people. The perfect young wife renovating
Vadim's eighteenth-century farmhouse in the south of France
hardly exists, even in memory. So one cannot totally trust her
word that this new life will be forever.

But it has already lasted seven years, and she speaks of it
with an evangelical fervor. "I grew up without a belief structure. There was a lot of emphasis on the way you looked, on
being slender, on buying your clothes in the right stores, on
being well dressed and popular. I reached the age of thirty-two
with nothing that guided my life. My choices were usually
haphazard and usually governed by what society said—jobs,
money, and upward mobility. A belief structure gives you a
reason for living. It allows you not to be tissue paper in a
stream."

Troy calls hoarsely from his bedroom under the eaves. He
is afraid of being left alone in the dark. Jane Fonda turns on
another light. He will never be alone in the dark, she says. Her
words are reality and metaphor. What she wishes for both her
children, she says, "is the understanding that they have a fundamental right to participate in the decisions that control their
lives and so does every single person who is alive."

She sits cross-legged on the floor and says matter-of-factly
—in her brusque, no-nonsense, English nanny voice—that she
has committed the rest of her life to the Campaign for Economic Democracy, an organization that her husband has
founded. There have been few men in Jane Fonda's life, but
each one has had immense influence not only over her emotions
but over her values. One is reminded of the way her Lillian
Hellman in *Julia* sat at the feet of Jason Robards's Dashiell
Hammett, a dutiful pupil tearing up her play when Hammett

tells her it isn't good enough. Fifteen years ago there was drama coach Andreas Voutsinas and her own burning passion to be the best and purest and most dedicated of actresses. Voutsinas was followed by Vadim, and she became a fashionable Parisian wife. Now she fits equally snugly into Hayden's life as a visionary and labor organizer.

By the time Jane Fonda met Hayden in the spring of 1972, she had an FBI file several inches thick, had been denounced by a number of senators and had earned a reputation as an abrasive agitator against the Vietnam war. She had even been taken into custody by the United States government for bringing dangerous drugs—which turned out to be tranquilizers—into the country. She thought she was totally dedicated. A year earlier, driving to Denver for an antiwar rally, she had realized "that I couldn't be a political activist in one part of me and continue to live like a movie star. I've never been able to do anything partway, and I didn't want to see myself as one of those do-gooders, those social ladies who come down out of their Beverly Hills houses and administer to the underprivileged." She tore up the lease on her Beverly Hills house and "moved into a house in the valley that was a far cry from what I'd been prepared for. It was a very modest house—at least I thought it was—and I was quite proud of myself."

She stopped being proud of herself when she met Hayden, a homely man with an enormous nose and a scarred face, who almost always wears a pair of torn blue jeans and a white T-shirt. In casual conversation, he is polite and quiet and gives no hint of the charisma that has already made him, at the age of 37, the leader of two political movements. In 1968 Hayden —an organizer of the anti–Vietnam war movement—had been arrested for disrupting the Democratic Convention in Chicago. In February 1970, he was convicted under the antiriot provisions of the 1968 Civil Rights Act. Two years later his conviction was overturned. By 1975 he would be losing in the

Democratic primary for United States Senator from California.

Her idea of modest living, Jane Fonda discovered, was considerably grander than Hayden's; he even had to borrow a tie from his lawyer whenever he was required to appear in court. "If you grow up with privilege and, on top of that, you're a movie star, there are some cancers that work their way into your soul. You're in the center of things, and there are a lot of people around whose job it is to very cleverly make you think you're special because, if they don't, then you'll fire them. But what is most pernicious is the subtle internalizing of that sense of privilege."

She found that her *modest* house was intimidatingly large to the people with whom she was working. "One Vietnamese student said, 'The rooms are so big.' Well, it was a house that had insulation between the walls, and none of the people I now know live in houses with insulation between the walls—including me." The house had a swimming pool, which Hayden never used. "He never said anything. He never criticized me. But he didn't go near the pool. And one day we were walking in the garden and I said, 'Isn't it pretty?' And he said, 'Yes, but it isn't right.' "

Within a few months she had shed the house and the pretty furniture and the swimming pool. "Inside myself, I was beginning to feel the contradiction between the way I was living and the way the people with whom I was working and who had become my friends were living. There was too much difference." With Hayden, she bought a two-story house in a low-income beach community and lent the bottom half to friends. (Ironically, the house, which cost them $40,000, is now worth over $100,000; real estate in Southern California, always expensive, has gone berserk during the last three years.) The house sits on a narrow street a block from the ocean. All the houses are old and neatly painted. They are owned by plumbers, hippies, and aircraft-factory workers. At 7:00 p.m. half a dozen

men wander from front porch to front porch drinking cans of
beer.

"It's important for me to live here," Jane Fonda says ear-
nestly. "Obviously, there's no way I can totally understand the
problems of a man or woman working on an assembly line. I
am famous, with the money and mobility that comes with fame.
But if you're a political organizer—which I am—you can't deal
with people unless you're trying to share their problems."

She even tries to share their problems through her work.
She insists that the producers of the movies hire any blacks,
Chicanos, and women who are on the rosters of the craft unions. On her last three films her make-up has been done by the
only black woman who is a member of the union. And several
years ago she decided "not to make any more films that lie. My
first concern is, 'Is the film about something that has any rele-
vance to our lives?' " In 1977 she made a comedy, *Fun with Dick
and Jane,* partly because she was tired of people saying she had
no sense of humor but also because "the script, with all its
faults, was about an absolute reality in American life: Middle-
class Americans are going broke. The layoff comes and the
bottom falls out." She followed *Fun with Dick and Jane* with
Julia, Lillian Hellman's memoir of a remarkable friendship
between two women. Her next film, *Coming Home,* is about
paraplegic Vietnam war veterans and the woman who falls in
love with one of them. And she has also completed *Comes a
Horseman,* a post–World War II Western about a woman and
a man (James Caan) who join together to fight for their lands
against a man obsessed with empire building.

If there is an inherent contradiction in this lean, independent woman with eyes as blue as marbles—who is unquestionably the most wooed and petted and desired American actress
at the moment—yoking herself to the oxcart of the common
man, her commitment is too great for her to feel it. "I've
committed my life to a very, very, very long struggle. We're

building a movement that will last fifty years. We'll lose and lose and lose again before we win, and I may not be around to see us win."

Winning, to the Campaign for Economic Democracy, means restructuring the economic system. "We have certain political rights. We can vote. We have freedom of the press, freedom of religion. But when it comes down to what makes our lives what they are—which is the economy—we have no democratic control at all."

She excuses herself and goes to make the bed. Nor does she feel any contradiction between the domestic gesture and the larger social canvas. Both allow her "to feel comfortable inside my own skin." Her marriage is an extension of the Campaign for Economic Democracy, CED a part of her marriage. In public she and Hayden rarely touch. Even when their engagement was announced in Norway in 1972, they did not kiss or hold hands.

She will, Jane Fonda says, remain married to Hayden for the rest of her life. "It would be indulgent for us to allow something to happen to our marriage. It's important to the children. It's important as an example to other people. When two people share a vision and have a sense of responsibility beyond themselves, it's important that their marriage work out."

There is another reason. "In order to make a long-term commitment, you have to have a stable personal life. I don't think you can work to achieve social justice or social change without sustenance and support—and children, who are the future. I am not prepared to give up love or friendship or my children. Beyond that, I learn more and more to give up all the other things that I was taught one ought to want to have."

She has painfully reduced her "want quotient" by 75 percent. It hasn't been easy. The bed in Vanessa's room is the most beautiful and expensive bunk bed sold in Los Angeles, a purchase Jane couldn't resist. She envies Hayden, whose desire for material possessions is limited to books. (And yet Hayden says ruefully that he never had to be concerned about the alternatives to poverty before he met his wife. And that he is finding it too easy now to make long-distance telephone calls when a letter would do.)

She sits beneath a bunch of balloons hanging from a pink ceiling. There are balloons and colors that assault the eye everywhere. The hall is orange, the kitchen pink, the bathroom fire-engine red. Like the plants that dangle from every ceiling and sit on top of every surface, the bright colors are "a cheap way to decorate." Fonda touches a Boston fern tenderly. She is surrounded by ficus, spider plants, onion, a sweet-potato vine curling across the stove, philodendron, a fat ivy trailing down the bottled water, and rhododendrons. She loves plants, she says. And, in the next breath, "Plants cost too much money. I should be able to do without so many."

It is Jane's money that supports the marriage. In a good year, she can make a million dollars. Hayden has never earned more than $6,000 in a year. Tonight he is speaking at a nearby college. His fee will be used to pay CED organizers. It was decided a long time ago that the day-to-day operations of CED, the salaries of the organizers, the money it takes to build a movement, would not come from Jane. "If we can't raise our own money, there's something wrong with what we're doing; and my money can't be a crutch to that. So the question became, 'What do I do with this ridiculous amount of money that I earn?' "

The answer was to buy a 120-acre ranch near Santa Barbara with a $100,000 down payment and a mortgage on her future earnings. The $500,000 ranch is "a way of putting down roots for the organization, a way of bringing our people together in a human community." In the summer it is used as a camp for an interracial, intercultural group of black, brown, white,

Asian, and handicapped children—including Vanessa Vadim, who arrived from Paris with a piggy bank full of money and a suitcase of new toys. After a certain amount of agonizing on the part of the counselors over how to treat the daughter of Jane Fonda, the piggy bank was taken away and the toys were made communal.

She is determined that her children will not be emotionally short-changed. There is, she says, "nothing militant about our life-style. The kids have as many toys as anyone else on the street. Vanessa complains about the lack of privacy because our house is small, but she does have her own bedroom. What counts is who puts you to bed, who gets you up, who teaches you to live. My main contact was with servants. There was the governess, the chauffeur, the gardener, and a German cook I was convinced was trying to poison us."

During the year Tom Hayden ran for the Senate, it was Jane Fonda who cleaned the house, cooked the meals, and put the children to bed. During *Coming Home* and the five months she spent in Europe for *Julia,* it was Hayden who cleaned the house, cooked the meals, put the children to bed, and worked one day a week in the community nursery school he had helped to establish. "Tom's commitment to his child is very, very deep, and he puts hours a day into it," Jane says. When she told him to have his mother come to help out, he refused. "I took a year away from them to run for office. I owe it to my family to put in this kind of time," he said.

In Colorado last summer, when Jane was making *Comes a Horseman* and Hayden was writing his autobiography, they juggled the care of Troy. (Vanessa was with her father in Paris. Completely bilingual, she spends some school semesters at a conservative girls' school in France and the rest in a free-form, experimental public school in California.) Provided with new cheap toys—a cowboy hat, a set of magnets, a box of crayons —Troy played in the fields among the cow dung outside his mother's trailer. But when he was sick with an unexplained fever, it was his father to whom he clung.

The telephone rings. Jane Fonda answers it in a tone so curt as to be almost rude. And yet there is no lack of politeness in her words. She has beautiful manners and a physical grace that she could not shed, even if she wanted to. But she has no leisure time, not even time enough for unnecessary courtesy on the telephone. If she misses anything from her old lives, it is not a garbage disposal or silver platters but the time to indulge herself in doing nothing.

The phone call is from someone who needs information about SolarCal, CED's attempt to keep the sun out of the hands of the gas and oil companies by making solar energy a public corporation in California. Next week she will start a speaking tour for SolarCal. Tomorrow she will go to the ranch to act as hostess at an explanatory breakfast for some state legislators.

Her style has changed since 1971. She has breakfast with congressmen rather than standing outside the gates of army camps denouncing them. But her anger spurts out at the people who have sanitized her, made her respectable during the last year or two. "I hate the isn't-it-wonderful-she's-come-back-to-her-senses-and-joined-the-fold. I'm more profoundly committed to what I believe in now than in the days when I was considered a traitor. Today I'm polite because it's possible. You couldn't be polite six years ago. It wasn't until Watergate began to be exposed that we could work through the system. And we did immediately. We came off the streets and into the halls of Congress to lobby."

The anger subsides. She rubs her toes and looks at the balloons on the ceiling. The word for her life, she says reflectively, is *joyful.*

"Joy is having a reason for living. Joy is having belief. Joy is knowing that you are part of an historical force that can make life better for people. There's this funny thing that I get told all the time. 'You sacrifice so much!' If you felt empty most of your life and you don't feel empty any more, if you've felt irrelevant and apathetic and numb and you don't feel like that any more, then what have you sacrificed?

"I've sacrificed emptiness and numbness and irrelevance."

Time rarely stands still in Hollywood. Fashions in faces are ephemeral. Careers are, most often, toys of the moment, not durable, neither mar-proof nor skid-proof. In Hollywood, five years can be a decade.

Yet nothing has disintegrated for Jane Fonda in the last five years—not her commitment, not her success, not her body. She won her second Academy Award as best actress for her performance as the mousy wife of an army officer who is radicalized by a paraplegic veteran of the Vietnam war in Coming Home. In such delicate ironies are life and art intermingled. And 9 to 5, a silly comedy which she insists was a tribute to American secretaries, earned more than $100 million.

Perhaps the most surprising turn her life has taken is that, as she approaches her forty-fifth birthday, her beauty has become its own industry. She owns a chain of trendy and moneymaking health clubs, Jane Fonda's Workout. The video cassette, videodisk, and book versions of her exercise program are best-sellers. She has also admitted publicly her most shameful secret, that for more than 20 years she vomited up each meal in a fanatic attempt to keep her figure. But she is so much a part of the mainstream now that even the confession of her bulimia did not shock. Bulimia, it seems, is a middle-class sin, a guilty secret shared by millions of American women.

When I last saw her, in the fall of 1982, she was spending her afternoons *walking door to door in west Los Angeles, passing out literature in her husband's successful campaign for the California State Assembly. "Hi," she said to each startled housewife, "I'm Jane Fonda."*

Video Wars: Hollywood's Corporate Rollerderby

There is always turmoil in Hollywood.

Big-budget movies like *Dr. Dolittle* or *Heaven's Gate* collapse at the box office, dragging their studios partway down with them. A blizzard buries the Northeast or a drought parches the Southwest, crippling January—or June—theater attendance. The extravagantly expensive $15 million remake of *Ben-Hur* in 1959 brings MGM $96 million, starting an avalanche of expensive epics. *Rocky* costs $1 million and earns United Artists $74 million, and every studio scrambles to make inexpensive movies about the ordinary guy. Filmways buys American International Pictures; Orion swallows up Filmways. A star is born in *Superman,* and ten other movies about comic-strip characters are planned; a star dies in an icy ocean at midnight, and her studio and its insurance companies fight over finishing her uncompleted movie. A dozen films fail and the man who chose to make them is swept out of his baroque office and barred from the studio lot as though his lack of luck were contagious.

But the turmoil that began three years ago, and will last for the next three years, is a different order of chaos. Today, the winds of change are blowing cold air at Hollywood's neck. "In my thirty-five years in the business, business has never been more dead," says one actor's agent. "The studios seem immobilized when it comes to saying yes to anything."

There are other signs of distress. In 1981 and 1982, more than 50 percent of the 22,000 members of Hollywood unions were out of work. "We've had serious unemployment for over two years, and we see no hope for much improvement until the fall," says Mac St. Johns, spokesman for the International Alliance of Theatrical Stage Employees. What is particularly ominous is that more than half of the art directors are unemployed. The 300 art directors are the first craftsmen hired on a movie or television production, so "the signs don't bode well for the summer," St. Johns adds.

In less than three years, Hollywood has suffered through a 10-week strike of 60,000 actors, a 13-week strike by its writers, and a threatened strike by its directors. Studios have changed hands like trading cards. At the box office, there is little middle ground. *Superman, Raiders of the Lost Ark,* and *Stir Crazy* are massive hits; *Sphinx, All the Marbles,* and *Cannery Row* are in and out of theaters in a week.

The men who now occupy the ornate offices and enjoy the titles of chief executive officer or chief operating officer at the six major studios recognize that most of their industry's current convulsions are part of something larger—call it an evolution or a revolution, a transition or a takeover—that will change the movie industry as dramatically as television did some 30 years ago.

"This precise time, this historical moment, the actions we take in the next year, will dictate the make-up of this industry twenty years from now," says Barry Diller, 41, chairman of Paramount Pictures. "In twenty years," Diller adds, "I don't believe all the same major movie companies that have been around for the last fifty years will still be here."

Diller's words are echoed by at least two other chairmen, each of whom feels his own company will prosper. But Hollywood has guessed wrong in the past and at least some of these gentlemen may very well be guessing wrong again.

Nevertheless, the film industry—like some primeval amphibian taking its first heady gulps of air—is waddling onto the shores of yet another great technological revolution, like those which introduced sound, color, and television. That analogy is offered by a well-tailored executive, who quickly coughs and replaces the thought with something more suitably technical.

Quite simply, the whole range of new technologies—basic advertiser-supported cable television; pay-cable television (Home Box Office and Showtime); direct-broadcast satellite television; over-the-air, subscription pay-television; video cassettes and videodisks—mean tremendous new worldwide markets for Hollywood films. (The actors and writers were willing to endure long, bitter strikes in order to get some share in the profits of original programs made for these new technologies.) Let three incompatible kinds of videodisks fight with two incompatible video-cassette recorders. Let the wires of cable television win over direct broadcasts from satellites to a disk no bigger than a saucer placed in your bedroom window. Or let the satellites win. "I have absolutely no interest in the hardware," says Frank E. Rosenfelt, 61, chairman of Metro-Goldwyn-Mayer. "I don't own a screwdriver. I don't even know how my television set works. All I know is they need programming and I have the programming. All I care about is that it's my product and I get paid for it."

Alan J. Hirschfield, 46, chairman of 20th Century-Fox, is more succinct: "I don't care if the milkman brings the disk. You can't sell milk without cows, and I've got the cows!"

By the summer of 1985, according to one studio's research, a blockbuster movie from a major studio will earn $25 million from the various pay-cable and subscription-television systems.

"Nonsense," says Hirschfield, the most fervent investigator of how to turn the new technologies to his studio's advantage. "A blockbuster will get $40 million."

Yet that $40 million is only a stopgap, a way station on what Diller describes as "the path to the future. We're all trying to see as far down that path as possible. At the moment, the end of the path is pay-per-view."

"Right now," says Hirschfield, describing pay-per-view, "the equipment is going in that will enable a cable subscriber to order programming on a per-view basis and have the cable operator bill him."

In pay-per-view, a movie will earn $40 million or $80 million or $120 million in a single night. And the means of getting that money—so-called addressable cable, the technical term for the equipment behind pay-per-view—dots the conversation of each of the studio chairmen like raisins on a sticky bun.

It's not that pay-per-view is a new idea. It has been available for years to the million subscribers of over-the-air pay television. In January 1978, Columbia's movie *The Deep,* starring Nick Nolte and Jacqueline Bisset, was shown pay-per-view over ON-TV in Los Angeles. Of ON-TV's 20,000 subscribers, well more than half paid $3 to see the movie, which had already played for several months in theaters. In the fall of 1981, subscription-television customers could buy both a Rolling Stones concert and the Sugar Ray Leonard–Thomas Hearns welterweight championship fight ($15 per subscriber, for a total gross of $7.5 million). A year later, in September 1982, *Star Wars* became the first movie to be shown nationally on pay-per-view. Despite the fact that *Star Wars* had just been released on video cassette and was also playing a reissue run in movie theaters, approximately 30 percent of subscribers hooked up for pay-per-view paid up to $8 apiece to see the film. The rub was that only the one million subscribers to over-the-air pay-television and

500,000 subscribers to newly built cable systems had such hook-ups.

What Hollywood is impatiently waiting for is not the concept but the screws, wires, and bolts that make it financially feasible to play a $20 million movie over television *before* it plays in movie theaters. And such an explosion in the number of homes capable of paying per view is not far off. The new 55-channel cable systems now just beginning to be installed will have the necessary addressable cables that were missing in most previous cable systems.

Hirschfield waves his huge cigar and throws figures into the air. Of all the studio heads, he is most in love with the new technologies, and his pockets are figuratively crammed—like the Mathemagician's in *The Phantom Tollbooth*—with glittering numbers from his numbers mine. "We'll have a population of twelve to fifteen million homes by 1986," he says. "By 1990, all homes that have cable will be capable of pay-per-view."

Never mind 1990. From his office on the fifteenth floor of Universal's Black Tower, Sidney J. Sheinberg, 48, president of MCA Inc., Universal's parent company, says, "We're estimating that by the end of 1982, there will be two million homes that could get pay-per-view. If we had an attraction that 50 percent of them would buy, and if we were charging $10 a home for it, we as distributors would get 70 percent or 80 percent of $10 million."

As yet, however, mocks a vice president of production at one of the studios, "we talk a lot, but we're all still virgins."

Just barely. Sheinberg was not idly throwing figures into the air. After vacillating for months in the spring of 1982 for fear of a boycott by theater owners, Universal made a decision to put its $14 million *Pirates of Penzance* on pay-per-view in February 1983, one day before it opened in theaters.

The Pirates of Penzance is, in many ways, a special case—

a musical made from Joseph Papp's successful production of the Gilbert and Sullivan operetta with the Broadway cast of Rex Smith, Linda Ronstadt, and Kevin Kline, and thus somewhat presold. Yet it makes it obvious that the changing technologies are already changing priorities in Hollywood.

"In a real sense, every movie that is being made today is being made for pay-cable," says Sheinberg. "If you took away the extra revenues we get from cable, no one would make any movies." Columbia's chairman and president, Frank Price, 52, who is jokingly called Hollywood's $10 million man, since that is the minimum amount of money Columbia will pay him over the next four years, has been quietly buying foreign films, ostensibly to distribute in small art-house theaters. But the real reason, he grins, was to get the cable and home-video rights. He can shout it to the world now because he has formed a joint venture with Gaumont, a major French film company, that will bring him films by Ingmar Bergman, François Truffaut, and other European directors whose names, he feels, are golden to cable viewers and cassette buyers.

In 1980, Alan Hirschfield inflamed theater owners by announcing that Fox would sell video cassettes and disks of *9 to 5* for home use within 90 days of the time the movie opened in theaters, thus taking advantage of the huge amounts of money his studio spent in advertising the film. "We backtracked because we got enormous pressure from exhibitors at a time when we were weak in the marketplace," Hirschfield says. "But already, what was once very daring is now standard, putting movies on cassettes and disks within ninety days of theatrical release."

Simultaneous opening of a movie in a theater and on cassettes is probably not more than two years away. Although no studio has yet made a movie specifically for pay-cable, every studio is waiting nervously on the edge of that pond. Once someone dives in, the water will suddenly become very crowded. "Virtually every week, we relook at the possibility of producing for cable," says Robert A. Daly, 46, chairman and chief executive officer of Warner Bros. "We could start tomorrow." Those first pay-television movies will be remakes of—or sequels to—successful movies. "You'll need some kind of name recognition, some kind of hook," says Alan Ladd, Jr., of The Ladd Company. "So you'll make *The Exorcist III* or *Alien II.*" "Ultimately," says Price, "you'll see an influence of cable on the kinds of movies that are being made. There will be more older-appeal themes." And, adds Hirschfield, cable will be a training ground where unknowns will have "an opportunity to write, direct, and act."

What will all this mean to the average moviegoer? David Chasman, vice president of production at MGM/UA, has as good an answer as any: "What did the automobile mean to the average horse-and-buggy driver?" What it means to Hollywood in the long run is self-evident—millions of people across the world watching a single Hollywood movie in theaters and in their homes.

Still, almost to a man, the chairmen of the six major studios insist that for the foreseeable future most movies will continue to play first in theaters—even though they also admit that by 1985 most of a movie's revenues will be coming from what Hirschfield calls "the electronic fireplace." "Theaters are the goose, even if pay-per-view is the golden egg," says Columbia's Price. "You need the theatrical run to create demand for your movie, to make it an event." "I don't care how big and wonderful television screens become," says Universal's Sheinberg. "People will always go out. Whether they go to movies, concerts, or video-game arcades, they will go out!"

The comedian Mel Brooks hopes so. "What am I going to do?" he asks. "Sneak into someone's living room to watch two people laughing?"

The chairmen also point out that the audience they will get

at home is an audience that was lost to movie theaters 20 years ago. The average moviegoing audience today is only 14 to 24 years old, they say, and the electronic fireplace will draw away more viewers from the television networks than from movie theaters. The feeling throughout the industry is that at least one television network will eventually be destroyed.

But the next-lower echelon of executives tells a different story. "The new love that dares not speak its name," says one vice president, "is Hollywood's love for cable. What no executive in Hollywood is willing to say out loud—but what everyone is discussing behind closed doors—is that theaters are going to be obsolescent, if not obsolete. Think of the advantages for us. There will be no delayed payments and no exhibitor cheating and we'll get our money at the end of the month without hassles."

Although theater owners bluster in public, they are frightened enough to begin laying off their risks. One of the largest chains in the country, U.A. Theaters, has bought heavily into cable systems. General Cinema, another massive chain, has purchased 10 percent of Heublein, which owns Smirnoff Vodka and Kentucky Fried Chicken, among others. Wometco, a major chain in Florida, has bought subscription-television systems. Richard H. Orear, president of the National Association of Theater Owners, has warned his fellow exhibitors that, whatever the studios say, pay-per-view is closer to reality than any theater owner suspects.

"The whole business of having to establish a track record in movie theaters before going to cable is a crock," says marketing expert Charles Powell. "Of course, there will always be some theaters, because my nineteen-year-old son is not going to sit home and watch movies with his parents. But pay-per-view will cause a marketing revolution. There will be no $7 million marketing costs. It will no longer be necessary to send Clint Eastwood on a whirlwind, twelve-city tour in a private plane with limousines waiting on the airfield and the presidential suite in the best hotel. Paramount made twelve hundred prints of *Raiders of the Lost Ark.* That's $1,680,000 no one will have to spend." Chimes in Gene Secunda, president of a marketing firm that specializes in the new technologies: "The advertising will be done on the cable systems themselves. Every study shows that viewers will accept such commercials so long as they don't interrupt the programming."

But the long run isn't here yet. "Right now, the studios are in a time warp where the ancillary revenues haven't caught up with costs," says Hirschfield. Most of the studios have cut back on the amount of money they are spending on making movies in 1982 and 1983, and have made private arrangements or public offerings to raise money by sharing ownership of their films. Warren Beatty's *Reds* is, it turns out, owned by Barclays Bank. Universal is actively soliciting rental tenants for its sound stages. The studios are thus putting a pillow under their down-sides, in case a big-budget movie collapses. "If we can just get through the next year or two . . ." is a constant refrain.

The kinds of movies that Hollywood is making to get through the next year are much the same mix that has proved more or less successful for the last few years. The dozen or more science fiction films include *The Blade Runner, Tron, Krull, The Dark Crystal* (a collaboration by the producer of *Star Wars* and the creator of the Muppets), the third in the "Star Wars" trilogy, *The Return of the Jedi,* and, of course, the movie that has dislodged *Star Wars* from its position as the most successful movie of all time, *E.T. The Extra-Terrestrial.*

There are also a dozen sequels to successful movies, including *Grease II, Rocky III, Star Trek II, Psycho II, The Black Stallion Returns,* and *The Sting II.* Along with the usual assortment of comedies and musicals, Paramount tried something different—a string of six or seven low-budget—under $8 million —films. The success of one of the movies, *An Officer and a*

Gentleman, made the whole slate profitable, despite the failure of several of the films at the box office.

In 1981, such a mix gave the movie industry its best-grossing summer in history, with ticket sales for the whole of 1981 amounting to nearly $3 billion, 7.9 percent higher than in 1980. But almost all the increase came from ticket-price inflation. "Movie attendance hasn't increased for twenty years," says Sheinberg. "It's silly to argue whether it goes up a bit or down a bit any given year." But it went up considerably in 1982, to $3.4 billion, nearly 10 percent more than ticket price inflation.

In its search for a new audience, one of the obstacles Hollywood must get past is Home Box Office's virtual monopoly on pay-cable. Because it is by far the largest system, HBO offers less than half the money per subscriber than is given by Showtime or The Movie Channel. Such "pittances," as Hollywood calls HBO's prices, average approximately $3 million per film.

Late in 1982, the studios tried two different techniques to overcome HBO's head start. On the theory that, if you can't beat them you should join them, Columbia joined with Home Box Office and CBS in forming a new studio which will undoubtedly make movies for pay-per-view. Home Box Office agreed to invest heavily in Columbia theatrical films that start production before July 1986, winning in return exclusive pay-cable rights to some of the films.

MCA, Paramount, and Warner Bros. bought The Movie Channel, which had previously been owned by a partnership of American Express and Warner Communications. Early in 1983, MCA, Paramount, Warner Bros., American Express, and Viacom formed a joint venture to own and operate both The Movie Channel and Showtime, which was formerly owned by Viacom.

Although the Justice Department will certainly scrutinize the joint venture, the studios are avoiding the mistake that made the U.S. Court of Appeals destroy their earlier attempt to get into the pay-cable business. In 1980, Columbia, Fox,

Universal, and Paramount tried to form their own pay-television channel, Premiere. Because the studios intended to show their movies exclusively on Premiere, the venture, which also included Getty Oil, was declared in violation of the antitrust laws.

In addition to the pay-cable wars, the recession, high interest, production and advertising costs, the increasingly large number of films being released during the summer and at Christmas (which means a smaller share of the choicest pie for any single movie), competition from the $6 billion-a-year video-game industry, the current tendency of a film to be a big hit or a big failure—all these are whipping the industry into a froth.

Already, MGM has swallowed United Artists, a $380 million meal which Hollywood thinks may give MGM terminal indigestion. There are rumors, which are denied, that MGM's controlling stockholder, Kirk Kerkorian, has put it up for sale. There are rumors, also denied, that MCA, which owns Universal, may be purchased by Getty Oil. Columbia has been bottled by Coca-Cola. Two mini-majors, Filmways and Embassy, also have new owners. Twentieth Century-Fox has become the private toy of Denver oil magnate Marvin Davis. Although Fox announced that it would be releasing 16 movies a year, observers believe that Davis bought Fox for its real estate and that he will sell the picture company sooner or later.

Only Warner Bros. can afford to be placid. Its corporate parent, Warner Communications, shares ownership of a major cable system, Warner Amex, and has sole ownership of Atari, a computer and video-game manufacturer. "Our company has an unbelievable amount of expertise in the new technologies," says Warner Bros. chairman Robert Daly. "And our movie company is about to do things that will be good for Atari, and vice versa."

In the short run, there will almost certainly be more turmoil and tension—brilliant moves, incredible mistakes—as all the studios attempt to get "positioned" for the future, to spread umbrellas against a rain whose nature they do not yet know.

"With the least amount of information—because there is none, it's all noise—everyone is trying to get sheltered from the dangers of the new technologies," says Diller. "We think we're making alliances, but I'm terribly afraid a lot of them may be misalliances. If everyone missed the transition to television, *and they did*—and that transition was simple, a little box in your home, and this transition is vastly complex—I shudder about this transition."

Behind the frantic grabbing for partners—of CBS and 20th Century-Fox, of Columbia and RCA, of Orion and Home Box Office, of Disney and Group W, of Paramount with Universal and Time Inc. to buy the USA Network basic cable channel as a way of positioning themselves for pay-per-view—is the specter of Hollywood's decision to ignore television 33 years ago, when, in Frank Rosenfelt's words, "We were too dumb to take over TV."

Irving "Swifty" Lazar, a ubiquitous agent, tells an instructive story about the way executives can miss the new forests growing beneath their feet. "L. B. Mayer said to me that he knew television couldn't be successful because the American public would never accept a Joan Crawford without her hair coiffed."

By 1951, 10 million American homes had television sets. Louis B. Mayer resigned from Metro-Goldwyn-Mayer, over which he had ruled for 27 years. Most of the other pioneers—those Eastern European immigrants who loved the movie industry with a passion that few of the agents and businessmen who came after them would feel—sat, bewildered, on their crumbling thrones.

Some malign fate—and the Justice Department—chose that moment to give Hollywood a second blow. The studios were forced by a 1948 Supreme Court antitrust ruling to sell off their theater chains. No longer could they shore up a weak movie by shoving it into their own picture palaces.

Rosenfelt, who entered MGM's legal department as a young law-school graduate in 1950, thinks there was a third, almost equally devastating blow to the studio system. "The income-tax rate had gone up drastically during the war years," he says, "so a star or director under contract and earning a large salary was paying huge taxes. To avoid taxes, their advisers started independent production companies for them." A few years later, those independent companies were supplying the studios with most of their films.

During the 1950s, when the studios were beginning their evolution into what they are today, the film companies won time by selling their pre–1948 movies to television. That money served as a financial bridge to the future while they experimented with wide screens and tried to force their way into television production.

By 1965, the moguls were dead or disinherited, and a dozen extraordinarily successful movies (including *The Sound of Music, Mary Poppins, Dr. Zhivago, Goldfinger,* and *Thunderball*) made movies seem a sensible corporate investment—particularly since there was a huge jump in revenues from foreign markets. Thus, *Thunderball* earned United Artists $28.5 million domestically and $26 million abroad; *Dr. Zhivago* earned MGM $47 million at home and $56 million abroad.

The patriarchs gave way to the corporate managers. In 1962, MCA—a talent agency that had had the wisdom to get into television production early—acquired Universal. In October 1966, Gulf & Western bought Paramount. The next March, Transamerica bought United Artists. Avco bought Joseph E. Levine's Embassy Pictures in 1968. Warner Bros. went to 7 Arts and then, in 1969, to Kinney National Services, which later changed the parent company's name to Warner Communications Inc. Also in 1969, MGM wobbled first to Edgar M. Bronfman, the liquor magnate, and then to the airline and Las Vegas hotel magnate Kirk Kerkorian. At the same time, two of the three television networks, CBS and ABC, decided to move into the lucrative business of making movies.

In essence, instead of creating movies, studios now bought a package of script, director, and stars put together by a talent agency. Since agents had the magically important "relationships" with Paul Newman or Barbra Streisand, they were invited to become studio presidents. Since most of the packaged movies were independent productions shot abroad—Hollywood had discovered that lush foreign locations couldn't be duplicated by television—the vast studio lots became white elephants. Under the leaden weight of *Cleopatra,* Fox sold its back lot cheap, the land being developed by Alcoa into a complex of office buildings, a shopping center, and luxury condominiums known as Century City. "We sold Lots 2 and 3 in 1970, but we would have sold them earlier if we could have gotten anyone to buy," says MGM's Rosenfelt. MGM also sold off all the brass beds, gilded clocks, and costumes that had dressed the sets of its movies, including Judy Garland's red shoes from *The Wizard of Oz* (they brought $15,000).

The corporate managers didn't have an easy time between 1969 and 1973. They had hurried into the movie industry because of the gigantic revenues of the mid-1960s, but they were already one step behind. By one of those sudden reversals that have always made Hollywood more of a gamble than an investment, movies stopped making money.

In 1946, 44 million people went to the movies each week. But by 1973, Hollywood's low point, only 14 million people were going to the movies weekly. CBS and ABC withdrew from the movie business, licking their wounds. Columbia was on its knees. "But," says Diller cheerfully, "you can't kill a movie company with a stick." Nine years later, Columbia is so prosperous that Coca-Cola paid around $780 million for the privilege of owning it.

By the mid-1970s, the wheel of fortune had turned. *The Godfather, The Exorcist,* and *Jaws* made hundreds of millions of dollars. *Star Wars* earned nearly $300 million and bought Fox a Coca-Cola bottling plant, a ski resort, miles of Pebble Beach, and some television stations. Every sound stage in Hollywood was booked up, mostly for television production (sometimes studios were making more money from successful television series than from feature films).

Once again, "There was a perception by the investment analysts that the movie industry was one where you couldn't lose money, and some people were prepared to believe that felony," snorts Sheinberg.

Actually, as Diller has phrased it, "There *was* a brief period when there was no way to lose money making movies. The average cost of a movie was only $5 million. The network television sale covered $3.5 million of that, and investors seeking tax shelters covered the other $1.5 million. Syndication was worth $1 million. Exhibitors paid huge, unrefundable guarantees." So, in came a dozen new companies during the late 1970s, crowding over each other to reach a golden trough. Even CBS and ABC came back to try again.

Old-line Hollywood executives scornfully call those new companies "boutiques." "There is a feeling that making movies is an easy job," says Rosenfelt. "Anyone who has made a hundred million dollars making ladies' dresses or selling insurance thinks he can make movies."

Almost every one of the boutiques has fared poorly. "The boutiques opened a motel along the old highway just before the freeway went in," says Powell. The average cost of making a movie soared to $10 million and the cost of marketing to $8 million. Tax shelters were tightened; television stopped buying films when it discovered that a made-for-television movie could earn higher ratings than a film that had already played theaters and pay-television; the box office turned sour; and pay-television revenues are still around the corner.

In addition, the major studios start one giant step ahead of the boutiques, since the best scripts and packages are offered to them first. "Why go to Lorimar unless the majors pass?" asks Price. General Cinema, Time-Life Films, American Cinema, Lord Grade's A.F.D. are already out of business. Filmways had to hang up a for-sale sign. Lorimar and Melvin Simon have retreated as gracefully as they could.

During the last year, however, five more studios have been gobbled up. At a time when only a few hit movies are making money, why are people rushing to buy studios? "The takeovers reflect the growing potential value of software," says Rosenfelt.

That is certainly the explanation of Coca-Cola's purchase of Columbia, which has been at the top of Hollywood's wheel of fortune for more than a year. Fox, bought largely as a real-estate investment, is an anomaly. Marvin Davis, its new owner, is now generally considered to have gotten a great bargain for $725 million, almost none of it his own cash.

When Norman Lear, the television producer, and A. Jerrold Perenchio purchased Embassy from Avco for $25 million, Perenchio had just sold, for $55 million, his 49 percent interest in the company that owns ON-TV. "I don't want to have to guess which technology is going to win. I want to be in software, not hardware," he says. "I will make razor blades for any kind of razor."

"Software"—the word has a trendy, tartly technical sound —has been borrowed from computer language, and nearly everyone in Hollywood now uses it to refer to the new movies and the thousands of old television series and movies that cable will need to fill its multiple channels. MGM purchased United Artists partly so it could once more distribute its own films and partly to acquire United Artists' immense film library.

"If we had tried to sell *The Wizard of Oz* outright to CBS for $4 million in 1956, when we leased it to them for $250,000, we would have been laughed at," says Rosenfelt. "Since then, we've made more than $10 million leasing *The Wizard of Oz* to television. Our 'Tom and Jerry' cartoons were dead, lying in our vaults. Between 1976 and 1980, we made $20 million on them from television syndication. And now we have not one but two of the finest libraries in the world." Rosenfelt points out, as do other chairmen, that a major studio's library enables it to ride out a bad year at the box office. "We have that steady source of income to carry us along when we guess wrong," says Rosenfelt. "The people in those new boutiques are naked."

MGM needs the cushion of its library right now since almost all of its recent pictures have been horrendous disasters at the box office and it is heavily in debt because of its purchase of United Artists in May 1981. It has recently reorganized, and Frank Rothman, 56, a Hollywood lawyer, has been brought in to head a combined company that changed its name to MGM/UA. David Begelman, former president of MGM, was shunted over to the chairmanship of United Artists and then, in the summer of 1982, fired. Of the 12 or 14 pictures Begelman had initiated, only *Poltergeist* was a major hit. Rosenfelt, 60— a courteous man who looks a bit like a leprechaun and has a reputation for being a gentleman—says that he was asked to head the combined company but chose to bring in his friend Rothman instead.

Orion—financed by Warburg Pincus, with a little assistance from Home Box Office—bought Filmways for much the same reasons MGM bought UA. Orion is owned by the former management team of United Artists. Of its 25 films, only *"10,"* *Caddyshack, First Blood,* and *Arthur* have been particularly successful, and Warner Bros., its distributor, was not displeased to get rid of it.

There are some people who question whether buying a distribution apparatus is an intelligent investment when such an apparatus, with its hundreds of employees and at least 20 offices, is necessary only to sell films to theaters—not to cable or television. But maybe it is, since nobody knows how pictures will need to be distributed ten years from now. After all, the studios expected to sell video cassettes of their movies, but customers have chosen to rent cassettes instead. RCA and MCA put hundreds of millions of dollars into manufacturing and advertising videodisk players, and consumers chose to stay with the more versatile video cassettes that can not only play a prerecorded movie but can also record programs off television.

"The first rule of marketing is that the consumer will decide what he wants," says MCA's Sheinberg, "and people did not rush out to buy our disks."

Could all of the future goodies, for which the movie companies are now waiting in line, be as much of a mirage as the huge anticipated market for videodisks? Probably not. "It's certain that all the new delivery media will chew up software at an incredible rate," says Fred Anschel, entertainment industry analyst for the brokerage firm Dean Witter Reynolds.

That the six major studios will get all they expect is less certain. A lot of software suppliers are sure to challenge them. ABC and CBS, for example, have vast financial resources and are in the race for good this time. Although CBS recently scaled down its film program and chose not to go into distribution immediately, the company insists it is still going to make theatrical films.

"Once they smell profits, anybody can start making films," says Anschel, although he thinks that the cable companies are more likely to go into partnership with the major studios than compete with them: "They want the majors' expertise and their ability to turn out a high-quality product." Home Box Office, Hollywood's bête noire, has already assured itself access to "product" by putting $10 million into Orion's purchase of Filmways and by its relationship with Columbia putting up what has been estimated to be $30 million.

But perhaps there is a limit to the number of movies and cable-television series people will tolerate in their living rooms. Perhaps they will switch off their 55 channels and their big-screen television sets and turn to a new form of amusement not yet invented. After all, five years ago video-game arcades didn't exist. And Charles Powell, the marketing expert, puts into words a different fear that is troubling more than one executive: "Maybe Hollywood is making all the same mistakes today that Hollywood made in the 1940s. Perhaps we're all going to wake up in five years and realize we should have owned the hardware."

The "I own the product, they have to use it" attitude of some of his peers also disturbs Paramount's Diller, a careful man who always wears a faint air of exasperation and is likely to formulate serpentine sentences that eddy back on themselves. "If there is no competitive market, your product will be sold for what *they* say they'll give you, not what you want or what it's worth," Diller warns. "If you had oil around the turn of the century, Mr. Rockefeller prevented you from getting it to the consumer because he owned all the barrels, flatbed railroad cars, and trucks."

In an office that seems all Lucite and smoked glass, Diller spoons honey into his tea and continues to sound the alarm: "If there is one wire and a monopoly in a city—depending on what happens, *which no one yet knows*—there are dangers for everybody. If you own a cable system, you're afraid of direct-broadcast satellite. If you own a television station, you're afraid of D.B.S. and cable. If you own a network, you're afraid of pay-cable and fragmentation. If you own product, you should be afraid of everybody, because your avenue to the consumer may well be blocked by a big bad Goliath who swats you down because he owns the access."

How do the other five chairmen view the future?

"The main strategy you have for the future is to be sure you're there," says Universal's Sheinberg. Where Diller is subtle and Price is jolly, Sheinberg, who looks somewhat like Abraham Lincoln, is inclined to knock you down with the bluntness of his personality. A lawyer, he is the second in command of a conservative, debt-free company. "We've tried to avoid being caught up in the crazy hysteria of cable," he says. "In the last months, the glamour has quickly begun to fade from the cable business. Just as it's cost a lot of money to put wires down, there's a disturbing feeling that maybe it won't be necessary because technology now exists to split a broadcast signal. If you can get three to five signals from over-the-air subscription television, why buy cable?"

He wonders, too, how long the movie industry will remain in Hollywood. "We don't have a monopoly of anything, including good weather," he says, "and if Hollywood doesn't cut costs, Texas or Florida will."

"By the end of 1982, you're seeing that sides have been chosen up," says Daly, who now occupies Jack Warner's old office. The former president of CBS's entertainment division and a newcomer to movie studios, he says emphatically, "When somebody looks back at this moment from 1984, he'll see how everything was formed."

Hirschfield is considered suspect because he started his career on Wall Street and because of his wholehearted embracing of the electronic fireplace. Hirschfield, after all, is the man who once said, "If people want to see movies on soda crackers, I would be all for gluing them onto crackers." Yet Hirschfield is surprisingly optimistic about the future of movie theaters. "I've been one of the big doom-sayers about theaters," he says, as he munches a handful of sherried walnuts from one of several well-stocked jars and tins in his Fox office. "But now I think that theaters will always occupy a big place. I suspect they will be larger, more elaborate theaters with movies transmitted by satellite, and with the ability to present a film in 3-D or multimedia."

He adds: "The big issue of next year is going to be productivity. Otherwise, the industry won't be based in this country. There's something wrong when you can make a two-hour television movie in three weeks and it takes six months and six times the cost to make a two-hour movie. But if we can keep costs down, cable will enable us to experiment with new subject matter and groom a new generation of film makers."

Rosenfelt holds his fingers over the bowl of his pipe and gestures into the air. "Technology is being developed that will be obsolete before it's finished," he says. "But our celluloid will not be obsolete." Rosenfelt escaped from what he calls "the worst slum in the Bronx" because a violin was put into his hands when he was four years old. Until World War II, when he was seriously wounded in the Battle of the Bulge, there was nothing in his life except music. Afterward, there was nothing but MGM. He has spent his entire working life there, and he now occupies the office that once belonged to L. B. Mayer. "Hardware becomes obsolete," he repeats. "Software increases in value."

In the dining room of Frank Price's brick mansion is a cardboard cutout of Columbia's lady with a torch holding a Coke bottle aloft instead of her torch. The legend reads: "Things go better with Coke."

Coca-Cola has bet a lot on Hollywood's future. Price, always an expansive man, is now grinning from ear to ear. "If I had to pick one business to be in, one business of tremendous growth and fewest problems, it would be making movies," he says. "There are 4.6 billion people on the face of the earth and most of them in one way or another are potential customers. It's not like automobiles, where suddenly the Japanese make a better product. The Japanese are successful at taking a product developed elsewhere and improving it and pricing it down, but movies can't be made with one successful design that is repeated. You can't keep making *Kramer vs. Kramer.*"

With one foot in the uncomfortable present and one eye on the rosy future, the studio chairmen await what Sheinberg calls "the inevitability of change." "The average filmgoer will dictate, as he has always done," says Diller. Sheinberg and Daly use the same words. They are, they say, "bullish about the movie industry." Price goes further. "Today, movies are a cottage industry," he says. "Tomorrow, they'll be one of the biggest industries in the world."

The Man with No Name
Is a Big Name Now

It was all dismayingly civilized: the dainty swimming pool no larger than an ordinary movie star's bathtub; the conventional ranch-style house riding the backbone of the Santa Monica Mountains like a paper clip on the edge of an ashtray; and Clint Eastwood dressed in Carnaby Street slacks, bedroom slippers, and a 102-degree fever, feeding rose petals to a turtle named Fred.

One expected more from the antihero of *Coogan's Bluff,* *Hang 'Em High,* and three psychedelic Italian Westerns than a copy of *Parents Magazine* on the coffee table, a cup of hot tea, an urgent telephone call to the doctor, and a face so sensitive that it could belong to one of Dostoevski's tortured characters.

Slouched against a nondescript couch, Clint Eastwood was suffering intimations of mortality. Being sick was an uncommon enough experience to be brooded over. "Every three or four years I go on a tour or something. I eat rich foods; I take a drink or two; nobody gives me a chance to exercise. So I get sick."

He was annoyed that, over a trivial weekend of playing golf in the rain, his body had broken down on him. He handles his body as a different man might handle an expensive car, tuning it to a peak of performance. He has never smoked a cigarette. He rarely drinks. He denies being "a health-food nut," but he refuses cake, ice cream, and frozen vegetables; searches diligently for organically grown carrots; and considers Japanese food "the healthiest food going; all that raw fish, not greasy, low in fat." On location in Mexico for *Two Mules for Sister Sara,* he never had a sick moment while gorging himself on pineapples and papayas, "fantastic fruit, just fantastic."

His exterior—the sensitive face, the 6-foot 4-inch, 190-pound body sinuous as honey dripping from the hive, the ragged dark gold hair—suggests a contestant in the Apollonian games at Delphi. But the interior seems more Spartan than Athenian, more the soldier at Thermopylae than the naked runner. In the garage of his Los Angeles house, he works out an hour a day, lifting weights and pitting himself against a regulation punching bag. At his "escape hatch house" in Carmel, he runs three or four miles along the beach. ("Clint usually exercises an hour a day," says his wife, Maggie, a solid and intelligent woman who seems uncontaminated by 16 years of marriage to a movie actor. "It makes his machinery feel better.")

Despite the facts that Clint regards himself as machinery to be honed and that his dapper business manager, Irving Leonard, pairs "Clint's fussiness about his body and his cars," the metallic taste is misleading. When—afraid of a parking lot attendant stripping the gears on his Ferrari—he drives to the Beverly Hills Hotel in his Chevy pick-up truck, he is neither playing the Paul Newman game of backward status nor protecting a $15,000 investment. He is shielding a delicate animal from mistreatment. He has changed his twentieth-century toys into something more primitive. The three motorcycles he stables in Carmel—a Norton 750, a Triumph 650, and a nostalgic Honda —are iron horses.

"You're riding something rather than being surrounded by something. It's an exhilarating feeling. When things close in, I ride up Highway 1 to San Francisco, have a couple of beers, and ride back."

The couple of beers cost him four hours, but he no longer has to question the prices of things. At 38, Clint Eastwood is the controlling stockholder of the Malpaso Company and also Malpaso's most salable commodity. Malpaso produces or co-produces all of his pictures, pays him $1,000,000 for his services, gives him his choice of director, writer, and co-stars, and tries to arrange deferred payments from which the Internal Revenue Service will take a nibble rather than a bite. Malpaso also owns several hundred acres of land that Clint found appealing on his trips up Highway 1.

A modestly successful television actor on "Rawhide" in the early sixties, Clint Eastwood has become a monumentally successful movie actor, beginning with *A Fistful of Dollars,* the Italian Western he made in 1964. From the moment of its release in Italy, "El Cigaro" was Italy's most popular American movie actor. By a quaint set of ethics, the producers of *A Fistful of Dollars* had never quite managed to buy the rights to the Japanese film on which it was based. For two years, while the rage for Clint Eastwood swept Europe like a fever, America was off limits for the film. When the litigation was settled in 1967, *A Fistful of Dollars* and its two sequels—*For a Few Dollars More* and *The Good, the Bad, and the Ugly*—were released here in a flood. Eastwood had been paid $15,000 for *Fistful.* The picture made four times that much in its first seven days in one midtown theater in one Midwestern city.

By 1968, Clint Eastwood was number five on the *Motion*

Picture Herald box-office list, an unsentimental election by theater owners based on how much money they find in the cash drawer each weekend. *Hang 'Em High,* a low-budget but superior Western, returned profit checks in ten weeks, the fastest return in United Artists history. He moved on to *Coogan's Bluff, Where Eagles Dare, Two Mules for Sister Sara,* and *Paint Your Wagon.*

Why?

Why should this laconic television cowboy who spent 14 unnoticed years nibbling at the edge of the Hollywood cake become the first genuine star since Julie Andrews?

Eastwood's three Italian Westerns have been dismissed as sadistic, violent, senseless travesties. They are much more. Even the worst of the three, *The Good, the Bad, and the Ugly*—in which an attempt to create the friendly enemies relationship of Clark Gable–Spencer Tracy *Boom Town* days becomes a hideously obscene parody—has a sense of space. American Westerns are cluttered with saloons full of cowboys and decipherable codes. In these Italian Westerns, the West is empty of everything except sand, ritual murder, and the sun chopping like an ax at adobe houses. They are sparse, nihilistic, weird fragments of an LSD trip, cold-blooded as a reptile creeping out of the desert night, beyond good and evil. The codes are indecipherable. The hero is no different from the villain, the victim no more innocent than the victimizer. It hardly matters that much of the weird quality comes because director Sergio Leone spoke no English and shot much of his film from the wrong angles. There is no longer that much space in the world, which is perhaps why men reach out for it on the screen.

Eastwood's audience is composed predominantly of men. A young black militant marking time in a trade school responds to his brutality and calls him "James Bond of the eighteenth century." A weekend hippie says, "He's a real one, all right. The real ones were screwy-looking, stinky types." And uncountable 40-year-old restaurant owners, barbers, and real-estate salesmen have "never missed a single one" of Eastwood's films.

"Clint gives," says his wife, "the feeling of a man who controls his own destiny."

But Eastwood's unlimited "Man with No Name," draped in a serape, an unlit stogy between his teeth, unsinged by conscience or neurosis, is as much a figment of a drug dream as Coleridge's Xanadu. No one controls his own destiny when an ounce of nerve gas can kill a civilization—not even Clint Eastwood.

"My appeal is in the characters I play," Eastwood said, hunched over with a spasm of coughing. "A superhuman type character who has all the answers, is double cool, exists on his own without society or the help of society's police forces. A guy sits in the audience. He's twenty-five years old and he's scared stiff about what he's going to do with his life. He wants to have that self-sufficient thing he sees up there on the screen. But it will never happen that way. Man is always dreaming of being an individual, but man is really a flock animal."

Clint Eastwood is not the character he plays—a fact that was obvious as he searched for photographs of his son, Kyle, and sipped tea to stop his sandpaper cough. Eastwood is encumbered by a wife, a baby, and the rules of civilization. Yet Eastwood is not *not* the character either. And a half-lie is also a half-truth. If his success has come because of his roles, it would not have come to another man struggling to fit himself into the same roles. Sitting uncommitted, holding himself in reserve, even in what should have been the safety of his own living room, Eastwood echoed the caverns of the man he portrays on the screen.

He shares the curious passivity that is the most interesting component of his characters. "Arizona," Coogan answers monotonously over and over again to "You from Texas?" in

Coogan's Bluff. Wordlessly, stoically, the man with no name endures—as though his energy is too precious to spill on the ground—until there is one thing too many to endure. Then he strikes back in the only quick gesture he ever makes—the revolver rising in an arc out of its holster.

When Eastwood reported to Paramount for *Paint Your Wagon,* driving the pick-up truck he had equipped with air-conditioning and stereo, he was refused entrance by a suspicious gatekeeper. He shrugged, turned his truck around, and went home. "What the hell, I was getting paid." His calm surface masks a volcanic interior. Like his character, he stores things up until the storehouse is full and then explodes in a paroxysm of violence. ("I talk obscenely, but I don't usually hit anyone any more.")

The drifter of his movies, defiantly wearing aloneness as a cloak, is based on half a lifetime of drifting. He grew up in the Depression trailing a father who pumped gas in all the small towns along the West Coast. From Seattle to San Diego, Eastwood never spent more than one semester in the same school. His one rooted memory is of his grandmother's chicken farm near Pleasington, California, which was near Niles which was near Hayward which was a stone's throw from Oakland. He went on the road the summer he graduated from high school. He started as a logger and drifted south. He stoked a furnace on the night shift at Bethlehem Steel, pumped gas on a dozen lost highways, and ate at a thousand roadside stands where the hamburgers were drowned in ketchup and flies settled like raisins on the cherry pie.

The army stretched a wire fence across his road. He settled down to two years at the Fort Ord swimming pool where his assignment was to pull out the recruits who flunked their swimming tests, preferably before they disappeared for the third time. Afterward, in Los Angeles, he "tripped across the movie business. I just decided to give it a try."

Like most Western heroes and the movie stars who play them, Eastwood is a political conservative. Unlike most, he does not hunt. He even refused to kill a rattlesnake for a scene in *Two Mules for Sister Sara.* "People are always asking me to go on hunting trips. I don't find it necessary to kill living things. I just don't get knocked out over killing animals." In a tone so soft it is almost a whisper, he admits to "having got hung up on the animal thing . . . at my grandmother's farm. Identified with them . . . Dr. Dolittle style." In a seemingly unattached next sentence, he describes the grown-up Clint Eastwood as "less complex, less introverted" than the child. His love for animals is tied up with a feeling that "civilization spoils things."

He can afford to buy almost any civilized thing he wants, but he squirms trying to think of anything worth his desiring. "I could buy a small jet," he says. Although his tone has not changed, everyone is expected to know this is a joke based on the preposterousness of Clint Eastwood's wanting an airplane. He cannot imagine why he should want anything larger or more elegant than the unpretentious house he bought nine years ago. In a forest overlooking the ocean at Carmel, he is building a house on land which cost a fortune. Yet the house will be "ordinary, a little on the rustic side. Like I am."

He is not unintelligent despite the pauses between words that last so long they can be measured in inches and despite the vocabulary that stays resolutely on the surface—as though to go underneath were to drown in unwanted knowledge. He can only describe himself as what he is not. "I certainly wouldn't be considered glossy or sophisticated." Or, in defiance of his friends' unanimous insistence on his loyalty, generosity, and kindness, "I'm not good, kind, and decent. That's for sure." Yet he is amazingly shrewd about picking his roles. He knows exactly what he is capable of doing. He fought for the filthy, unshaven image he presented in his Italian films, delighting in "rolling out of bed and going to work being a slob, taking a nap on the set and knowing no guy would wake me up with a powder puff."

It is difficult to guess what will happen to Clint Eastwood's appeal when he is prodded into acting. So far his films have simply required him to be the monolithic center of an environment. All the words he spoke in his first six films would barely make half an hour's reading for a beginning reader. But, as the budgets of his films get higher, more is demanded of him.

The future did not seem to bother him at all as he sat in his imitation ranch house watching the sun rise over his miniature swimming pool. It was only the present that gave him trouble.

He went to the doctor that afternoon. After a few days on tetracycline, he was fine, just fine.

For an actor, movie stardom is a gift of the gods. And like most such gifts, it is capricious and ephemeral. For a time, the jut of a jaw, the tilt of a head, matches the audience like some lost piece of a jigsaw puzzle. But audiences change and yesterday's perfect fit is today's embarrassment. The word "star" remains attached to the actor's name as an appositive and the salary is still good, but the reality has disappeared.

Yet for over a decade, Eastwood has been what movie studios label "bankable," one of perhaps five actors whose names alone are enough to sell a project. Money can be borrowed on his name, and his movies fail at the box office only when he flaunts a character completely at odds with his audience's expectations, as he did with his Civil War soldier in The Beguiled, his shoe salesman turned Don Quixote in Bronco Billy, and his dying singer in Honky Tonk Man. With equal box-office success, his tight-lipped, deadly hero became a policeman in Dirty Harry and Magnum Force and a criminal in Escape From Alcatraz. He is even able to mock his screen persona successfully, co-starring with a chimpanzee in

Every Which Way But Loose and *Any Which Way You Can. Every Which Way But Loose* was a blockbuster, Hollywood's term for the 30 movies that have earned more than $50 million in film rentals in America and, thus, $100 million or more at the box office.

He has been equally successful as a businessman. Unlike most major stars who fall into the trap of waiting for a script or a character worthy of them and are not seen on the screen from one year's end to the next, Eastwood, year in and year out, stars in two movies. His company produces them. He often directs them. At 52, he is divorced, extremely rich, and famous.

When I first wrote about him, 13 years ago, Clint Eastwood was a curiosity, still vaguely unrespectable, an eccentric taste on the part of a small segment of the public. If one anticipated anything of him, it was that he would disappear in a few years as quickly as he had come.

How a Hollywood Rumor
Was Born, Flourished,
and Died

On August 18, four days after his forty-sixth birthday, Norman Garey, a successful Hollywood entertainment lawyer, canceled his lunch date, went into his den, and shot himself in the head.

Norman Garey's suicide had unexpected and dismaying consequences for the 20th Century-Fox Film Corporation and several prominent movie industry figures because it was the catalyst for a number of rumors of malfeasance and embezzlement that swept through Hollywood in the next two months. The rumors accused Garey's client, Daniel Melnick, the executive producer of *All That Jazz* and *Altered States,* of embezzling as much as $50 million from Fox. They also pointed to James Bridges, the director of *The China Syndrome;* Steve Roth, Bridges's agent, and Sherry Lansing, the former president of 20th Century-Fox, as Melnick's confederates. And they touched off a highly publicized investigation by the Los Angeles

District Attorney's Task Force on White Collar Crime in the Entertainment Industry.

On November 19, six weeks after its investigation began, the task force said there had been no truth to any of the rumors. The District Attorney's statement read in part: "We have found no evidence to support any type of criminal investigation. No evidence has been found to support any of the rumors. Moreover, none of the key persons involved have made any allegations that criminal activity took place."

What remains, however, are bruised feelings and damaged reputations and a singular case history of how rumors feed on rumors in the insular world of movie making in Hollywood. The anatomy of this incident offers a crash course in the pathology of a community united chiefly by its fear of failure and its envy of success.

"Hollywood is a town that is dying for the next disgrace," says Michael Maslansky, a friend of Melnick's and a partner in Pickwick, a well-connected public relations firm here. "It is a town of intense rivalries and jealousies, a town that is not civilized about other people's successes or failures."

Adds the producer and record entrepreneur David Geffen: "The uglier the rumor, the more people relish it. A lot of people dislike Danny Melnick simply because he's successful."

Melnick, who is most often described as "sophisticated," has one of Hollywood's best cooks and most bravura houses. In the upper levels of Hollywood, such things count a lot. Strewn with pieces of modern art and banks of white chrysanthemums in silver planters, his house is as dramatically black-and-white as a chessboard. Handsome, fiftyish, lithe and tanned, he wears with grace the $100 Turnbull & Asser shirts that are custom-tailored for him in London.

He also is widely perceived to be, in Maslansky's words, "Hollywood's first queenmaker." Sherry Lansing, the first woman to become president of a movie studio, is considered to be Melnick's protégée. Miss Lansing began her career as his employee at Talent Associates, she was executive story editor when he was head of production at MGM, and she followed him to Columbia, where she was his vice president of production. Although they dated at one time, that relationship no longer exists.

When Melnick was head of production at Columbia and MGM, he initiated such movies as *Straw Dogs* and *Network.* If his movies have sometimes faltered at the box office, they usually are regarded by his peers as literate and carefully crafted.

Daniel Melnick's deals are considered even more carefully crafted. When he resigned the presidency of Columbia in 1978, he had already put his independent film production company, IndieProd, under a lucrative contract to the studio. Two years later, he reached an arrangement in which his company would develop films for 20th Century-Fox. The nearly 200-page contract provided for a minimum of $5 million just to cover his overhead between 1980 and 1985. Depending on what movies he developed or produced, the contract could be worth as much as $14 million. Even by Hollywood standards, Melnick's arrangements were considered extraordinary.

Moreover, by moving to Fox he was reunited with Miss Lansing and with Alan Hirschfield, his former boss at Columbia, who was now the chairman of Fox. But the following year Marvin Davis, the Denver oil millionaire, bought the studio. Davis was appalled at what he called "the rich deals" of several Fox producers and he insisted that Melnick's contract be renegotiated.

If *Making Love,* a movie with a homosexual theme that Melnick's IndieProd produced for Fox, had been a success, the renegotiation might never have taken place. But *Making Love,* which starred Kate Jackson, Michael Ontkean, and Harry Hamlin, was a critical and box-office failure.

Norman Garey had negotiated Melnick's contract with Fox in the first place and it was Garey who was to renegotiate it. Within the movie industry, he was regarded as a star among the powerful group of lawyers who represent Hollywood's top actors, directors, and producers.

"He was my brother, my support system, my surrogate father," said a well-known agent, Arnold Stiefel, of Garey. Sherry Lansing remembered him as "a strong father figure to many of us. He was always in control, always stable, always calm."

"The Rock of Gibraltar," added Robert Wrede, a lawyer who was brought into the Melnick-Fox negotiations by Garey. "Whenever it looked like there was going to be a fight, I was essentially Norman's fighter. Norman and I had breakfasts, constant phone calls. I felt I knew him well, but apparently I didn't."

That feeling of somehow having failed Norman Garey "by not being sensitive to his pain" would be a constant refrain among his friends in the weeks after his suicide. The rumors against Melnick and the others would be fueled, in part, by Hollywood's search for some secret dreadful enough to have caused the lawyer to put a gun to his head. But that spring Garey seemed the same as always, an unruffled workaholic who was, said Wrede, "compulsively organized with such incredible retention of detail that he could remember every point in a forty-page deal."

The negotiations that he conducted with the studio eventually ended with Melnick's selling his IndieProd company to Fox for approximately $2.5 million. But they began early in May in an atmosphere of suspicion. Alan Hirschfield, the chairman of 20th Century-Fox, has been quoted as referring to "a disgruntled former employee of Melnick's" as the source of negative rumors about the producer that contributed to this hostile atmosphere.

According to highly placed Fox officials who declined to be identified because of corporate policy, a former important executive in Melnick's company came to them and hinted of improprieties at IndieProd, most particularly improprieties concerning a contract with James Bridges. The contract had to do with Bridges writing and directing *Manhattan Melody,* a musical that subsequently was abandoned by Fox.

According to Melnick, early in April agents and executives with other studios began to phone him and repeat what they said his associate had said about him.

After the former Melnick executive had talked to Fox, the studio scrutinized the Bridges-Melnick arrangement anew. If his story that there was something unsavory about the arrangement was true, Fox would then be able to end Melnick's contract on terms favorable to the studio.

"Garey brought in six drafts of the various agreements between Melnick and Bridges," said Burton I. Monasch, Fox's executive vice president, who handled the dealings with Garey. "We were satisfied because the deal clearly went back a year and a half and wasn't a last-minute thing. It was not inappropriate for creative people to share compensation, and the manner in which they shared wasn't our concern. Their arrangement was neither illegal nor improper and it imposed no additional expense on Fox."

And what were those arrangements? For *Manhattan Melody,* Bridges had wanted "gross participation"—a percentage of each dollar Fox received in film rentals. The studio refused. However, Melnick's contract provided him with 10 percent of the movie's gross film rentals. Melnick traded Bridges 5 percent of his 10 percent for all of Bridges's $750,000 directing fee and $160,000 of his $500,000 writing fee. This represented a pooling of stakes. Bridges was willing to gamble much of his salary because he was confident that his pet project would eventually be a big success. Melnick wanted the writer-director badly enough to agree to his terms. As it happened Fox rejected their film and the two are trying to sell *Manhattan Melody* elsewhere.

Meanwhile, Garey's stability apparently had begun to crumble. A year earlier, he had walked out of Los Angeles's most successful entertainment law firm, Rosenfeld, Meyer & Susman, taking with him 130 clients, including Marlon Brando and Gene Hackman, to form his own firm, Garey, Mason and Sloane. His new offices, overlooking the Pacific Ocean in Santa Monica, "were exquisite," said Arnold Stiefel, the agent. The rent for the penthouse suite was more than half a million dollars a year.

But at the same time he was negotiating with Fox on behalf of Melnick, Garey, for some reason, was convinced his new firm was failing.

"There was no truth to it," said Barry Haldeman, one of his partners in the firm. "Norman was operating under a number of delusions and nobody was aware of it."

Melnick added: "Norman left the comfort of a big firm where he was the star to form his own firm where everything was on his shoulders. The pressure became too much."

Garey was depressed enough to be seeing a psychiatrist, another fact of which none of his associates said they were aware. Seemingly with no provocation, he insisted on having Melnick's offices checked for a wiretap. On July 14, during the Fox negotiations, he blacked out twice, perhaps because of stress or perhaps because of the effects of an antidepressant drug, Desyrel, that he was taking.

"He leaned over to get his briefcase, suddenly stiffened, and fell unconscious on the sofa," said Monasch, recalling the episode. "I thought he was having a heart attack or a stroke. He came around a few seconds later and passed it off as 'a little hot in here.' I ran to get water. He put the glass to his lips and fell to the floor. That's when I summoned emergency help."

Two months later, Garey's fainting spells would be distorted by the rumor mill as the moment when he made a fatal "mistake" in Melnick's settlement. That rumor would be particularly damaging to Melnick because it would tie his contract negotiations to Garey's suicide. Many influential people in the movie industry would then believe that the lawyer killed himself because of something illegal in the sale of IndieProd to Fox.

Everyone connected with the negotiations now insists that Garey made no mistake, but simply failed to win a negotiating point he desired on behalf of Melnick.

"Norman didn't make a mistake," said his associate Robert Wrede. "There is a provision of the I.R.S. code that provides for a company that is being sold to file a document known as a consent. Norman felt it desirable to have a consent for Melnick's tax purposes and saw Fox's refusal to allow it as a failure. It wasn't. It was simply one of many negotiating points he didn't win."

However, by the beginning of August, Garey himself was so convinced that Melnick was going to sue him for malpractice for failing to get this consent that he informed his insurance company. Melnick said he was not even aware of Garey's concern about this point until after Garey had killed himself. He said that he would not have sued in any event.

By the week of August 16, Garey's concerns about money had become obsessive, according to his associates. "The day before he died, he phoned me to say that a client of mine owed his firm $5,000," said Melinda Jason, an agent. "He sounded distraught and terribly nervous. I checked and the bill was less than a week old. It hadn't even gotten to the accountant yet."

The report of the Los Angeles County Coroner in respect to Garey's suicide that week reads in part: "Decedent was concerned over a mistake he had made in an important contract he did legal work on for 20th Century-Fox Studios. During the discussion with his wife, Decedent stated that maybe 'he should shoot himself.' "

"We thought he had it all," said Sherry Lansing. "When we heard how he died, we were sure someone must have killed him. Suicide would mean none of us knew Norman Garey. It would mean that our father, in a sense, betrayed us. Why? Because none of us could accept not knowing the answer. We started looking for one."

The partners in his law firm were so convinced that Garey would not have taken his own life that they even hired a private detective to investigate.

"The more prominent the person the larger the network of pseudoexplanations," said Dr. Robert Litman of the Los Angeles Suicide Prevention Center. "First there's a denial, an effort to make it an accident or homicide. Then, for a forty-six-year-old man, there would be an explanation of disease or frustration in love or work."

New rumors vainly attempting to explain Norman Garey's suicide circulated and they rapidly became enmeshed with the gossip that had already surrounded the lawyer's contract negotiations on behalf of Melnick all that spring.

It was Sherry Lansing who heard the first rumor early in September, that Garey had killed himself because she had broken off an affair with him. Her response was anger.

"The first rumor I heard," said Melnick, "was that Sherry had loaned me $1 million of Fox money interest free and I gave it to Norman to save his firm. The rumor had it that Marvin Davis found out and demanded it back and Norman killed himself."

A few days later, Arnold Stiefel called Melnick. A new rumor had inflated the $1 million to $50 million. Even more, the rumor said that Melnick and Miss Lansing had embezzled the money from Fox and had stashed it away in ten different banks in London. "My God, what are the Swiss going to say?" was Melnick's response. Sherry Lansing joked, "They should know how much trouble I have getting money to get pictures made!"

"There was no one to fan the rumor that Norman and I had had an affair," explained Miss Lansing, "so it was overtaken quickly by something more juicy. A love affair is not nearly as interesting as a financial scandal."

By late September, the $50 million rumor was still alive in Hollywood, but with the refinement that Steve Roth, then James Bridges's agent and now a producer at Columbia, was one of the conspirators. The questions Fox had had about Bridges's contract with Melnick were distorted into a $500,000 discrepancy between what Fox had paid Bridges and what Bridges actually received. The $500,000 siphoned off was supposedly split by Melnick, Roth, and Garey.

"It was so fantastic," said Roth. "You can't steal money from a studio during the development process. People can pad production budgets on a film, but not development money." Development money is given to a producer to hire a writer and perhaps a director to begin work on a script, and the disbursements are made directly by the studio.

In what he said he thought was an off-the-record conversation, Melnick denied all the rumors to a newsman from the Hollywood *Reporter,* an industry trade journal. On September 29, the Hollywood *Reporter* published a story under the headline: "Melnick denies fund misuse, connection to lawyer's death." This was the first time that the public learned about the rumors.

Melnick said his first reaction was that his lawyer, Robert Wrede, "would kill me." To his surprise, Wrede thought that it might be just as well to get the rumors into the open. "It may make the heat a little hotter in the short run, but if there's no truth in them, light will make them go away," he advised.

Fifty or sixty people called Melnick to commiserate about

the Hollywood *Reporter* article. "Probably half of them were secretly gloating," he said. "For the last twenty years, I've been in a position to say yes or no. Does this actor get hired? Does that picture get made? There has to be resentment."

He was to fly to New York on October 1 for meetings with some bankers. He said he was attempting to get a $100 million line of credit so that he would not be dependent on studio financing for his movies. The banks canceled the meetings.

In her gossip column in the *Daily News* a day earlier, Liz Smith hinted at aspects of the rumors, concluding with "Garey was a lawyer for producer Danny Melnick, who recently departed 20th Century-Fox. Watch for this story; it could be bigger than Columbia and David Begelman! In other words, more 'indecent exposure.' "

Two months earlier, the pirated galleys of David McClintick's not-yet-published book *Indecent Exposure* had circulated to every Hollywood executive suite. The book was an account of corporate infighting in 1977–1978 at Columbia Pictures following the disclosure that David Begelman, the company's president, had embezzled money from the studio by forging checks. Among the figures in the book were Alan Hirschfield and Melnick, who had succeeded Begelman as president of Columbia Pictures.

"Those galleys started a feeding frenzy," said Melnick. "The people the reporters questioned about me then repeated the questions as statements of fact, spreading the rumors even further."

Several anonymous phone calls were received by the Los Angeles District Attorney's Task Force on White Collar Crime in the Entertainment Industry and an inquiry was launched. This task force was created following the Begelman scandal and has prosecuted several middle-level executives in the movie industry, mostly for embezzlement.

The ultimate triumph of the rumors came with the entrance

of the law-enforcement agency into the affairs of Melnick and Fox. Newspapers began to publish stories about the inquiry as a result and Melnick and his colleagues became the focus of national attention. "D.A. task force to question Fox on rumors of mishandled funds" was the headline in the Los Angeles *Herald-Examiner* on September 30. "D.A.'s Office, Studio Clash on Financial Probe" wrote the Los Angeles *Times* on October 1.

Al Albergate of the District Attorney's staff said the task force inquiry into the rumors was mainly based on the assumption that where there's smoke there's fire.

"But," said Melnick plaintively, "in this business, where there's smoke, there's more likely to be a smoke machine."

Although the task force cleared Melnick and his associates, the producer is convinced that people will continue to believe he must have been guilty of something. "If I died tomorrow," he said, "there would be less attention paid to the movies I'm proud of than to these rumors about me."

Burton Monasch summed it up this way: "There's such a small amount of success to be had in Hollywood. Even the most successful people have one failing or aborted project after another. In sports, one athlete revels in another's success. Here everybody's happy when a new picture is rumored to be terrible. Everybody wants to believe the worst because the failure of somebody else lets you know you're not alone."

Barbara Stanwyck:
Still a Golden Girl

It was after the third or fourth letter came asking where she was buried that Barbara Stanwyck ended a self-imposed retirement to appear in a "Charlie's Angels" television segment in 1980. She had starred in more than 80 movies, but the last was 16 years ago, and Hollywood makes little room for stately age.

"You have to know when you've had your hour, your place in the sun," Miss Stanwyck said on a springlike day in her seventy-third year. "I pity an actor who doesn't understand that."

Her hair is silver—but it has been silver for more than 30 years. When it turned prematurely gray, she refused to dye it, just as she refused to lie about her age. "Everybody said, 'Oh, my God, no actress can have white hair. No one wants to make love to a gray-haired lady.' Everybody said, 'To be over forty isn't possible.' Tó be old is death here. I think it's kind of silly. Be glad you're healthy. Be glad you can get out of bed on your own."

March 1981

Ironically, on the eve of being honored by the Film Society of Lincoln Center for 35 years of achievement, she looks extraordinarily lovely, with porcelain skin and a figure that has not varied one pound or one inch for nearly 50 years. A golden horse with a flaming mane is pinned to her magenta jacket and its bridled vitality is echoed in her own chiseled features. She started the day, as she always does, by walking half a mile on the slanted treadmill that dominates her bedroom. An exercise bicycle is now relegated to the garage because it was "too easy." The uphill treadmill is more satisfying work.

Barbara Stanwyck withdrew into Hollywood shadow a decade ago, after her Western television series, "The Big Valley," ended. Recluse? She shakes her head determinedly. "I'm not a yesterday's woman. I'm a tomorrow's woman. If I don't have a job, what am I going to give interviews about? 'And then I did . . . And then I did . . .' Who the hell cares?"

Having reluctantly agreed to be honored by the Film Society, she has something to give interviews about now. On screen, she was, most often, fiercely independent. The titles of many of her 82 movies can be strung together as a portrait of a wise-cracking strident dame of easy virtue from the wrong side of the tracks. *Shopworn, Illicit, A Lost Lady,* a *Gambling Lady,* one of those unsavory *Ladies They Talk About* paying *The Purchase Price* of *Ten Cents a Dance,* and always, always, in *Jeopardy* for her *Crime of Passion.* Two of her four Academy Award nominations came in classic Barbara Stanwyck roles—as the tough-talking but soft-centered mother in *Stella Dallas,* sacrificing everything for her daughter, and as the ruthless slut who orchestrates her husband's murder in *Double Indemnity.*

Reel life bearing no arithmetically calculable resemblance to real life, Miss Stanwyck is noted for her generosity and modesty. "She's atypical of actresses," says her close friend Shirley Eder, the columnist. "She has pride in her work, but I don't think she realizes her worth as an actress or as a person.

She thinks she's average; she thinks it's an imposition to ask her friends to come help honor her."

"At first I said no to Lincoln Center," agrees Stanwyck. "Talk about insecurity. I can go up on stage for Hank Fonda and for my Golden Boy, Bill Holden. When I told Lincoln Center I couldn't go through it for myself, they very artfully asked Shirley to convince me."

There was always a hard edge of candor in her screen performances. The same no-nonsense, forthright appraisal is part of her personal baggage. She sparkles, in the sense of giving off sparks, and her energy level is unexpectedly dazzling.

Sitting straight as a ramrod, she takes a cigarette from a gold Art Deco case decorated with the sunburst of her face and a ruby, her birthstone. It was a present from Robert Taylor, early in their marriage. That marriage ended in divorce, as did her first marriage, to Frank Fay, the comedian who starred at the Palace Theater in New York but shriveled in the shadow of his wife in Hollywood. She caresses the cigarette case. "Losing somebody you love by death or divorce is hard. But if they decide they want to be free, there's nothing to battle for. You have to let go. Bob and I didn't stay friends. We became friends again." She lifts her chin in a jaunty gesture, and the husky voice is a remembrance of dozens of films. "Time does take care of things."

Time has, she says, been good to her. "I had my job, my work. People talk about 'my career,' but 'career' is too pompous a word. It was a job, and I always have felt very privileged to be paid for doing what I love doing. I still look forward to living. I wake up looking forward to each day. Whatever comes, I'm alive! I'm existing. I'm part of it."

Shirley Eder says of her that "Barbara has learned to make do with life."

Born Ruby Stevens in Brooklyn, orphaned at four, on her own and wrapping packages at a department store at 13, a nightclub dancer at 16, she is still grateful for the bounty that came afterward. She responded to fame with neither demands nor tantrums. Even now she is ten minutes early to any appointment because "I'd rather wait for people than have them wait for me."

The women she played through four decades were active, even physically daring. "I couldn't stand being passive," she says. "I couldn't play the placid girl." According to film historians, that cocky independence appealed more to men than women. It appealed to the men on her sets, too. She was the favorite co-star of Robert Preston, William Holden, and Henry Fonda. "The love of my life, I absolutely adored her," said Fonda; and Holden sent her roses every year for 42 years in gratitude for her kindness to him when she was a star and he was an untried actor who was cast as her *Golden Boy.*

To the men who worked in the crew, she was known as "Missy" and that endearment became her nickname. Even today, if a grip or cameraman she worked with 20 years ago is having problems, Missy is there with money enough to make the situation easier.

She tosses her head in a typical Stanwyck gesture of impatience. "I'm not Lady Bountiful," she says. "There's no halo around my head. But there's always someone in trouble, and if anyone needs any help I'm there."

If she has one regret, it is that she didn't return to the stage decades ago. She had become a minor stage star in *Burlesque* before United Artists brought her out for *The Locked Door* in 1929. "But I fell in love with film," she says. "Besides, how do you keep a marriage together if you're back there and he's here? Now I'm scared to try. Now I'm a coward. They keep asking me, and I wish I had the courage, honey."

Unlike many actors of her generation who no longer bother to see films, she can still respond passionately to movies and "absolutely adored" *Ordinary People*. But she prefers the Hollywood that used to be—when she was "an interloper, a usurper from the theater in 1932, and Ronald Colman, walking toward me, was the most beautiful man I had ever seen.

"The amount of security that the star had—Crawford, Gable, Tracy, Taylor—was wonderful. Two or three pictures a year written for them by the top writers. It was like a baby being bathed and all wrapped in a blanket. You were safe. Today it's catch as catch can. Today someone buys a book or a play and asks, 'Who can we go to the bank with?' not 'Who's right for it?' It was a good system for a while, but Hollywood today is like a series of Mobil or Standard Oil stations leased to a distributor.

"And the salaries! In my wildest dreams, I never believed any actor would get a million dollars. All I could think of when I saw Marlon Brando with his white hair in *Superman,* knowing he had gotten $3 million, was 'Why him? Why not me? I could use my own hair!' "

There are no bitter memories. She remembers Preston Sturges saying he was going to write her "a marvelous comedy because you're funny." And adding, "Then I'm going to the front office and insist they let me direct it." She smiles. "A lot of people said that sort of thing, and fifteen minutes later it was forgotten. But, two months later, Sturges handed me *The Lady Eve.* He was marvelous. He loved actors. Some directors get along with actors, but they don't really like them."

Barbara Stanwyck was, with rare independence for a star of the thirties, never under exclusive long-term contract to a single studio. Her few years at Warner Bros. "didn't work out. I was suspended a lot. If you were a bad girl, you were punished at Warner Bros." She characterizes Warner Bros. as "cheesy," Hal Wallis as "fair," and Sam Goldwyn as "a man who had class." "Make all the jokes you want of the way Sam talked, but he instinctively knew what was right. He wanted real flowers on his sets because he didn't want an actress to have to put her face in a piece of wax."

She is, she says, "contented" with her life today. Even excited. "I'm excited by learning how to cement pins into driftwood. I love to spend time watching people." Although she has given away her library of first editions because their value made her nervous, there are two or three new books to read each week; and she is supervising Spanish lessons for her eight-year-old great-niece because "this is going to be a bilingual world." She wants to see as much of that world as she can, and there was a recent summer trip to Alaska.

And—"like an old warhorse"—she is always open to the right offer. Even, she laughs at herself, from "The Love Boat" with its constant cargo of aging stars. She has turned down the producer of that television series but added, "When you go to China, count me in. I've never been to China. It's high time I went."

Martin Ritt:
Survivor Extraordinaire

The coffee tastes like burnt rubber. It slops over the edges of the plastic cup and dribbles down director Martin Ritt's jumpsuit. He hardly bothers to wipe it away. There is snow on the mountains and the track is fast, a parlay potent enough to drag him away from his other passion, tennis.

"What'd'ya like in this race, Marty?" "Anything look good to you in the third?" They climb to his box like pilgrims, ruddy-faced old men lusting for a sure thing.

Martin Ritt likes the number II horse, but the odds are 6–5 and it is, he says, "against my religion to bet at that price."

But then, he has directed 20 movies in the last 23 years, and despite his success with *Hud* and *Sounder,* he learned long ago that there is no such thing as a sure winner: "When I saw the first preview of *Conrack,* I said to my wife, 'Our grandchildren will live off this.' I thought *Casey's Shadow* would be a big hit. I still don't understand why *The Molly Maguires* got no audience."

February 1979

He is not really bewildered by the box-office failure of the three pictures. "I've never had a runaway hit," he says. "It's not likely I ever will. Because of the subject matter I choose. I don't agree that anything first-rate can be pure entertainment."

Martin Ritt works on small canvases in a business where most of the big successes are billboards. It is not merely that his pictures are serious. Such massive hits as *The Godfather* and *One Flew Over the Cuckoo's Nest,* directed by others, are serious films. It is more that Martin Ritt does not usually concern himself with madness, suicide, grandiose heroic gestures, or war.

Two of his movies have been about exploited workers, one —*The Front*—about blacklisting, five about the tenuous relationships between blacks and whites. Critic Stanley Kauffmann once wrote that "all Ritt's pictures stem from a genuine concern with the way people live together and how it might be improved."

In his nineteenth film, *Norma Rae*—which opened on his sixty-fifth birthday—"the themes are the themes I've always been involved in," he says. "Exploring the human condition." And they are played out in his usual arena, the rural South. "I'm an urban Jew, but I'm as American as apple pie or chopped liver. I've always felt related to rural America. I like the pace of the rural South and Southwest, the work of it, the fair shake of it. The people are tough and funny. The heart of *Norma Rae* is similar to the heart of *Conrack*—affirmation about struggle."

Based on a *New York Times Magazine* article by Henry P. Leifermann, *Norma Rae* deals with the attempt of an intellectual Jewish New York labor organizer (played by Ron Leibman) to form a union in a cotton mill in a small southern town. In the process of helping him, an uneducated young woman whose underarms stink of mill sweat and who will unzip her pants in return for a steak dinner is transformed into a superior human being. Months after that day at the racetrack, Sally Field would win an Academy Award as best actress of 1979 for her performance as Norma Rae. The movie, while not a blockbuster, would earn a pleasing $25 million in ticket sales and would be nominated for an Academy Award as best picture. Although the director of a nominated picture is most often nominated as best director, Ritt would, as usual, not get a nomination. He has been nominated only once, in 1963, for *Hud.* Again typically, his next movie—*Back Roads* starring Sally Field as a good-hearted prostitute—would be scorned by both audiences and critics.

Ritt uses terms—"affirmation about struggle," "human equation"—that are antiseptic and abstract. But his movies are abrasively concrete. In *Conrack,* a white southerner manages to teach a little geography to black children so abysmally ignorant that they do not know the world is round. In *Casey's Shadow,* a father must pit his need to win against his son's love for a horse. In *Norma Rae,* Reuben, the alien Jew, is tangibly out of place on the streets of the backwater southern town. The savage environment of the mill thunders with deafening, dehumanizing noise. The savagery is deliberately implicit. "I've been overtly polemical before," says Ritt, "but not in *Norma Rae.* It's the first film about unions that has no goons, no Mafiosos. There was one scene in the script when Reuben's brakes were cut by the mill management, but I didn't shoot it."

Ritt shakes his graying, bulldog head and smooths out a crumpled racing sheet. In order to make *Norma Rae,* he gave up half his salary, working for $250,000. "That doesn't sound like a hardship case and indeed it isn't," he says, "but nowhere except in the arts would people who could make half a million dollars work for less." The project was turned down by Warner Bros., Columbia, and United Artists. When the producers, Tamara Asseyev and Alex Rose, brought it to 20th Century-Fox, it was almost turned down again. "They all thought it would be depressing," Ritt says. "I told them I didn't want to start a film that had no chance of making money. I asked them what was depressing about a girl who turns into a woman who can work, who can love, who can fight, who is as close to a complete woman of superior dimensions as any woman in film history."

It is nearly post time. Ritt stares at his racing form. "One good thing about growing older," he says. "Success is not that important. My family will not hunger nor will I." It is doubtful whether he believes what he is saying. "Marty always wants to win," says Jon Voight, who starred in *Conrack*. "He was the best tennis player on the *Conrack* location. Two young guys challenged him and maybe they won once or twice. But Marty's always got that one step extra that comes from wanting to win. Marty plays tennis the way he directs, with a nice, clean touch. He doesn't overrun the ball, doesn't make the grandstand play, the extra frill."

Ritt chews a thin cigar and, sighing at the odds, tosses the racing form aside. He has a bad track record at predicting the success of his films. Of *Sounder* he warned his wife, "It's a lovely picture, but it won't do ten cents at the box office." On the other hand, there was *The Molly Maguires*. The commercial failure of that expensive, somberly beautiful film about Irish immigrant coal miners who sabotage the mines in which they work was, he says, "the most painful experience of my professional life."

"An impressive failure," Pauline Kael called it, a film that "feels like a reminder of a bitter, tragic past, and when you come away you know you've seen something." Ritt's own bitter past, the most painful experience of his personal life, was subliminally printed on the celluloid. The central character of *The Molly Maguires* was a company spy, an informer. Ritt, who was blacklisted a quarter of a century ago because he refused to be an informer, made the spy "so attractive that audiences didn't even know I thought he was a villain. The irony is that I confused audiences because I made a conscious effort to be as fair as I could, considering my own prejudices about the nature of an informer."

The muscles in his weatherbeaten face tighten when he bites out the word "informer." Jon Voight says of him that he "is always judging your actions, watching you to see how you *behave.*" "He is," say Irving Ravetch and Harriet Frank, Jr., the screenwriters of *Norma Rae* and five of his other movies, "a man you would have to kill—literally—before he would abdicate his principles."

In sentence after sentence, he uses the unfashionable word "moral." His own rules of right conduct are uncomfortably rigid. They include a fierce sense of loyalty. When he read in the papers that the head of Columbia Pictures, David Begelman, had forged his name on a $5,000 check, he did not volunteer to help the police. "I am not a vigilante," he says. "David was a friend of mine." Although he wonders why Begelman forged his name, among others, he has never been indelicate enough to ask.

Ritt agrees that his personal values are reflected in his films, which "are conceived on a very moral note." *Hud,* he says, "was intended as a deeply moral film about the American heel-hero Clark Gable used to play for half a film before he got converted. The Ravetches and I wanted to carry the character to its logical conclusion. I was shocked when young audiences idolized Hud and wrote letters telling me they hated 'that stuffed shirt old man.' I should have sensed that Haight-Ashbury was just around the corner."

Despite the fact that Ritt was blacklisted in the early 1950s, he was, he says, never a member of the Communist Party. He started as a Jewish kid from the Lower East Side who never had a serious thought in his head until he joined the Group Theatre as an actor and overdosed on the class struggle. He was a jock

—a barrel-chested, tough battering ram with bruised knuckles whose goal, if he had one, was to coach football when he was too old to play it. The family in which he had grown up had neither political nor religious interests. It was devoted to making money. While his immigrant mother cleaned other people's houses, his immigrant father—a complex, secular, greedy man —hustled newer immigrants and became the richest man in the neighborhood.

The Group Theatre accepted him, he thinks, "because I had certain abilities all those intellectuals didn't have. They were doing *Golden Boy* and they needed someone to take care of Luther Adler when he went to train at a gym, and punch the punching bag offstage."

He became a director in the army during World War II. He honed his craft by directing over 100 plays on live television, acting in nearly 150 during the same time. Then, one day, his name was on a list.

"It was guilt by association, I suppose. I was never subpoenaed, never named by anybody. I had a lot of job offers if I would only go before a committee and name a lot of people who had already been named or who were already dead. I thought it was all incredibly cynical on the part of the people offering me those jobs. I told them, 'If you're not looking for information, why ask me to debase myself?' "

His chunky body moves restlessly back and forth in the narrow orange chair in his box at Santa Anita. He is wearing a blue-checked jumpsuit and a blue-checked cap. If he owns a pair of pants, no one has ever seen them. He has 40 jumpsuits —maroon, yellow, plaid, checked, all custom-made at $42 each from a single pattern. When he gains weight, they are tight against his muscular thighs. When he loses weight, they sag. Right now, as usual, he is dieting. Eating the large green apple he has brought with him and staring at the track, he seems stolid, pragmatic, the possessor of a rough but serviceable vocabulary and a brain unlikely to be stirred by flights of fancy. "Don't believe any of it," say the Ravetches. "He role-plays the tout. He puts on a donkey's head, but underneath it is a subtle, complicated mind."

When the horses reach the post, he quivers, although he has not bet on the number II horse or any other horse in this race. Racing is a passion. When he was blacklisted, his wife's small paycheck and the classes he taught at the Actors' Studio paid the rent but Aqueduct and Belmont kept him sane. And the winnings from his daily visits to those tracks bought dinner. Now he owns the Martin Ritt Stables—brown silks with a gold cap and $150,000 worth of weanlings, yearlings, and brood mares.

The number II horse runs third. So much for sure things. Although he is considered an expert handicapper, he has lost all three $10 bets he has placed today.

One of the four horses he has at Santa Anita is running in the next race—a four-year-old mare, Flick Your Bick, that he claimed for $25,000 at Del Mar last summer. Martin Ritt is now, by all but Hollywood standards, a wealthy man. It was his father who had an appetite for success and yet, he says, appreciating the irony, "I make more in a single year than my father made in his lifetime."

People have warned him that America is turning conservative, that nobody wants to see serious movies, that his liberalism is out of date, that he should find frothy subjects about which to make movies. "There's no way for a director to be a little bit of a whore," he says. "I am what I am and I'm not about to change. I didn't change when not changing had real meaning for my survival. If you give up your balls, you give them up forever. I would have nothing to make pictures about. The one thing an artist can't do is be a gelding."

In the focused sunlight of late afternoon, his face seems a road map of nearly two dozen movies made on location in small southern and southwestern towns with unpronounceable names. He shakes his head. "Hell," he says, "let's go see the race."

Flick Your Bick finishes second to Viking's Joy. Martin Ritt is not dissatisfied. For the moment, the winner's circle has eluded him, but "I thought she ran well. She'll run again."

There's always next time.

The Anatomy of the
Sneak Preview

For the last hour, the seven executives have sat silent and glassy-eyed in front of the television golf match. No one is drinking the beer or eating the sandwiches or taking a shower with the perfumed soap. At 4:00 p.m. on a day in April 1981, the expensive Dallas hotel room might as well be the Sahara.

"Oh God, I feel so parched," mutters Alan Ladd, Jr. "You think it doesn't affect you, but it does."

The Dallas *Morning News* has advertised an 8:00 p.m. sneak preview of The Ladd Company's *Outland,* starring Sean Connery and Frances Sternhagen. The $14 million movie is the first real fruit of the studio's 20 months of existence. There was a less-than-successful Bette Midler concert film last fall, *Divine Madness.* But *Divine Madness* was just to fill space. *Outland* is the first major test of The Ladd Company's sorcery. Has Alan Ladd—who, as president of 20th Century-Fox, chose to finance *Star Wars* and *Alien*—retained his magical ability to pick movies that audiences want to see?

May 1981

For the last 50 years, sneak previews have been an important part of the process of making films. Studios have shown their not-quite-finished movies to one or two paying audiences and then used the audience reaction to fine-tune the films. But, despite this Dallas hotel room and the seven men sweating out the afternoon, the sneak preview system is now on the verge of a radical change.

According to Barry Diller, chairman of Paramount Pictures, "You can still have a sneak preview on an ordinary film, but you can't on any film to which attention will be paid. Today, movies being sneaked are no longer considered works in progress. Judgments are made and those judgments turn up in the press the next day."

After an unfinished version of Francis Coppola's $25 million Zoetrope production *One From the Heart* was shown in San Francisco for bidding purposes to a group of exhibitors, their negative comments were reported in an article in the San Francisco *Chronicle*.

"Paramount and Zoetrope made a mistake," Diller says. "We should have realized we didn't dare take the risk. We didn't," he adds, "make the same mistake with *Reds*." For the $33 million *Reds*, Paramount "hunted around for an obscure place in Canada where we could have a preview," Diller says. "But we realized if we didn't have an audience of Eskimos who didn't speak English, word would be all over the place the next day. With a high-visibility, expensive picture, you can't take that risk."

"The concept of previews evolved out of the picture makers' need and desire to verify their judgments with an audience," says Daniel Melnick, executive producer of *Making Love*. "If you're setting out to entertain and an audience isn't entertained, you had better rethink what you've done."

Yet Melnick never previewed *Making Love* publicly. "The growing sophistication of exhibitors means that the theater chains send men out to Denver where I might be trying a cut with an off-the-wall emotional scene," Mr. Melnick says. "They see an imperfect film and the next morning everyone in distribution says, 'Boy, was that a bomb in Denver.' "

It was Irving Thalberg, the creative head of Metro-Goldwyn-Mayer, who shaped the ritual of the sneak preview. Thalberg, the movie industry's frail *boy genius,* was fond of insisting that "movies aren't made; they're remade." Thalberg once ordered a set for *Tugboat Annie* rebuilt at a cost of $35,000 so that Wallace Beery's shoes would squeak in a crucial scene. When an early MGM talkie, *The Big House,* met a hostile reception, he kept previewing the movie until he understood that the audience was reacting negatively to Chester Morris's romance with a married woman. The movie was reshot to make the woman Robert Montgomery's sister instead of his wife.

The classic case of a sneak preview's saving a movie was Frank Capra's *Lost Horizon.* Although the 1937 movie played well to a small audience of Columbia studio employees, it was jeered off the screen in a large theater in Santa Barbara. Capra eventually understood and solved his problem by taking out and literally burning the first two reels of the movie, which went on to be nominated for seven Academy Awards.

He later wrote in his autobiography, *The Name Above the Title:* "The line between the sublime and the ridiculous is rather wide and indefinite to an audience of one; thinner and sharper to an audience of many. No proper judgment of a motion picture can be made without the vital 'third dimension' of a large audience being present. And, may I add, the collective opinion of a large group of normal individuals is generally saner and more correct than the opinions of individuals, singly or in small groups. In short: 'The audience is always right' is a safe bet."

On this humid April night in Dallas, *Outland,* a thriller set on the third moon of Jupiter in the not-too-distant future, is

being shown to a paying audience for the second time. Much
of the movie's own future will depend on the result of tonight's
sneak preview and last night's preview in Minneapolis. Changes
will be made; they always are. How severely *Outland* will be
cut or restructured will depend on the laughs, silence, or ap-
plause of tonight's audience; on the number of trips to the snack
bar and bathrooms during the film; on the hundreds of 6-by-10-
inch yellow cards filled out before the audience leaves the theater.

A few years ago, during the preview of *Rolling Thunder*—
a bloody Paul Schrader movie in which William Devane had his
hand chopped up in a garbage disposal—audience anger was so
intense that Ladd and the other Fox executives literally hid in
their seats. Their black limousines were sent away "so the
audience couldn't identify us and stone us," says Ladd. The
next day he sold the movie outright to American International
Pictures.

In an earlier era, Thalberg and the other MGM executives
rode a special Pacific Electric trolley car to the unsophisticated
cities two hours south of Hollywood—Santa Ana, Riverside,
San Bernardino, or Pomona. But superhighways and half a
century have tainted the megalopolis of Southern California.
Now the favorite preview cities are far away from either coast
—St. Louis, Denver, Dallas, Minneapolis—and the entourage
travels by airplane. Warner Bros. distributes The Ladd Company movies, so today's flight was made in Warner's Grumman
Gulfstream jet.

There are other changes between the 1930s, when Thalberg's
ear alone detected the moment of disbelief, and the 1980s. One
hundred members of tonight's audience—carefully selected as
to age, sex, and frequency of moviegoing—will be telephoned
during the next few days and questioned in depth on their
reactions to *Outland*. Six single-spaced research reports will be
sent to Ladd and Warner production and sales executives to

guide them in "fine-tuning" and selling the movie. The interviews will also identify "a prime prospect audience."

An even more decisive change is that no preview today is a classic "sneak" preview. In the days when nearly everyone went to the movies every week, the title of the evening's preview was never announced until the lights in the theater dimmed and it flashed on the screen. With today's smaller, more fragmented audiences, part of the game is to see if the star or title or advertisement can fill a theater in middle America.

Readers of the Dallas *Morning News* know nothing of all this, of course. They know only what the advertisement has told them—that *"even in space the ultimate enemy is still man."*

"Is it enough? Will they come?" Richard Roth, the producer of *Outland,* remembers that he "actually threw up" at the sneak preview of his first movie. Last night in Minneapolis, sitting in his theater seat waiting for the movie to begin, he had a fantasy "of buying twenty-five candy bars and staying in the men's room eating them until someone said I could come out because the picture was over. But I didn't want Mr. Ladd, the president of the whole company, to see how nervous I was. Afterward, he told me he was dying to get up, but he couldn't afford to show me how nervous *he* was."

Roth, at least, has one advantage. He is not afraid of flying. Peter Hyams, the director of *Capricorn One* and *Outland,* who crouched in a corner of the theater lobby throughout last night's preview, is. So are Alan Ladd and Ashley Boone, who has been Ladd's marketing expert since his early days at Fox. Yet the two men will be carrying the other Ladd Company films —*Looker, Chariots of Fire,* and *Body Heat*—out to preview nearly every weekend from the end of May to June 18.

Alan Ladd is a quiet, self-contained man. Wearing jeans, loafers, a black pullover sweater, and a half-smile, he seems a casual California yachtsman sailing on a smooth sea. Yet his wife of 22 years, Patti, describes him today as "crazed." The only external sign of inner turmoil, however, is the perspiration that drips down his face as he shoves the script he has been trying to read back into his briefcase. "As if I could read a script," he sighs.

The ritual of the sneak preview is as full of omens, portents, and superstitions as any pagan fertility rite. For those who can find proper ways to propitiate the gods, there will be full theaters.

Movie makers demand that their films be previewed in specific cities and even specific theaters where audiences applauded a previous film. For five or six years, most Fox sneak previews were held in Minneapolis because the Zanucks had had such good fortune there with the previews of *The Sound of Music.* After the disastrous preview of *Dr. Dolittle,* Minneapolis was no longer their favored city. On the other hand, Steven Spielberg demanded that all his movies be previewed in Dallas after the success of *Jaws.* His superstitious trust in Dallas was shaken by the hostile preview of *1941.* Most studios prefer to preview on a Friday or Saturday because audiences are larger. However, if a director has had luck with a Thursday preview he will continue to demand Thursday previews.

Sometimes there are less symbolic reasons for choosing a preview site. For four years, Honolulu was one studio's favored city; the president's son was attending the University of Hawaii. And some executives even choose a city because of a favorite restaurant. At least one executive, David Weitzner, former vice president of advertising at Universal, feels that studios would still have no problem previewing their movies secretly if they used such cities as Madison, Wisconsin, or Lansing, Michigan. "But they want the comfort of easy airplane rides and good restaurants," Weitzner says. "And so previews are stacked up in Dallas and everybody goes to San Jose."

In every case, however, so private is the ritual and so frightened are movie makers about the possibility of any negative word leaking out that it took this reporter two years to find a company brave enough—or foolhardy enough—to allow her to participate. It is doubly reckless of The Ladd Company, because *Outland* bears an extra burden. "Every preview of every picture I've been involved with has been terrifying," says Ladd. "But we feel *Outland* has the potential to do something extraordinary at the box office. That increases the possibilities—and the tension. What if we've been fooling ourselves?"

The courteous, intelligent men in the Dallas hotel are trying hard not to fool themselves. "We don't preview to confirm for ourselves that we have a triumph on our hands," says Ladd. "We preview to see what work still needs to be done."

There are a considerable number of producers, however, who do fool themselves. Although the cards that Robert Dingilian, The Ladd Company's vice president for publicity, will pass out tonight will allow audience members to rate *Outland* "fair" or even "poor," some producers limit the range of responses from "excellent" to "good." And any Hollywood publicist can cruelly mimic his producer's excuses for a sour preview: "What do you expect of a Long Beach (or San Jose) (or Cincinnati) audience?" "Look at the day of the week." "It's not a true test because these boobs can't appreciate our picture." "It's Easter vacation and the kids are out of school." Or, a week later, "Of course we couldn't get a good preview on this picture when the kids are back in school." As a last resort, the pain from any hooting or catcalls can be soothed with the balm of *Shampoo.* That Warren Beatty comedy was treated savagely by a hostile preview audience in Santa Barbara but, almost unchanged, was released to critical and commercial success.

"Too often previews are used to demonstrate how much an audience likes a film," says Gareth Wigan, Ladd's production vice president. "*Alien* previewed very well. But afterward we took out a whole sequence where Sigourney Weaver found Tom Skerritt in the Alien's lair and he begged her to kill him. And we shortened and simplified the final sequence."

In retrospect, it seems obvious that the breakup of the sneak preview system started on November 7, 1977, when *New York* magazine published a devastating review of a sneak preview of *Close Encounters of the Third Kind,* which had been held in Dallas two weeks earlier. Columbia stock plunged three points that day and the race to be first with news of controversial movies had begun.

The race was exacerbated by the growing curiosity and sophistication of theater owners. Since 1975, blind bidding has required exhibitors to bid on and sometimes pay large unrefundable advances for movies they have not seen. They have retaliated by sneaking into previews.

Sometimes movies are not finished in time to be tested with an audience. Two recent examples are *The Shining* and *Heaven's Gate. The Shining* was released with a banal and anticlimactic hospital scene which destroyed the tension at the end of the movie. Three days later, after Stanley Kubrick had had a chance to see audience reaction to his movie, he cut out the scene. *Heaven's Gate* was demolished by the critics and withdrawn to be re-edited at a cost of nearly $2 million.

It is 5:00 p.m. now in Dallas. The golf match is over. Someone suggests dinner. No one responds. Then, somehow, the room is full of gallows humor—half a hundred awful moments dredged from the painful past.

For example, *Lucky Lady.* "We previewed the movie nine times. The two-hour, thirty-minute version was wonderful. Burt Reynolds and Liza Minnelli died at the end and everything was set up for them to die. But market research told us they shouldn't die, so we started chopping a bit here, a bit there. We took the seriousness out. The only good preview we had was when the film broke, and Stanley Donen, the director, did a dance for the audience while it was being spliced."

The gallows humor trails off around 5:30 when tonight's first omens are announced. The theater manager has told Dingilian that people started buying tickets for *Outland* at 1:00 p.m. Since the theater, in the North Park Shopping Center, has 1,100 seats, the early line is unexpectedly good news. By 8:00 p.m., when *Outland* starts, the news is even better. The theater was sold out at 7:00, and 1,000 people have been turned away. Last night's preview in Minneapolis was sold out, too. Since Ladd and his cohorts have refrained from using a lot of radio advertising to pack the theaters, they consider the response unadulterated.

A few minutes before the picture is to begin, Robert Daly, the new chairman of Warner Bros., and *his* cohorts sweep into the theater. They have arrived in Dallas on the smaller Warner's jet and will return to Los Angeles the moment *Outland* is over.

The theater lights dim. Ladd whispers, "The ending doesn't work. The last third of the picture has no punch. But it's fixable. The problem the second night is that you want to have already made all the changes you decided on the first night."

It is an unnecessary disclaimer. *Outland* plays well. "I don't need this plane to fly home; I could fly by myself," says Peter Hyams on the 11:00 p.m. flight back to Los Angeles. "You spend two years working for one day—the day you show the movie you've directed to the paying public. My goal was a specific intensity. The audience's reaction was stronger than I allowed myself to think it could be. I couldn't believe the cheering. When you go through the process of making a film and you see it over and over, you really begin to detest it. I was attempting to make a picture set in the future that had emotion. But I never dreamed people would respond so affectionately to the friendship between Sean and Frances."

Now everyone is eating and drinking. Rumpled and exhausted and nestled into the brown velour seats of the jet, everyone is king of the hill. "When it goes well," says Wigan, "there is a wonderful sense of camaraderie. We brave men have ventured out and won."

Tomorrow the euphoria will wear off. *Outland* will be taken back to the editing room, and the last third of the movie will be pulled apart. It has been agreed that, from the moment two hired gunmen arrive at the mining colony, the movie is overlong and lacks surprises. A few scenes and characters will be repositioned to add suspense. Four and a half minutes will be cut out. What Wigan calls "endless tracking shots down long corridors" will be edited out. He adds, "There will be more sense that the cats are stalking the mice."

But that is tomorrow. Tonight, there is only the taste of victory. The men spill out of the plane into the warm Los Angeles night, each to his separate car, his separate home. Alan Ladd stands on the empty runway and shakes his head. "What's amazing," he says, "is that I've never seen the city. I've been in Dallas four times, and all I've ever seen is a hotel room and a movie theater."

Despite the euphoria of that Dallas night, paying audiences were perverse when Outland opened in May 1981. The movie actually started out quite well in major cities. "In less sophisticated cities, places that weren't hotbeds of science fiction readers, it was just another movie," says Ashley Boone. But even where the movie opened well, word of mouth was, at best, fair. Somehow the last third of the movie never quite got fixed properly. The final consensus among the executives of The Ladd Company was that the movie lacked a satisfying confrontation with the chief villain.

Outland cost $14 million to make and another $12 million for prints and worldwide advertising costs. Then there were a few million in indirect costs, including interest and assorted distribution fees. The movie brought The Ladd Company $9.8 million in film rentals in the United States and Canada and another $8 million from film rentals abroad. Sales to pay-cable have netted $7 million and CBS has paid $5 million for two runs on network television. Videotape and videodisk sales are just starting and, so far, total $200,000.

In the end, *Outland*'s costs and income will cancel each other out. The Ladd Company will *"get our cash back."* What it will not get back is the squandered energy and high hopes.

Today's Hottest
Movie Stars

Scuttling across the desert of a mediocre planet like an upright gold crustacean, See Threepio (C3PO) worries about being lost and Godforsaken and getting sand in his machinery. See Threepio is a robot who would be comfortable at a cocktail party, a domestic droid hopelessly out of place amid the wars of George Lucas's *Star Wars* and longing only for a bath of fresh oil.

"It was like a sauna bath inside my costume," says Anthony Daniels, the 31-year-old British actor who spent five months encased in Threepio's 50 pounds of aluminum, steel, fiberglass, vacuform plastic, and vulcanized rubber. "I used to look at the other actors in their flowing robes and feel the bitterest envy. The first day they saw me it was like they had all seen God for the first time. In a week, they were used to Threepio. People would come up and stand near me and say the most outrageous things as though I wasn't human. They forgot there was a human inside, that I needed a drink or some food. I couldn't turn my head more than twenty degrees to the right or left, so I had tunnel vision. I felt totally alone. People could be standing by my side and I could hear them but I couldn't see them. I felt so isolated."

Threepio and his plucky, cheerful fellow robot, Artoo-Detoo (R2D2)—the vacuum-cleaner-shaped Lou Costello to Threepio's Bud Abbott—are, in fact if not in name, the stars of Lucas's $9 million space fantasy, which opened to unanimous critical praise and box-office lines over three blocks long. "I'd tease Mark Hamill," says Daniels. "I'd say, 'You can act if you like, but you don't really stand a chance in this scene. Because I'm gold, I glitter.'"

Threepio does more than glitter. A gilded cross between Jeeves and Noël Coward, he is more painfully human than the farm boy (Mark Hamill) and space adventurer (Harrison Ford) with whom he shares an intergalactic quest. In fact, the character played by Mark Hamill—the stalwart, fair-skinned human hero of *Star Wars* who rescues a princess and defeats a galactic empire—did not even exist in writer-director George Lucas's first script. "My first centered completely on the robots," says Lucas. "Only when my friends told me that I was crazy, that it wouldn't work, that no one would make the picture, did I add Luke Skywalker."

It is midnight, seven days before *Star Wars* opens in New York, and George Lucas sits in a dubbing room in Hollywood. Despite his thick black beard and burning eyes, he seems to melt into his seat, such a vastly shy man that he is hardly more substantial than a silhouette. During the last year he has worked 361 days, 16 hours a day. For the last six weeks, he has been in a dubbing room from 8:30 p.m. to 8:30 a.m., pulling picture and sound apart and putting them back together again. In four days, 20th Century-Fox will take his picture away from him, will freeze it in a form so imperfect that he sighs with despair. He wants another week, another month, another year.

He has asked 20th Century-Fox to give the picture back to him after its first run so that he can polish and refine one hour and fifty-seven minutes of celluloid on which he has already spent four years of his life.

It was in Lucas's obsession that See Threepio and Artoo-Detoo began. They are his "strange creatures in a strange land"; his transmutations of mythological animals; his elves, dwarfs, Cyclops, and dragons placed in "an environment that makes them believable." He wanted, he says, "to create a world for them to step into." It is a lived-in world where the space-ships need polishing and the sand of the desert planet has pitted the tools. The sun is warped and the cool plastic dishes are slightly too large to fit a human hand. "Most science fiction films reek of overdesign," Lucas says. Their worlds are new, cellophane-wrapped spaces awaiting the arrival of the actors. Lucas's universe is, he hopes, "not so unusual that it sticks out. The little things are different. Every sound in the movie was created. When a door slammed, we didn't use the sound of a door slamming on earth. There are two hundred sound units in an ordinary film. We had two thousand. We cut a million feet of film containing sound effects."

The stylistic thread of *Star Wars* is not the inhuman hardware of outer space but the Art Deco of the 1930s. "Even Threepio is a thirties-type art deco robot whose strongest influence is the robot in Fritz Lang's *Metropolis* [1926]," says Lucas. "We spent months sculpting Threepio's face to get a neutral enough design to convey any expression. We went through mask after mask after mask. There would be a ridge on a cheek-bone or a twist of the mouth that might have been boring. I didn't want the robots to be inhuman. I wanted them to be people you could relate to."

Lucas wrote Threepio as "an overly emotional, fussy robot." Anthony Daniels—who shares with Threepio "a slight fussiness; I like everything to be orderly"—saw him as "a crazy

English butler who happened to be made of metal. He was so busy being efficient that he was really slightly incompetent. Always getting hysterical and terrified of being melted down."

Daniels, best known as Guildenstern in the Young Vic's London Production of *Rosencrantz and Guildenstern Are Dead*, was chosen for Threepio because he was also a mime. "When you put anybody in a robot suit," says Lucas, "he ends up walking like a robot. Because the robot joints oppose human movement. I wanted a robot who walks like a human, a graceful robot, and I needed a mime to bring grace."

The bringing of grace was more painful than Daniels likes to remember. The robot in *Metropolis* moved only a step or two. Threepio shuffled down long corridors. "The first day I put the costume on in Tunisia, I walked ten paces and couldn't walk any more. The whole weight of Threepio's fiberglass legs was across my feet. The weight of the arms rested on my thumbs. For months I lost almost all feeling in my thumbs." Eventually a series of bandages took some of the stress from Daniels's neck and shoulders. But all movements "except tiny head movements" remained incalculably difficult. "I was wearing Mickey Mouse shorts made of plastic. If I turned the wrong way, they cut me like a pair of scissors. There were wheels inside the knees. If I moved more than thirty or forty degrees, those inner wheels would hit me on the kneecap. You get tentative knowing you might be pinched, cut, or hurt when you move an arm or take a step. Two or three times I got very, very angry because the whole costume hurt so much."

Kenny Baker, the midget who played Artoo-Detoo, was more comfortable. In the first place, he was able to sit down inside his costume. In the second place, he played Artoo sporadically. Seven Artoo-Detoo models were built for the one role. Only one fiberglass and one metal model housed Baker. Four of the other five copies were unoccupied lightweight or radio-controlled models. The fifth was a shell with special arms for the scenes in which Artoo had to extend his arms or plug into equipment. Essentially, Baker only played Artoo when the robot was standing still. All of the scenes in which Artoo rolled forward were done using one of the remote controls. One of the most disorienting things for Daniels was to start a conversation with Baker and discover that he was talking to a radio-controlled piece of machinery.

Although the relationship between the two robots was obviously an emotional one—"Threepio has absolute affection for Artoo," says Daniels, "but he also got cross with the dumpy robot because he was stupid. I was really able to get angry at Artoo after standing in my costume for two hours while they tried to get a radio-controlled model to perform properly"— Artoo's personality came almost entirely through his cleverly cylindrical shape and his electronic voice, which says no comprehensible words but only speaks beeps and whistles. And it took George Lucas and his sound effects man, Ben Burtt, six months to develop that personality.

"Robots have always spoken English with human voices warped mechanically," says Burtt, a 28-year-old graduate student in film whom Lucas plucked off the University of Southern California campus and who then spent two years creating voices and languages for the strange creatures of Lucas's galaxy. "But George decided he wanted an electronic language. Many of the nonhuman creatures in the film speak invented languages. For the Jawas, those rodentlike scavengers of desert scrap metal, we created a combination of exotic languages— partly Zulu, partly Swahili—that would serve as pidgin English. For Greeto, the thug who started the showdown in the bar and whose speeches were subtitled, we invented a gibberish based on ancient Incan. But Artoo was more difficult because he had to express human feelings with inhuman sounds. First we had to decide his mentality and his personality. We decided he was intelligent but, emotionally, a five-year-old kid. Frightened but brave. Then George and I hammered his language out syllable by syllable. We went through the script. What would Artoo be saying at this point? 'I'm frightened'? 'I'm hungry'? His first line in the picture was, 'Yes, I did.' "

"By the time we were halfway through," says Lucas, "we had a vocabulary. For certain emotional situations, he used excited whistles. Sighs showed he was distressed or frightened. Eeeks meant he was conveying information."

To create the actual electronic sounds that were used for Artoo, Burtt started with a music synthesizer. "Chirping. Tweeting. A plausible approach but not enough character. I had to add the organic." To add the organic, he spent days squawking onto tape, making rude noises, sighing, or rubbing bits of dry ice against metal. "I would coo into the microphone or sigh and then slow the tape down or speed it up to get a baby-doll quality. The hardest thing was to put all those isolated sounds together to make a language. I began to see Artoo as Harpo Marx, who could convey all the feeling necessary through his horns or whistles. By the end of the picture I knew I had succeeded. Because the film editors began to cut to Artoo for a reaction. If you think about that, it was like cutting to a lamp or a drinking fountain, a prop brought to life by the baby birdlike sounds."

Getting a voice for Threepio was considerably less difficult. That Threepio's voice caused any problem at all was due entirely to George Lucas. "I liked Tony Daniels's voice," says Burtt. "George didn't."

Everything in *Star Wars* had to look and sound exactly the way George Lucas wanted. This was not an intellectual decision on Lucas's part but an emotional one, and Threepio, like most other elements of the film, was both a re-creation and transformation of his adolescent fantasies. Lucas's insistence on putting on the screen the precise vision inside his head caused several fierce quarrels with his special photographic effects supervisor,

John Dykstra. Burtt had no power to quarrel with Lucas. In fact, he thinks that "the reason George likes to work with young people is because they don't have much experience or power. With me, he could still be in charge."

"Anthony Daniels had one of the few strongly British voices in the film," says Lucas. "I didn't want that, even though everybody else liked it. I wanted something more neutral." Daniels's voice was taken out, and 30 other voices were tried in his place. "Some were sleazy, some oily, some used-car deal-erish," says Lucas. "And I couldn't find anything I liked better. His voice had the most character." So, reluctantly, Lucas agreed to use Daniels's voice. Then, to give Threepio some slight quality of a machine, Daniels's voice was recorded through a television speaker. "That didn't work," says Burtt. "So we ran it through an electronic circuit where a little bit of the original voice was held for a second and then added to the original voice again. That was phasing, making the voice rub against itself."

Since Threepio's face was a metal mask, there was no visual correlative to his speaking. Because his lips did not move, "I moved," says Daniels. "Every time I spoke. As a human actor, you keep still when you're saying an important line. As a robot, it was important to move or people wouldn't know I was there. Then, when I was dubbing, I discovered I had to speak to the body movements I had made." Lucas had *2001: A Space Odyssey* screened for Daniels so he could listen to the voice of the computer, Hal. "There was no way that calm voice would work for Threepio, who went to pieces most of the time," says Daniels. Daniels, who was the voice of Legolas in Ralph Bakshi's animated film of *The Lord of the Rings,* had had considerable experience as a radio actor. On his graduation from drama school in 1973, he won a competition in which the prize was six months as a member of the BBC Radio Drama Repertory Company. Yet he surprised himself "by giving a very visual performance inside my mask. You would imagine that when you're faceless, you would stop smiling. But I didn't."

It is doubtful whether the human characters in *Star Wars* will be long remembered. It is equally doubtful whether the Jawas and Sand People, Chewbacca the furry seven-foot-tall Wookie, See Threepio, and Artoo-Detoo will be forgotten. One of the boldest things in *Star Wars*—Lucas's decision to start the movie with two robots talking—sets the stage for their place in his galaxy. "After all," says Daniels, "the only difference between the humans and the robots was their station."

From A(dolph) to Z(ukor)

The morning sunlight streams in, painting the old man's face. His eyes are rheumy and almost sightless, and he does not close them against the glare. He is a hundred years old now, Adolph Zukor, and who is there to question what he sees as he sits motionless every morning in the same chair in the same room in the same sunlight?

Hollywood has buried its creators. Of all those who had fame or money or power at the beginning, there are left only Mary Pickford, Allan Dwan, Samuel Goldwyn, Colleen Moore, Minta Durfee Arbuckle, John Ford, Raoul Walsh, Jack Warner, Henry Hathaway, Gloria Swanson, Blanche Sweet, King Vidor, Lillian Gish, Charlie Chaplin, and Adolph Zukor.*

Zukor is a generation older than the rest. Ulysses S. Grant was president of the 37 United States when he was born in Hungary, January 7, 1873. He came to America by steerage in

*The list is considerably shorter now, a decade later. By the beginning of 1983 only Colleen Moore, Minta Durfee Arbuckle, Blanche Sweet, Gloria Swanson, Lillian Gish, and Henry Hathaway remained.

January 1973

1888 with $40 sewn into the lining of his second-best waistcoat; made, lost, and remade a modest fortune as a furrier; became a partner, almost by accident, in a penny arcade with its *moving picture* machines in 1904; gave up the safety of manufacturing ladies' furs for the dangerous exhilaration of exhibiting those moving pictures in 1905; gave up the safety of exhibiting one-reel melodramas for the dangerous exhilaration of producing hour-long features of "Famous Players in Famous Plays" in 1912.

It seems a simple idea now, 60 years later, that audiences, like himself, craved more complexity and emotional satisfaction than could be gotten from a 15-minute film. But Zukor was considered crazy when he imported Sarah Bernhardt's four-reel *Queen Elizabeth* in 1912, crazier when he hazarded the $500,000 his 25 years in America had brought him to film successful Broadway plays the same year.

The party to celebrate Zukor's one-hundredth birthday— paid for by Paramount, the studio that he founded—was over four weeks ago. Planning for the $100,000 party began ten months ago. To an indelicate question about the dangers of planning nearly a year ahead in the life of a 99-year-old man, vice president of studio publicity Bob Goodfried responded that he would guarantee Zukor's existence to January 7, 1973—and beyond. On meeting Zukor, it is easy to understand Goodfried's certainty. The teeth are twisted and yellow, but they are his own —and strong enough to chew a daily luncheon steak. The hands tremble as they pick up a coffee cup, but they do not tremble enough to spill the coffee.

He is at a loss in crowded conversation, unable to hear well enough to sort out which of a group of people is talking. But —one to one—with his companion's mouth close to his ear, he has no difficulty. And there is no quaver or hesitancy in his voice as he responds.

At 96, he lived alone in a winter apartment at the Beverly

Hills Hotel. At 97, he spent two hours at the studio every day, and the first thing he asked for each Monday morning were the weekend grosses on all Paramount films. At 100, he lives with a young black housekeeper in a high-rise apartment building built, ironically, on what was, only a few years ago, 20th Century-Fox Studios. It takes him ten minutes to walk the 50 yards from his apartment to the elevator, another ten minutes to walk the 50 yards from the parking lot of the Hillcrest Country Club to the room where he lunches every day and later watches "the old-timers"—men in their late seventies, like Jack Benny and George Burns—play bridge. He has never, except for the night of his birthday party, used a wheelchair.

The men in charge of the dinner convinced him that the wheelchair was necessary to get him to the dais at the exact moment his 14-foot birthday cake was wheeled in—some three and a half hours after the black tie dinner had begun. He ate his own dinner in a suite above the Beverly Hilton ballroom—chopped steak instead of chateaubriand, tea instead of French wines. He tucked his napkin into his shirt collar as a bib, and his skin was as softly pink as a baby's.

He had had during the early evening a constant stream of visitors. At one point there were nearly 20 children, nephews, grandchildren, and great-grandchildren in the room, although his three great-great-grandchildren were too young to come to so late a party. The real understanding of Zukor's age comes obliquely, with such knowledge as the fact that his 75-year-old son, Eugene, has been retired for five years and spends his own days painting.

What Eugene Zukor remembers best from his childhood are "the evening meals. I can hardly remember an occasion when the four of us—my father and mother, my sister and I—didn't sit down to dinner together. My father would discuss all the events of the day, good and bad. And if disaster was ahead, we would know it and be prepared for it. And if he had made a mistake in judgment, we would know it. We were always moving from an apartment with an elevator and servants to an apartment over a candy store, from Riverside Drive to Broadway. There were four or five such moves. They never bothered my father. 'I can lose money,' he would say, 'but they can't take what I have in my mind. What I created once, I can create again.' "

In the suite above the ballroom there were also photographers and movie stars and security guards and a man from Italy come to give Zukor an award. "Luigi," the man introduced himself. "Luigi."

Halfway through the endless photographic session, Zukor leaned forward. "You know Luigi . . ." he said.

Gently, Luigi said, "No, Mr. Zukor. I *am* Luigi."

Zukor continued as though he had not been interrupted. "I know. You know, Luigi, I was going to talk to Charles Bluhdorn about you, but when I saw him, he said he had already met you." (It is one of the penalties of old age to be constantly misinterpreted.)

His baked potato devoured, his caramel custard untouched, Zukor is alone now, except for a security guard and two caretakers. The rest are downstairs in the ballroom where the dinner had raised $100,000 for charity and where, at one moment early in the evening, Jack Benny, Anne Baxter, Liv Ullmann, Jimmy Stewart, Barbara Stanwyck, and Bette Davis were jammed against one wall of the crowded room.

Zukor lights his ritualistic after-dinner cigar and sits, bolt upright, in a tangerine chair to wait for the moment they will come for him.

At another moment—in the sun-warmed living room of his Century City apartment—Zukor will talk of movies and their audiences. Although his interests have narrowed—"When you live as long as I do, most of the time you don't mingle with the mob; you don't go out nights; you don't go to dinner"—within the scope of his interest, he is both lucid and articulate. The words are his, unretouched.

"If we knew in advance when we made any picture how it was going to be taken by the public, we'd have to hire a hall to hold the money. You make a picture you believe in. That doesn't mean the public will agree with us. I devoted my time and energy to selecting the material we were making. The story was always most important. At any stage of life, you cannot always do what you think the public wants, but if you study the trends of success in literature . . . A picture is a publication, the same as a book. If a book sells a million copies, there must be a reason for it.

"If you try to superimpose your own taste and feel the public has to like something because you like it, you will fail. I was fortunate. Failures were very few and far between, and successes were numerous. I always tried to make pictures that appealed to the young people. I always selected subjects the young people would be fascinated by. That's why we had more hits than the others. Because you know the public taste changes in time just like styles in clothes."

His fingers stroke his fingers as he talks. He cannot—today at least—remember the emotions and events of those early years when he stepped ashore at Battery Park—15 years old, barely over five feet tall, with no English and no prospects. "I could manufacture a lot of things," he says, but he does not. It is the moving pictures that occupy his mind today, and what he learned of them.

"I don't think a lot about the past. I just sit and watch the procession. I realize I have reached a stage where all I can do is watch and see what's going on as a bystander. I realize I live in another world. Time marches on. Taste and public feelings change faster than you do. The older you get the farther removed from present events. When you get to be my age, you slow down. If you think *you* are right and *they* are wrong, that's your first mistake. I cannot tell people how to make pictures any more."

Yet Paramount, the studio that he founded, saved itself in the 1970s in his style—by making a best-selling novel of a screenplay *(Love Story)* before the picture was released and by buying what would be a best-selling novel *(The Godfather)* before its publication.

On January 7, 1973, Zukor's first 100 years ended in the ballroom of the Beverly Hilton amid 70 packages of rose petals and 30 gross of balloons and a 14-foot cake made, appropriately, of frosted plywood.

It was, Zukor said afterward, "very hard to visualize in advance the heart-warming feelings you get from people you haven't seen in years. Your emotions happen in a way you can't mentally prepare yourself for. All the heartbreaks and sufferings fade away. All the unpleasant things that happened are unimportant. It makes living to be a hundred worthwhile."

The Great and Powerful
Wizard of Lucasfilm

At 38, George Lucas has become an institution.

It is the greatest of ironies that Lucas—who fled from Hollywood because he was afraid his art would be stifled by its commerce—is the sole owner of one of the most successful movie factories of all time.

Of Hollywood's five box-office champions between 1903 and 1983, Lucas has a share in three. He created, wrote, and directed *Star Wars*. He created and financed, and his company, Lucasfilm, produced *The Empire Strikes Back*. He created the story for *Raiders of the Lost Ark,* and Lucasfilm also produced that movie. During its first three weeks the third movie in his "Star Wars" trilogy, *Return of the Jedi*, earned more than $100 million.

But a list of Lucas's successful movies—which would also include *American Graffiti,* currently among the top 25 box-office winners—comes nowhere near suggesting his impact on the movie industry.

Physically and financially, he is almost completely independent of Hollywood. *Forbes* magazine has estimated his personal fortune at $50 million and his net worth, including Lucasfilm, at more than $100 million. Lucas must still use the major studios' distribution apparatus to get his films into American theaters, but he can demand his own terms. The 3,000-acre ranch he is turning into a haven for film makers is in a valley hundreds of miles north of Los Angeles. By 1985, half a dozen or more writers and directors will be planning and editing their films on the ranch. Partly because of his presence, the San Francisco area is already a precursor of the regional film making that he thinks will revitalize the film industry by 1990.

Beyond Lucas's personal independence, he is creating and building tools—digital sound, computer graphics, computer-assisted editing—that will revolutionize the way movies are put together. A sprawl of converted warehouses in San Rafael houses his two-year-old research and development company, Sprocket Systems, and his special effects company, Industrial, Light and Magic. Because it is a research company, Sprocket Systems has been losing $200,000 a year, but a recent joint venture for Sprocket Systems to create and design video games for Atari should nudge the company into the black. Founded to do the effects for *Star Wars,* Industrial, Light and Magic is now the premier special effects firm in the movie industry. *Star Trek, Poltergeist,* and *E.T.* used ILM. So did *Raiders of the Lost Ark* and *Dragonslayer,* both nominees for the 1981 Academy Award in visual effects.

Symbolically, Lucas is one of the two most visible members of the film school generation that began infiltrating Hollywood in the sixties. (The other is his mirror opposite, Francis Coppola.)

"Once we got our foot in the door, we took over," he says of himself, Coppola, Steven Spielberg, Martin Scorsese, Randal Kleiser, John Carpenter, and the dozens of other film school graduates who are now among Hollywood's most successful directors, cinematographers, and film editors, although—except for Lucas and Coppola—they have not cracked its higher echelons of power.

"From my point of view, the film industry died in 1965," he says. "It's taken this long for people to realize the body is cold. The day I won my six-month internship and walked onto the Warner Bros. lot was the day Jack Warner left and the studio was taken over by 7 Arts. I walked through the empty lot and thought, 'This is the end.' The industry had been taken over by people who knew how to make deals and operate offices but had no idea how to make movies. When the six months was over, I never went back."

Sitting in an unpretentious office adjacent to Industrial, Light and Magic—which has been headquartered in San Rafael, 400 miles north of Hollywood, for nearly five years— Lucas points south. "Down there, for every honest true film maker trying to get his film off the ground, there are a hundred sleazy used-car dealers trying to con you out of your money. Going down there is like visiting a foreign country."

The director of quintessentially Hollywood entertainments is a country boy from California's hot inland valley. Although he is still a shy man enveloped in a privacy as tangible as brown wrapping paper, he has nothing of the rumpled, untidy look he had five years ago. With Hollywood success, he has trimmed his graying beard and cut his hair. But the small-town California childhood which he put on the screen with loving effectiveness in *American Graffiti* still lingers in the rural twang of his voice —and in his choice of clothes. The green polyester pullovers, the blue-and-red checked shirts, the Western shirts with pearl buttons seem fresh off a rack at K-Mart. He has always been painfully ill at ease among the deal-makers in three-piece suits and designer blue jeans who muscle their way to success bearing "Hot Properties" and neatly wrapped packages of director and stars.

Unlike the cosmopolitan Coppola who has a gambler's passion for risks, Lucas is a cautious and frugal man. His personal life is austere and almost reclusive. "Francis accuses me of not knowing how to spend money," he says. "Francis is right."

But frugality should not be confused with stinginess. Lucas has generously given "points," or percentages of his movies' profits, to key employees and has donated $5.7 million to the University of Southern California cinema school that trained him.

Coppola's creativity is unleashed by the threat of losing everything. "George," says Marcia, Lucas's wife of 13 years, "is methodical and ritualistic. He loves to feel safe and secure. Any kind of threat would make him so uneasy and uncomfortable he couldn't work."

Although he loves to play games, Lucas is too cautious even to play Monopoly well. "I'm a bad poker player," he says sheepishly. "I don't have the ability to bluff."

The word most often used to describe him is "serious." "Even when he's silly," says Marcia Lucas, "nothing is simply a fun moment. Everything gets logged. George's calling our enormous black-and-white malamute a 'furry co-pilot' when I would take him for a ride in the car turned into the Wookie in *Star Wars.*" Her husband is also, she adds, "the hardest worker I have ever seen." He would not deny the description. He has described himself as "not especially bright and not especially lucky" and credited his success simply to his diligence.

Until *The Empire Strikes Back,* George Lucas lived in Northern California but had to take the 9:00 a.m. Monday PSA flight south to make deals and do the postproduction work on his films. No longer. "The deal-makers will come up here for George," says Michael Ritchie, another of the cluster of directors who live in Northern California. "The rest of us must still pay homage at the court of money."

With the success of *The Empire Strikes Back,* Lucas was able to cut the fraying ropes that bound him to Hollywood. In the summer of 1981, the last unit of Lucasfilm, the sales and marketing division, moved from its offices across the street from Universal Studios to San Rafael. Lucas had begun shedding his Hollywood clothing a year earlier. After quietly resigning from the Academy of Motion Picture Arts and Sciences, which had nominated him as best writer and director for *American Graffiti* and *Star Wars,* he tore up his membership cards in the Writers Guild and Directors Guild of America in the spring of 1981.

But then he neither needs nor wants to write or direct his movies. To be allowed to direct, and thus to dictate absolutely the tone and motion of camera and actors, is the victory almost all film makers strive for. But whatever Lucas's needs for power and control, they aren't ordinary ones. "I dislike directing," he says passionately. "I hate the constant dealing with volatile personalities. Directing is emotional frustration, anger, and tremendously hard work—seven days a week, twelve to sixteen hours a day. For years my wife would ask why we couldn't go out to dinner like other people. But I couldn't turn it off. Eventually, I realized that directing wasn't healthy for me."

The passion dissipates. He says simply, "I don't have to work for a living any more."

Together, *Star Wars* and *The Empire Strikes Back* have sold more than $900 million worth of tickets. The $25 million *The Empire Strikes Back* was completely financed from the profits of *Star Wars.* The $32.5 million *Return of the Jedi* was financed out of the $92 million in *The Empire Strikes Back* ticket sales kept by Lucasfilm. In addition, Lucasfilm has earned another fortune from its share of the $1.5 billion in retail sales of the characters and artifacts of the two films. And games and toys based on Lucasfilm characters will continue to stock three or four shelves in every neighborhood toy store for at least the next five years.

It would be a mistake to sneer at Lucas or accuse him of hypocrisy because, even while he rails at Hollywood's sleaziness, his own movies are spectacularly commercial. He is simply one of the lucky ones—like Alfred Hitchcock, Preston Sturges, and David Lean—whose vision, however lightweight, coincides for a while with the inner needs and unspoken desires of his customers.

Nor is Lucas's often expressed desire to make experimental films—abstract shorts pulsating with color—simply a ploy or self-deception. "As a film student, he made marvelous abstract films," says Gary Kurtz, who was a few years ahead of Lucas at the USC film school and became his producer on *Star Wars.* "He was one of four students hired by the *McKenna's Gold* people to do some documentaries about the production of that film. George's movie was wonderful, but it was all about the light in the desert, not about the movie. I doubt the *McKenna's Gold* people thought it a useful sales tool."

Lucas's first commercial movie, *THX-1138,* was not very commercial. Produced in 1970 by Francis Coppola for $750,000 and filmed primarily in the unfinished BART subway in San Francisco, it was a longer version of Lucas's student film that had won first prize for 1967–1968 at the National Student Film Festival. *THX* was about a grim future, and it failed at the box office.

"After *THX,* I realized I had to make entertaining films or back off and release through libraries," Lucas says. "I didn't want to struggle to get $3,000. It was too limiting, like giving a painter one brush, a piece of hardboard, and tubes of black and white paint. You can do it, but . . . I didn't want to be a self-indulgent artist, and I didn't want my wife to support me forever. I started on the road to make a rock-and-roll cruising movie, determined to master that trade."

The "rock-and-roll cruising movie" was, of course, *American Graffiti.* Lucas may have intended to dash off an exploitation movie, but he created instead a film that evokes an un-reachable time and re-creates a lost innocence, a time and inno-cence before the choices of adulthood have to be made. An extremely specific account of adolescents prowling the streets of a small California city from dusk to dawn on a Saturday night in the fall of 1962, *American Graffiti* is about the moment of choice. By morning one of the protagonists has chosen to go away to college; another has chosen to stay at the comfor-table junior college at home. Each wins; each loses. And, despite its humor, *American Graffiti* is, in the end, a melan-choly film, pervaded with a sense that no choice can possibly be the right choice simply because choosing forecloses on the future.

"I was amazed when I saw *American Graffiti* and *Star Wars* together for the first time," Lucas says. "I thought to myself, 'Well, I have a certain talent at this.' The two movies shared a certain nice effervescent giddiness."

His eyes permanently fixed on the farthest wall, his body melting into his chair like some animal camouflaging itself in a tree, his voice as hesitant and soft as cat's feet, Lucas gives the impression of fragility. Diabetes, discovered during his in-duction physical, kept him out of the Vietnam war. And there is about him at all times a sense of physical limits beyond which he is not willing to go. "Marcia makes him a tuna salad sand-wich on white bread with the crust cut off, and he's under the covers at 9:30 every night," says his friend, director Phil Kauf-man, about Lucas's life-style.

He cannot tolerate face-to-face confrontations and almost never shows his anger. He demands neither service nor obei-sance, and his employees speak of his humility, but he has an obvious psychic strength. And he can be ruthlessly arrogant about his values and priorities. "That he cannot be turned from the vision inside his head nor corrupted by outside influences is the key to his success," says one of his vice presidents.

His resignation from the Directors Guild came because the Guild fined him for placing the director's credit at the end of *The Empire Strikes Back,* even though Irvin Kershner, the director he had chosen for *Empire,* did not object. For *Return of the Jedi,* he selected a little-known English director, Richard Marquand, who does not belong to the American guild.

"The Hollywood unions have been taken over by the same lawyers and accountants who took over the studios," Lucas says angrily. "When the Writers Guild was on strike, I couldn't cross the picket line in my function as a director in order to take care of *American Graffiti* when the studio was chopping it up. I quit the Directors Guild because the union lawyers were locked in a traditional combat with the studio lawyers. The union doesn't care about its members. It cares about making fancy rules that sound good on paper and are totally impractical. They said Lucasfilm was a personal credit, not a corporate credit. My name is not George Lucasfilm any more than William Fox's name was 20th Century-Fox. On that technicality they attempted to fine me $125,000. You can pollute half the Great Lakes and not get fined that much. The day after I settled with the Directors Guild, the Writers Guild called up. At least their fine didn't go into the treasury. Two-thirds went to the writers of *Empire*."

In May 1982, just before the twentieth reunion of Lucas's high school graduating class, several of his Modesto High School classmates recalled him as a high school "nerd." Lucas remembers himself—and wrote himself into *American Graffiti*—as the inept, hapless Terry the Toad, the passionate drag racer played by Paul LeMat, and the tentative, questing adolescent created by Richard Dreyfuss. Only Ron Howard's serene and secure class president bore no relation to George Lucas.

His father owned a stationery store, and George Lucas grew up on a walnut ranch, the third child and only son. "I was as normal as you can get," he says. "I wanted a car and hated school. I was a poor student. I lived for summer vacations and got into trouble a lot shooting out windows with my BB gun."

On a country road outside Modesto, one day in his seventeenth year, his own turning point came. "I was making a left turn and a guy ran into me. When I was pulled out of the car, they thought I was dead. I wasn't breathing and I had no heartbeat. I had two broken bones and crushed lungs. The accident coincided with my graduation from high school, a natural turning point. Before the accident, I never used to think. Afterward, I realized I had to plan if I was ever to be happy."

Is he happy?

The answer, like the man, is not uncomplicated. "I took the day off yesterday," he says. "I saw dailies at 9:00 a.m., had a meeting from 9:30 to 12, saw more film, had another meeting. I worked from 9 to 6 on my day off."

And, on another day a year earlier: "People have a perception that money will make everything wonderful. It doesn't make anything wonderful. You can live in a nicer house and choose what you want for dinner. But if your Mercedes Benz has a dead battery, it's even more frustrating than a dead battery in your Chevy. When you're rich, everything is supposed to work."

One thing his money could not buy was a child. Finally, in 1981, after 12 years of marriage, Lucas and Marcia, his wife and the Academy Award–winning film editor of *Star Wars,* adopted a baby.

"I was desperate to have a family," he says.

The admission is surprisingly out of character. It comes only because of a relationship built from a dozen long meetings over half a dozen years. "Yet I knew when I had a family I couldn't devote 98 percent of my time to the company. Since my daughter, the focus has changed. Thirty percent of my time now and in a year 50 percent will be focused toward the family."*

Saying he will extricate himself may be easier than doing it. "He has it all in his head," says Tom Smith, general manager of Industrial, Light and Magic. "When he's away, people wait for him to come back."

"He's asked five hundred questions a day," says Sid Ganis, vice president of marketing for Lucasfilm. " 'Should we make the banisters in the ranch house mahogany or green?' 'Should we start this sequence with an over-the-shoulder shot of Harrison Ford getting off the ship?' 'Would it be O.K. to reveal a certain story point in the Jedi trailer?' When we were shooting *Jedi* in the desert and the winds blew and we couldn't work, we were depressed. Until George said, 'It's good luck. I always have a day like this on a picture.' Then we weren't depressed any more. All of us think of him as our leader. At Lucasfilm every one of us is working for George and knows it. When I worked at Warner Bros., Ted Ashley was my boss. George is my leader. I watched one of the secretaries who met him for the first time look at him as though he was a deity."

Lucas's wife is equally doubtful. "Some people are nine-to-fivers," she says. "George is a five-to-niner. He leaves home at 5:30 in the morning and returns at 8:30 at night."

Nonetheless, Lucas says, with just a tinge of desperation, "With *Jedi* I have finished what I began nearly ten years ago with *Star Wars.* When *Jedi* is launched, I'll take a couple of years off. The company was created to serve me, but it's turned out the opposite. I serve it. When I was in film school, I had a dream of having my own company of one hundred people, to have facilities and talented people available to me so I could make the movies I wanted to make without considering the

---

*Soon after the release of the final film of the trilogy Marcia Lucas ended their 15-year marriage.

marketplace. The reality is that I have a company of three hundred and thirteen people depending on me. I've told them, 'I'm not going to make any more hit movies for you. I'm not going to carry this company on my back any more.'

"The original idea was to take the money my films make and put it into outside businesses—businesses like solar energy that don't pollute and aren't morally indefensible—and make money to fund more films. I wanted a financial base. I don't have it yet. Our profit of $12 million to $15 million a year is nothing. The big television producers—Tandem, Lorimar, Aaron Spelling—make more in one year than I've made in my whole career. 'The Jeffersons' outgrossed *Star Wars.* Pac-Man outgrossed *Star Wars.* If I really wanted to make money, I'd have been better off in the microchip business. The kid who started Apple has made ten times the money I have."

For at least five years Lucas has been weighed down by the immensity of what he started with *Star Wars,* and it is hard to distinguish the reality of his complaints from his psychological exhaustion.

"George can see the tape at the end of the race," says his wife. "Now he needs his last burst of energy, and sometimes he feels he doesn't have it left."

"A year and a half ago," Lucas says, "the company was run inefficiently. I was it and it was me. I rearranged it so that now I can walk out and it won't collapse."

He does not intend to walk very far. "George likes to do the same thing on the same day every week," says his wife. "I still can't get him to go out to dinner."

"I like to be in my own bed watching television," he has said. Routine comforts him, whether it is the routine of going to the office six days a week or the routine of spending the seventh day taking his wife to brunch, reading the Sunday papers, napping, watching "60 Minutes" on television, giving the baby her bath, and watching her fall asleep next to him on the bed. During his year off, he will still be at Lucasfilm two days a week. And there is always the ranch to oversee.

His $10 million plan, now nearly half completed, is to build a working retreat for film makers, an environment for creating on celluloid, which he has offered to share with such writers and directors as Hal Barwood and Matthew Robbins, John Korty, Michael Ritchie, and Phil Kaufman. "A lot of rock groups build backyard recording studios because they like to work at home. I'm building a backyard film studio," he teases.

George Lucas is a sober man—his wife's key phrase to describe him is "a serious fellow" and though she suggested on their first date that he "lighten up," he has not yet gotten around to it—and the joke is a measure of his pride in his Skywalker Ranch.

On the 3,000-acre Skywalker Ranch, he has the luxury of building a world in which he finds it satisfying to live—an odd mixture of the nineteenth and twenty-first centuries. In an extraordinary coincidence, Skywalker Ranch is located in a valley north of San Francisco that was named Lucas Valley long before George Lucas was born. Driving down the winding valley road two years ago on a day so hot that the steering wheel was painful to touch, Lucas looked out at the yellow hills. "We have two seasons here—the green season and the yellow season," he said. Having grown up in the dusty valley town of Modesto where summer days were 110 degrees, he loves the yellow hills and the stifling heat.

The ranch was empty land two years ago, except for the raw wood framing the first few buildings, and he reached down and picked up a clod of warm, dry earth, the bedrock of his empire. "From the valley floor, we own everything in sight," he said. "We own over the crest of the mountain. Over 90 percent of the land will be kept in its natural state. It's a totally controlled environment, and it's designed so that no building will be visible from any other building. Four to six years from now, we'll have all the amenities for film makers—editing rooms, mixing rooms, automated dialogue recording, a film research library, and a place simply to sit and think."

Now the buildings are rising. Through a redwood forest, over a newly built wood bridge, is a Victorian village—octagonal buildings with casement windows and glowing stained-glass grapevines, tongue-and-groove oak paneling that can rarely be found in homes less than 80 years old, gables, cupolas, immense flagstone fireplaces, leaded-glass doors—all of the quaint, eccentric buildings painted ice-cream white and blueberry gray. Inside, Victorian England seems to have been crossed with a lodge in the Adirondacks, and the huge, two-story rooms smell of fresh Douglas fir. Everything from the stained-glass fieldmice to the brass chandeliers have been designed and made in some Lucasfilm shop.

At the nursery up the hill there are two groves of redwoods still in their 5- and 15-gallon cans, and an assortment of six-foot-tall oaks, bay, cypress, maple, and cedar. There are meadows of wild flowers everywhere, and the tenth deer of the morning grazes on a hillside clotted with the frail orange petals of California poppies. The swimming pool and tennis court haven't been built yet and the gymnasium is only half finished, but the three-acre lake is dug and filled and stocked with trout.

There are softball diamonds, too. Lucasfilm is a playful company with softball leagues and ski trips, free movies, and a company roster in the form of a high school annual.

Below the lazy nineteenth-century landscape, in the basements of the quaint buildings, lie the conduits and wires, the circuits and computers of the twenty-first century. Those cellar computers will run the washing machines and irrigation system, sweep the 3,000 acres with closed-circuit television, and control the electronically operated gates that defend the roads from strangers.

If there is a touch of paranoia in his walled paradise, Lucas insists it is justified. "There are a lot of crazy people walking in the streets," he says. "Some guy came into our Los Angeles office claiming to be a Jedi Knight and pulled a knife on a secretary. Another real lunatic insisted he wrote *Star Wars* and came to pick up his $100 million check." Although Lucas's wife was ready to adopt a child several years ago, he hesitated because he feared his vulnerability as a person with "a well-known name."

The main house—George's house, it is called, although he will work, not live, there—will be completed in May 1984. Now a hawk swoops down on his prey in the bowl that forms the basement of the 43,000-square-foot house. At the company picnic in 1981, a time capsule full of *Star Wars* trivia was buried there.

When Lucas made *Star Wars,* he was hoping only for enough success to be allowed to make a sequel. *Star Wars* was actually "Episode IV: A New Hope" of a nine-film triple trilogy he had created in his mind. After the success of *American Graffiti,* he had tried—and failed—to launch the *Apocalypse Now* script (on which he was script consultant) for Coppola. No studio was interested. George Lucas's *Apocalypse Now* was more science fiction than the movie Francis Coppola eventually made from a script by John Milius. "I wrote a kind of *Dr. Strangelove,*" he says. "Francis went up river to make *Heart of Darkness.*"

Casting around, he brought out his *Star Wars* story. United Artists and Universal turned him down. Twentieth Century-Fox did not. "If people had laughed *Star Wars* off the screen, I'd have been less surprised than I was at what *did* happen," he says. "Until the day it opened, I felt it would do $16 million and, if I pushed hard, I could make *The Empire Strikes Back.*"

When *Star Wars* was first released in May 1977, Lucas spoke of having wanted to make the kind of movie he had enjoyed as a 12-year-old. Now he says that he "never enjoyed movies that much" as a child. "I started caring about movies when I went to film school and what I cared about was Kurosawa and Canadian Film Board documentaries."

He views film in a basic sense as a moral instrument. "Film and visual entertainment are a pervasively important part of our culture, an extremely significant influence on the way our society operates," he says. "People in the film industry don't want to accept the responsibility that they had a hand in the way the world is loused up. But, for better or worse, the influence of the church, which used to be all-powerful, has been usurped by film. Films and television tell us the way we conduct our lives, what is right and wrong. When Burt Reynolds is drunk on beer in *Hooper* and racing cops in his rocket car, that reinforces the recklessness of the kids who've been drawn to the movie in the first place and are probably sitting in the theater drinking beer."

"*Star Wars,*" he says now, "came out of my desire to make a modern fairy tale. In college I became fascinated by how culture is transmitted through fairy tales and myths. Fairy tales are how people learn about good and evil, about how to conduct themselves in society. Darth Vader is the bad father; Ben Kenobi is the good father. The good and bad mothers are still to come. I was influenced by the dragon slayer genre of fairy tale—the damsel in distress, the evil brothers, the young knight who through his virtue slays the dragon."

The deliberately mythic names of his *Star Wars* characters took months to evolve. "Skywalker" was originally "Darklighter" and then "Starkiller." "Darth Vader" was Lucas's careful blend of Deathwater and Darkfather. "Jedi" was chosen for its knightish echo of the samurai, while "Obi-wan Kenobi" seems to Lucas both ancient and hypnotically phonetic.

What must not be overlooked about *Star Wars* is that he succeeded. Even the most basic level of that success, commercial success, should not be underestimated. Lucas is absolutely correct when he says, "Everyone thinks entertaining movies are easy to make, that they're mindless and anyone can crank them out. It's not true. Most of what comes out under the guise of entertainment is junk. If it were easy, every picture would be a giant hit."

Beyond the money, his tale of The Force, with its light swords and noble sacrifices, is a modern fairy tale, even if it is not quite dark enough to be a modern myth. And Lucas himself is one of its captives.

He is spending ten hours a day with the film and sound editors of *The Return of the Jedi.* "The editing room is where a movie is made," he says. "Everything else is gathering raw material." He leaves at night torn between the "relief" he will feel at "getting it off my back" and the "sadness" of seeing it come to an end.

There will be a second trilogy, of course—dealing with the young Darth Vader and the young Ben Kenobi. The good and bad mothers will play their part, as will the robots—R2D2 and C3PO—the only actors who will bridge both trilogies. At the end of the first trilogy, Luke Skywalker will be four years old. "I'll develop the stories but somebody else will write and direct," Lucas says. "I'm ready to have a different life, to go off and do different things."

Exactly how different that other life will be is a matter of debate. "That he will even consider taking a year off is an immense psychological change in George," says Marcia Lucas. "He grew up with the traditional American values of hard work, earning your own way, and more hard work. It doesn't do him any good to have the money to indulge himself if he never indulges himself."

Comparisons between Lucas and the flamboyant Francis

Coppola, who twice mortgaged his house and private vineyard to make movies and who bought a nine-acre studio in Hollywood with borrowed money, are instructive. "There are no anecdotes," Lucas says of his calm life. "Francis's life is one big anecdote." Coppola won the throw of the dice with *Apocalypse Now*, despite the movie's bloated $32 million budget. But he lost his studio with the $25 million *One From the Heart*.

"Francis pyramids," says Lucas. "If you go fast enough, you can stay afloat but the minute you stop it collapses. I've built a concrete foundation."

It is hardly an accident that Lucas's favorite fable is "The Grasshopper and the Ant." For the last two years Lucasfilm's Sprocket Systems has been working on digital sound and computerized video sound editing, and Lucas estimates it will take another two and a half years before the system is perfected. "You simply can't do what Francis did," Lucas says with exasperation. "You don't buy things off the shelf, a couple of Sony TV sets, and put them in a trailer and say, 'Oh boy, I invented electronic cinema.' "

Lucas began his career as an assistant on Coppola's *The Rain People*, and it was Coppola's willingness, after his success with *The Godfather*, to act as producer on *American Graffiti* that convinced Universal to finance the movie. It was Coppola who gave the impetus to a Northern California film industry when he set up his Zoetrope in San Francisco in 1969. Then he plunged back into Hollywood with dreams of creating an old-fashioned movie studio there and lost everything except his formidable talent. Now it is Lucas who is the focus of the Northern California film makers.

"The technology of making movies," he says, "is getting more accessible. With a small, dedicated crew, you can make a movie with a very small outlay of capital. You could make a professional-looking film for quite a bit less than a million dollars. I think it's only a matter of time before one of the thousands of film-school-trained guys goes back to Kansas City and makes a *Rocky* or an *American Graffiti*. The distribution system will be located in Los Angeles for quite a while before it breaks up. But even that will break up eventually as cable TV and cassettes and other markets open up. You can sell to cable TV by making five phone calls out of your house.

"I've been saying for a long time that Hollywood is dead. That doesn't mean the film industry is dead. But for one region to dominate is dead, although it will take ten or fifteen years to have that visible. The film maker hasn't figured out he doesn't need the agents and the studio executives. What is Hollywood? An antiquated, out-of-date distribution apparatus, a monopoly, a system designed to exploit the film maker. The system is collapsing because of new technologies. The movie companies are structured inefficiently. In good times, it doesn't show. But they won't be able to survive the bad times."

Lucas has made a point of using film crews from the San Francisco area even when they are not as skilled as Hollywood craftsmen. "I'd rather take the knocks of not quite as good a movie in order to train people," he says. "That way, eventually crews up here will be as good as crews in Hollywood."

It is Lucas's hope that the films that come out of different regions of the United States "will be as different from each other as films from different areas of Europe. When film making is diversified across the country, every film maker won't be locked into thinking the same stale ideas. When you get film industries in Georgia, Texas, and Chicago, they'll stop copying the Hollywood product."

Most of the film makers headquartered in the San Francisco bay area echo Lucas. They include Michael Ritchie *(The Bad News Bears)*, Phil Kaufman *(Invasion of the Body Snatchers)*,

Saul Zaentz *(One Flew Over the Cuckoo's Nest)*, and John Korty *(The Autobiography of Miss Jane Pittman).*

"You can write a good script anywhere and you can shoot a good script anywhere," says Korty. "Just invest in some editing equipment. Arthur Penn cuts his films in his barn in Stockbridge, Massachusetts, Paul Newman in Westport, Connecticut," says Ritchie.

Ritchie, too, points south. "Down there," he says, "everyone is afraid of getting his newest idea stolen. We never worry about stealing ideas from each other since each one of us is interested in making films unlike anybody else's."

Phil Kaufman, who is editing his *The Right Stuff* in a converted factory in San Francisco, points to the unusual cooperation of the Northern California film makers. "George will come in and look at my film," Kaufman says. "So will his wife, Marcia, who is one of the best film editors around. Here, everything has the flavor of work in progress and directors share techniques."

Korty, who came to the area first, says, "In 1964, in all of San Francisco, there was only one place that had double-system projection—film on one track and sound on another. Now there are twenty. In those days people would treat me like I was crazy because I was making films in San Francisco rather than Hollywood. Now they ask how they can get in on it, too."

During his "year off," from the summer of 1983 to the summer of 1984, George Lucas will have to make a major decision. Will he move Lucasfilm to the next logical plateau? Will he enlarge it into a movie production company that produces five or six films a year created by other film makers? "Do I hire somebody whose taste is compatible with mine and try to become a Ladd Company?" he asks.

He has no answer yet. He sits inside one of the concrete block warehouses that currently form his empire. On a shelf a few rooms away sit Millennium Falcons in all sizes down to a spaceship the size of a half dollar. He has conquered outer space, and the stamp of *Star Wars* has shaped the decisions at every major studio during the last five years. It would be the ultimate irony if Lucas, who argues fiercely for Hollywood's obsolescence, should be the mogul to replace it.

A NOTE ON THE TYPE

The text of this book was set via computer-driven cathode-ray tube in a face called Times Roman, designed by Stanley Morison for *The Times* (London), and first introduced by that newspaper in 1932.

Among typographers and designers of the twentieth century, Stanley Morison has been a strong forming influence, as typographical adviser to the English Monotype Corporation, as a director of two distinguished English publishing houses, and as a writer of sensibility, erudition, and keen practical sense.

Composed, printed, and bound by The Haddon Craftsmen, Inc.,
Scranton, Pennsylvania
Typography by Virginia Tan